Books by Robert Bernard Martin

WITH FRIENDS POSSESSED: A Life of Edward Fitzgerald   1985

TENNYSON: The Unquiet Heart   1980

THE TRIUMPH OF WIT: A Study of Victorian Comic Theory   1974

THE ACCENTS OF PERSUASION: Charlotte Bronte's Novels   1966

VICTORIAN POETRY: Ten Major Poets (editor)   1964

ENTER RUMOUR: Four Early Victorian Scandals   1962

THE DUST OF COMBAT: A Life of Charles Kingsley   1959

A COMPANION TO VICTORIAN LITERATURE *(with T.M. Parrott)*   1955

With Friends Possessed

FitzGerald at piano, Cambridge, by John Allen.

With Friends Possessed

A LIFE OF
EDWARD FITZGERALD

by
Robert Bernard Martin

Atheneum   New York   1985

For K.B.

When in disgrace with Fortune and men's eyes
I all alone beweep my outcast state,
And trouble deaf heaven with my bootless cries,
And look upon myself and curse my fate,
Wishing me like to one more rich in hope,
Featur'd like him, like him with friends possess'd,
Desiring this man's art, and that man's scope,
With what I most enjoy contented least;
Yet in these thoughts myself almost despising,
Haply I think on thee, – and then my state,
Like to the lark at break of day arising
From sullen earth, sings hymns at heaven's gate:
    For thy sweet love remember'd such wealth brings
    That then I scorn to change my state with kings.

WILLIAM SHAKESPEARE

Contents

Illustrations

13

The author and publishers are grateful to the following for permission to reproduce pictures and/or for furnishing copies:
The Master and Fellows of Trinity College, Cambridge: Frontispiece, III, IV, V, IX, XIVb; Don Niccolo d'Ardia Caracciolo, III; Mrs Edward Norman-Butler, IV; Mr J. H. Fryer-Spedding, V; Mrs A. McK. Terhune, VII; Lady Anne Hill, XII; Mr Robert H. Taylor, XIVa; Ford Jenkins Studio, XV; the owners of three private collections.

Foreword

During his lifetime his affectionate disposition made Edward Fitz-
Gerald beloved by nearly everyone who knew him. In the century
since his death he has become one of those literary figures like
Cowper, Lamb, or Keats who are loved more than they are read.
There are plenty of reasons, including his great translation of the
Rubáiyát of Omar Khayyám and, above all, his published letters,
why we should feel affection for FitzGerald, but as in most such
affairs, there is more chance of its lasting if we really know whom
we are loving and if we love him for what he is, not for a sentimen-
talized image.

Because FitzGerald wrote with enormous charm, and usually
with consummate ease, it has been irresistibly tempting for many
biographers to assume that his personality was as simple as his
style. And since his writing so often reflects his deep love of the East
Anglian landscape in which he lived, the easiest way of dealing
with him has been to treat him as only a delightful, learned, and
eccentric recluse in funny clothes who lived in untroubled ease in
rustic surroundings from which he issued a constant flow of cultivated letters to the famous literary men who were his friends. In
that direction lies what might be called the 'Old Fitz' approach to
FitzGerald; it is the quickest way of disposing of him, but it seems
to me ultimately condescending in its refusal to recognize the com-
plications of his nature.

In one of the best essays about FitzGerald, Frank Kermode
questioned the adjectives 'charming' and 'childlike' that one critic
had used; he wrote that the 'second epithet is certainly odd. He was
excessively complicated, it seems to me.' If to be childlike is to be
free of guile, in so far as human beings are capable of such a state,

15

FitzGerald was certainly that (although it strikes me as singularly inappropriate for some children I have met). But if it has any hint of being morally uncomplicated, it could hardly be wider of the mark when applied to FitzGerald.

Leon Edel wrote of Henry James's letters in words that might be taken over without qualification to speak of FitzGerald's: they are 'lavish in feeling yet cautious in self-revelation'. The correspondence of any serious writer has to be approached with care, for his letters will almost certainly be artefacts created as deliberately as any other work of literature, attempts by the writer to reveal only what he wishes to give away, even if a good bit is going on beneath the surface that is not immediately apparent and that may even be something of which the writer is unaware. I doubt that FitzGerald tried very often to deceive others by what he wrote, but over and over there are hints in his choice of language, in the relative enthusiasm with which he approaches different subjects, most of all in what he leaves out, that tell us a great deal more than he intended. As much as any poem or novel, a letter may please by both the conscious and the unconscious intentions of the writer.

In nearly everyone we know in 'real' life, we find as much pleasure in what is unintentionally revealing as in his or her more deliberate gestures of communication, and it is the contrast between the two that I have found so appealing in FitzGerald. I had originally intended to write this book with as little quotation from his own writing as possible, but it took me only a short time to realize that his letters were the very fibre of his personality, and that to treat them solely as factual sources was to ignore what was individual about FitzGerald as well as to deprive both the reader and myself of a good deal of pleasure. Therefore, I make no apology for my lavish use of quotation to carry the burden of his life. I do believe, however, that the necessity of taking an attitude to what he wrote distinguishes the purposes of a biography from those of an edition of his letters; both provide pleasure if all goes well, but the qualities of that pleasure are different.

When FitzGerald was planning to write a biography of Lamb, he said it was necessary to include all the horrors of his life 'to show forth what the Man had to suffer' and thereby to love him more. FitzGerald's own life had few horrors, but there are areas of it that have not been investigated by earlier biographers; I doubt that he

Foreword

would have thought highly of their omissions. This book has been written in the conviction that we owe FitzGerald the serious recognition of a complicated personality, hiding nothing deliberately. If it is successful, the reader may come to love FitzGerald as much as the writer does.

Oxford
April 1984

With Friends Possessed

CHAPTER I

Family and Childhood

On one side of Edward FitzGerald's tombstone in Boulge, Suffolk, are his name and the dates of his birth, 31 March 1809, and of his death, 14 June 1883. On the other is inscribed part of a verse from Psalm 100 that FitzGerald himself chose because, he said, he had heard it spoken so often by a clergyman friend: IT IS HE THAT HATH MADE US, AND NOT WE OURSELVES. It probably slips harmlessly past the casual visitor and is forgotten, like most quotations familiar since childhood. Any strangeness in the words will assert itself only by an uneasy feeling that they are too conventional and facile, too glibly orthodox to have been intended in their traditional sense by FitzGerald: not words he would have chosen under which to sleep away the years. Like so many aspects of FitzGerald, the phrase ought to tease us into considering the delight he took all his life in the ambiguities of language, his mischievous pleasure in saying more than his words apparently intended, his thoroughly unmalicious joy in watching others reveal their predispositions by the meaning they attached to language or by the mistakes they made with it. For the overly pious or the unwarily conventional, the verse presents no problem, but it is easy to imagine FitzGerald's pleasure at their missing the point of his choice of the quotation.

On a windless spring day Boulge churchyard seems little changed since his death a century ago, a quieter enclave within the gentle Suffolk countryside. A few hundred yards away runs the road to Woodbridge, uninsistently reminiscent of the twentieth century, but there is little traffic except that of agricultural machines moving from field to field. The grass under the trees of the old park is spotted with daffodils, and hundreds of pheasants

19

sit in sculptured rows on the fences along the shaggy drives or perch with a proprietorial air on the tombstones in the churchyard itself. As it was put by one of FitzGerald's collateral descendants who had not inherited his restraint with words, Boulge 'on a moody April day' is full of 'hidden violets and pale knots of prim-roses, intoxicating us with their subtle perfume'. FitzGerald once said that it was among the ugliest and dullest places in England, but the uncharacteristic petulance was a reaction to persons, not landscape. Today the visitor is more apt to find it conventionally pretty, no bad place in which to risk the boredom of eternity.

At such times it is easy to forget that Boulge Hall was torn down years ago, leaving only a few of the extensive outbuildings. Cer-tainly there is little of the sadness that usually hangs over seldom used churches left behind in the grounds of vanished country houses, perhaps because the building itself is so neatly kept and the churchyard in such decent order. To sense that melancholy the visitor to Boulge should come back on an autumn day when the dripping trees keep out the light, and the sodden turf between the graves subsides into the earth. Suddenly one feels something of the quiet despair behind the amiable, eccentric front that FitzGerald showed to the world. He knew the loneliness of the churchyard well as a young man, but he could not bring himself to go near the place in later life, refusing even to attend the funerals of his own family.

In the south aisle of the church are the simple, handsomely carved tablets to other FitzGeralds of the nineteenth century, their lack of ostentation testifying to the monumental self-confidence of the survivors who erected them in the squire's pew, which is almost a small room, shut off by a gate from the body of the church. The remains of FitzGerald's parents and grandparents, his brothers and sisters, and other relations are not here, however, for most of them are buried in the family mausoleum, an ornate, spiky building outside the church. The flint with which it is faced is still in good condition in spite of the damp, and so are the steep steps down which one enters the mausoleum. It is an unpleasant little building, arrogant in manner, and it is somehow fitting that Edward Fitz-Gerald should be apart from the rest of his family, in an unlined grave across the low fence that surrounds the relatives who in life had seemed to him too concerned with country houses and furniture, hunting and a box at the opera, their places in the Government and in society: the blameless if not very profound considerations of money and position normal for members of the gentry who also happened to be extremely rich.

FitzGerald never wanted to be buried at Boulge, although his family lived in the Hall and for fifteen years his own home had been the cottage at the gates of the park. His first choice was burial at Geldestone, Norfolk, beside his sister Mrs Kerrich, the only one of his immediate family whom he unreservedly loved. If that failed, he asked that he be cremated or cast into the 'sheer water' of the sea off Suffolk. When all three options proved impossible, it was at his own wish that his body was put in a plain earth grave, not in the mausoleum. He wanted, he said, to be where he could hear the birds sing. And, he might have added, where he could not hear his family.

Only one of his seven brothers and sisters, Mrs Jane Wilkinson, survived him, and she was unable to come to his funeral from her home in Italy. Of all his nieces and nephews, only two sons of Mrs Kerrich appeared. At the head of the flat granite slab on his grave stands an attenuated rose bush in a wire cage, the descendant of one that grew near the tomb of Omar Khayyám, whose poetry has been best known for more than a century in FitzGerald's translation. The rose was grown from a hip brought from Persia, and then it was appropriately grafted on to English stock at Kew before being planted in the inhospitable soil of Boulge by the club named for Omar.

The quiet acceptance implied in the verse on his tombstone has often been mentioned as particularly fitting for FitzGerald, a gentle, acquiescent man whose life was taken up by kindness to his friends, who seldom rebelled against his own lot or that of others, who was content to take the world as he found it. It is a view of FitzGerald made explicit in 1893 by the Rector of Boulge, who is said to have been dismayed, when the rose bush was planted, that the plate accompanying it should name a heathen poet and philosopher, the mere mention of whom seemed to transgress the spirit of Christian resignation associated with his translator.

The Rector's opinion, which is after all the traditional one of FitzGerald, is understandable, but even a cursory look beneath the surface of his outwardly uneventful life makes it clear that there

21

was another whole side of his personality, one that is indicated by the ambiguity of the quotation and that seems to shrug off on to a Maker who is either indifferent or inimical the responsibility for his own existence. By most men's standards FitzGerald's life was guiltless enough, but to him his failings were so disastrous that he had to share the burden of his culpability. Presumably it would have been impossible to get the Rector's permission to inscribe a line from a pagan poet on his tomb, and one can imagine Fitz-Gerald's quiet amusement as he asked instead for the quotation from the Psalms, knowing that in truth it said nothing different from a line he had once translated from the Persian: 'We are helpless – thou hast made us what we are.'[1]

All his family were mad, FitzGerald used to enjoy saying, but at least he had the advantage of knowing that he was insane. The wryness of the statement nearly blinds us to its essential truth. All his brothers and sisters were, in one way or another, peculiar. Some of them suffered from periodic mental breakdowns, and one was so odd that he became the subject of a chapter in a book on English eccentrics.

The FitzGeralds had an enormous fortune and came from an ancient and distinguished Irish family, but their legacy included as many liabilities as it did advantages. Edward FitzGerald's own parentage was almost a pattern for ensuring emotional disorders in himself and his brothers and sisters.

Until he was nine years old, Edward's surname was Purcell. His father was the son of a wealthy Dublin physician; his mother was his father's first cousin and the heiress to one of the greatest fortunes in the kingdom. It is emblematic of their marital relations that when Edward's maternal grandfather died in 1818, Edward's father, John Purcell, should have taken his wife's name, Fitz-Gerald, although there seems to have been no requirement that he do so for his wife to inherit the family money. But by then the couple had already been married for seventeen years, and John Purcell had long since gone under to the imperious will of his wife. The change of name can hardly have surprised anyone who knew them both.

Henceforth Edward Purcell was Edward FitzGerald. One of his brothers later resumed the name of Purcell in addition to Fitz-

Gerald, but there is no indication that Edward ever considered doing so, although he hated his 'own scrolloping Surname' [IV, 309].* He constantly made up pseudonyms to avoid using it, and as late as the year of his death he was still objecting to the name which he said 'is for certain reasons distasteful to me'. [IV, 549] FitzGerald never wholly revealed those reasons, but it is obvious that they included a mixture of self-loathing and a hatred of what his family stood for. And, of course, it was his mother, to whom the name properly belonged, who was most closely associated with it in a complex web of deep attraction and constant repulsion. Her character, more than any other single factor, was to determine the conditioning of his own.

According to family tradition, his mother, Mary Frances Fitz-Gerald, had received a proposal from a young officer, Arthur Wellesley, who became known to history as the first Duke of Wellington. Since Wellington's biographers make no mention of the matter, it would seem improbable, were it not that the FitzGeralds owned a miniature of him, believed to have been presented to Miss FitzGerald on the occasion of their engagement, which was subsequently broken. Whatever the truth of the Wellington proposal, her commanding appearance and financial prospects far outweighed a rather too dominant personality, so that she received several offers of marriage; no doubt she felt there was less risk in marrying her well-to-do first cousin, John Purcell, than in chancing the fortunes of a soldier. The woman who married Edward Fitz-Gerald years later said of Mr Purcell that he was an 'inefficient, kindly man, big of body and hale of cheek.... It is, however, pretty sure because of his marriage, that he possessed a kind of dumb distinction, and the full quorum of passive virtues.'[2] Not much indication that Miss FitzGerald was swept off her feet by passion, although she was a woman of strong and impetuous emotion, but at least marriage to him kept her money in the family, and he was a good deal easier to manage than Wellesley would have been.

Large though he was, John Purcell seemed visually dwarfed by his wife's commanding presence, and his amiable, slightly fuzzy,

*Here and throughout the book numbers in brackets incorporated into the text refer to *The Letters of Edward FitzGerald*, eds. A. McK. Terhune and A. B. Terhune, 4 vols., Princeton, NJ, 1980.

I   FitzGerald's father. Copy from painting once in possession of his
daughter, Mrs Wilkinson.

manners and incurable absent-mindedness were no match for her domineering personality. He was a graduate of Trinity College, Dublin, and he had been enrolled in the Inner Temple, but he never took up a legal career. Instead, since he was always wealthy, he adopted the far more congenial life of a country gentleman. He loved to hunt and shoot, he kept his own pack of harriers, and he passed on to Edward his enthusiasm for the countryside but not his passion for country sports. From 1826 he served as Member for Seaford, Sussex, where he had bought a fine big house and enough influence to ensure his return, until the seat was abolished in the Reform Bill of 1832. There is little evidence, however, that he took his parliamentary duties more seriously than he did those of his commission as Lieutenant Colonel of the East Suffolk Second Corps Volunteers, or that he even particularly regretted it when he lost his seat. 'The question with him', wrote his son at the time, 'is, not whether the Bill is a good one, for he thinks it is: but whether he ought to vote for the disfranchisement of his own borough.' [I, 93] He also served as High Sheriff and as Deputy Lieutenant for Suffolk, where he was more at home than in Westminster. Had he married differently, he would probably have remained a placidly bemused country squire contentedly in harmony with his surroundings. As it was, he felt unhappy that his wife had considerably more money than he, and that, because of his unbusinesslike ways and his gullibility in dealing with unscrupulous stewards, she and her trustees were unwilling to turn its management over to him. Inevitably, he felt driven to show that she was mistaken in his abilities, and equally predictably she was proved to be quite right.

Edward FitzGerald's parents both came of good families, but they were scarcely of equal standing. The Purcells were well-connected, descendants of the Barons of Loughmoe, but John Purcell's pride was that his mother had been a FitzGerald, and it was presumably to consolidate that connection that he married his first cousin. Through Purcell's mother and Mary Frances's father, both were descendants of an Anglo-Norman family that had been in Ireland for more than six centuries, during which they had built up their position through reckless warfare and prudent marriages until they were one of the three great families in control of the country. Their own branch of the family had been distinguished since the fourteenth century as the heirs of the Earls of Kildare,

25

who were generally believed to have well-defined 'Geraldine' traits of haughtiness, intelligence, and complete disregard for any opinions save their own.

Mary Frances was doubly entitled to complacency at being a FitzGerald, since her own parents had been first cousins of that name, and in marrying a first cousin herself she was only emulating several other unions of the kind among her close relations. In such a family it is perhaps not surprising that at her wedding both her parents and the mother of the bridegroom should all have been FitzGeralds by birth, but it must occasionally have complicated the problem of determining exact consanguinities. Edward FitzGerald was well aware that intermarriage among relatives brought other problems, and he blamed the eccentricities of his family upon their in-breeding.

Mary Frances FitzGerald's father was named John FitzGerald (so, for that matter, were her grandfather, her brother, her husband, her eldest son, and several descendants), and it was from him that she inherited a great deal of her wealth. Much of his money came from land, since his legacy had included several large country estates in England, as well as the Irish family seat, Little Island, a decrepit but charming castle set in two hundred acres in the middle of the River Suir, near Waterford. Most of his adult life he moved between these houses and his London mansion, with frequent Continental trips to vary the routine, travelling with his own retinue, even carrying in his coaches the pictures he wanted hung on the walls of his apartments wherever he settled. He was High Sheriff of Waterford and of Flint, but the duties of those offices did not keep him long. He was old-fashioned in his habits, and one of his grandson's abiding memories of him was the smell of his hair-powder in the bedroom to which he was summoned to entertain the old man. He and his daughter shared a love of the arts and of the traditions of their family; at the death of her brother in 1807 while still a young man, Mary Frances became sole heiress to the family fortune. With his son-in-law old Mr FitzGerald had little in common except enthusiasm for shooting and for the two large cutters that the old man sailed off the coast of East Anglia.

Since the remote days when they were assiduously building up their dynasty, the FitzGeralds had been true to family tradition in considering marriage as primarily a matter of the acquisition and maintenance of property, with gentler emotions commanding less attention. Old Mr FitzGerald and his wife drifted apart, apparently after their daughter's marriage, and they finally occupied separate residences in town and country. As Edward FitzGerald told a young friend many years later, his grandfather, conventional even in his vices, used to keep an opera dancer in London, but four times a year he would be driven ceremoniously across the Park to make a formal call on his sharp-tongued wife, a lady so aware of her grandeur that she expected her own daughter to address her as 'Madam'. Long after he was grown, FitzGerald would speak of his grandfather as dissolute, apparently not because of his sexual morality but in reference to the coarseness of his sense of humour and the crudity of the practical jokes to which he was addicted.

Mary Frances FitzGerald and John Purcell were married in 1801, and at first were devoted to each other. She wore a bracelet made of her husband's hair, on the clasp of which was engraved *Stesso sangue, stesso sorte* ('same blood, same destiny'). Between them they produced eight children in nine years; Edward was the seventh child and the youngest of three sons. Some of the difficulties of the marriage undoubtedly stemmed from his mother's independent wealth. Even before her father's death she had inherited an enormous fortune: in 1810 she was left the major part of the wealth of a great-aunt whose estate amounted to something around £700,000.[3] It made her one of the richest commoners in the land, far wealthier than her husband was. There is probably more than simple coincidence in the fact that when she inherited the fortune she ceased having children, although she was only thirty-two at the time. After that she and her husband increasingly lived separately.

Most accounts of her emphasize her beauty, which is not quite borne out by the surviving portraits, but she must have believed in it herself, since she was said by a descendant to have been painted by Thomas Lawrence twenty-four times, and she sat on other occasions to such fashionable portraitists as A. E. Chalon, who managed the improbable feat of making her look a conventionally pretty young woman adrift in a troubled sea of ruffles. 'Vanity of person and of situation' was the beginning and end of her character as much as that of Sir Walter Elliot in *Persuasion*, and like that handsome baronet she was prone to judge other persons, even

other countries, by their looks. As the years progressed, her fine exterior owed as much to Art as to Nature. At sixty she wrote, 'Nothing produces *wrinkles* so soon as passion of any sort or kind; even the most legitimate affection in Woman, must be kept in subservience to reason. Let woman consider this if she value her beauty.'[4]

Not all the portraits of Mrs FitzGerald ascribed to Lawrence have survived, and modern experts have questioned the attribution of some. In old age Edward FitzGerald mused about his mother's appearance: 'as I constantly believe in outward Beauty as an Index of a Beautiful Soul within, I used sometimes to wonder what feature in her fine face betrayed what was not so good in her Character. I think (as usual) the Lips: there was a twist of Mischief about them now and then, like that in – the Tail of a Cat! – otherwise so smooth and amiable.' [III, 331] He thought, however, that Lawrence was the only painter who had succeeded in catching her true likeness, and, remembering the family story of her proposals, said wryly that she had a surprising resemblance to the Duke of Wellington.

The masculinity of looks suggested by his remark, and his use of the word 'fine', go further to indicate her appearance than anything implying conventional beauty. The surviving portraits show her as a big, slightly shapeless woman with strong sloping shoulders, intimidating bust, chin haughtily lifted but still insufficiently distinguished from the neck, lovely violet eyes, dark auburn hair, long and even nose, and the too-small mouth of which her son complained. Impressive, even magnificent, but not beautiful. After she had inherited Little Island she was in the habit, on her return to the family seat, of being rowed in state across the river with twenty-four musicians playing in the barge. One luckless boatman who had been part of the motive power on such an occasion encapsulated her appearance with admirable economy as 'a fine woman ... a fine broad woman'.

Among the family pictures thought to have been by Lawrence is a pair of three-quarter-length portraits of Edward FitzGerald's

---

II FitzGerald's mother.
   a. Reproduction from drawing by Thomas Lawrence.
   b. Engraving from painting attr. Thomas Lawrence.

parents. His mother stands solidly, looking loftily down her nose as she appears to ignore the scrutiny of the viewer. The rich satin of her gown leaves her powerful shoulders bare, with ropes of pearls hanging around her neck and threaded through her hair. It is the image of a woman of superb self-confidence. Her husband, however, has been posed so as to look diffidently over his shoulder at the painter, as if he were hesitant, almost afraid, about facing life. There is a startling resemblance between his cleft chin and tilted, startled eyebrows and those inherited by his son Edward. The two portraits are a perfect reflection, probably completely intentional on the painter's part, of the differences that divided this ill-assorted couple. Edward FitzGerald loved his father, but he could never have felt masculine identity with him or chosen him as a psychological model; he wanted to love his mother, but she seldom gave him the opportunity. It is no surprise that FitzGerald's own marriage was a complete disaster, or that most of his brothers and sisters married unsuitably and were unable to establish stable homes for themselves, since they had never had the normal opportunity to learn at first hand the ways in which a happy marriage works.

Edward FitzGerald (or Purcell, as he then was) was born in the White House, Bredfield, two or three miles from Woodbridge, on 31 March 1809 and baptized on 7 May, the next to last of his parents' children. The others were Mary Frances, who died when she was only eighteen; John, the heir to the family fortunes and easily the most peculiar of an eccentric lot; Andalusia, to whom Edward was close in spite of the paralysing fits of depression into which she was occasionally plunged; Eleanor, whom he loved without qualification and whom he tried to help in her difficult marriage to a man who was desperately unstable even by Fitz-Gerald standards; Jane, who disapproved of Edward's bohemian ways and wrote distantly after his death, 'I was never very intimate with him'; Peter, a simple and lovable child of nature, full of animal spirits and next to Eleanor in Edward's affections; and Isabella, who married a penniless Italian teacher who Edward said was a 'converted Catholic Monk', after which she largely dropped out of her brother's life.

The family already owned more than its fair share of houses, but presumably old Mr FitzGerald, his estranged wife, and (until his death in 1807) their son needed them all, for on their marriage the Purcells had settled in the White House, which was rented from a friend and neighbour, Squire Jenney. The plastered Jacobean brick house was alternately called Bredfield House and Bredfield Hall. It was somewhat gaunt and charmless, but there was plenty of room for a big family and a large staff, and it stood in a good park with fine gardens and ponds, handsome stables to accommodate all Mr Purcell's hunters and his wife's carriage horses, and kennels for hounds and harriers. The interior was rich with the trophies of Continental trips: family portraits on brocaded walls, gold plate, and gilded satin furniture sinking into the deep carpets. 'No one can imagine the state in which my Grandfather and Grandmother lived,' wrote Edward FitzGerald's nephew, 'but it was State chastened with pure nobility quite devoid of vulgarity.'[5] Such a fine distinction was not often made except by members of the family.

The other attractions of Bredfield were probably less responsible for the Purcells' tenancy than its proximity to Boulge Hall, a mile away across the fields. Old Mr FitzGerald had bought Boulge for them at the time of their marriage, but it was still held by a sitting tenant, Mrs Short, the widow of the former owner, who at the time of the sale had reserved the right to live there until her death, which from the point of view of the Purcells had been unduly postponed. As it turned out, her longevity was to prevent their taking possession of the house for almost thirty-five years after its purchase, by which time the family for which it was intended had been dispersed. The Purcells knew that Mrs Short was not an easy woman, and Bredfield was a handy vantage-point from which to keep an eye on her and Boulge.

The nursery at Bredfield in which Edward was brought up was in a gable at the back of the house, some distance from the gilt and satin of the state rooms. In spite of his love for Eleanor and Peter, he was lonely, since he felt little sense of community with the other children, and he was cut off from his parents. Jagged fragments of memories of Bredfield used to recur to him throughout his life, and usually the language he used to record them is shot through with images of isolation and loneliness. Solitary and unobserved in his gable window, he liked watching his father and Squire Jenney in hunting caps coming across the lawn with their harriers, cracking their whips as they walked, or seeing the horses as the hunt met around the house, the riders unaware that they were silently watched from above. More often he strained his eyes at the sea a few miles away, trying by the strength of his imagination to forge communication between Bredfield and the men-of-war lying in Hollesley Bay: 'I like the idea of this: the old English house holding up its enquiring chimneys and weathercocks (there is great physiognomy in weathercocks) towards the far-off sea, and the ships upon it.' [I, 235] His childish emotion was so strong that its memory could suddenly overwhelm his vision decades later as if it were an 'almost obliterated Slide of the old Magic Lantern'. [III, 331]

Part of the loneliness Edward was feeling was inevitable for the child of a marriage in the process of dissolution. Mrs Purcell had no real love of country life, however luxurious, and the boredom she felt in Suffolk was like the ennui of being married to a dull man whose attraction had vanished. Unfortunately, she could no longer be a good mother without having to dwindle into a rural wife. Her solution of the problem was to transfer the centre of her life to London, where she could now easily maintain another household without worrying about the money. There was no formal separation yet, and occasionally her husband accompanied her to town, but the emotional break was nearly complete. She frequently came to Bredfield, where her role became almost that of guest.

In London she put into her social life all the energy that had seemed wasted in Suffolk. Her position was somewhat anomalous without the support of a resident husband, and she was not taken into all the circles to be expected from her birth and wealth; instead most of her intimates were painters, poets, musicians, architects, even superior actors such as the Kembles and, later, Macready. Her love of art in almost all its manifestations was genuine, and her artistic friends were certainly respectable, but her world lay on the fringes of the great houses of London. She gave splendid dinners in Portland Place, at which the gold plate and the decorations and the food became ever grander, but the guests did not. The glimpses we get of her in the memoirs of her contemporaries are usually of her public appearances, most often in her box in the third tier at the Haymarket Opera, where her magnificent gowns and jewels caused astonished comment, but there is seldom indication of her being personally known to the writers. Some of the hatred of her London life that Edward FitzGerald expressed when he was an adult must have been for the pain that it undoubtedly caused her, but he loyally never mentioned the pretentiousness, even vulgarity, into which she had slipped as her position became more uncertain. One young woman, a friend of her daughters, fixed her with a less charitable eye and called her an 'elegantly ostentatious woman of the scentless-rose sort'.[6]

For her trips between London and Bredfield Mrs Purcell was driven in a splendid glittering yellow carriage drawn by four perfectly matched black horses, an equipage that was hardly designed to preserve her anonymity. Following her would come other carriages with maids and footmen and mounds of luggage. Edward and his brothers used to hide in the shrubbery of the drive to watch her arrivals and departures, too intimidated by her magnificence to wave at her in greeting or farewell.

When she came to Bredfield, Mrs Purcell tried hard to be a good mother, but if she had once had the knack, she had lost it by now. Something of both the love and the fear Edward felt for her is shown by the letter written after his death by his only surviving sister: 'I remember when my Mother read to us any thing interesting he used to creep under the Table to *feed* on & enjoy what she read.'[7] The depth of his disappointment clouds his account, when he was more than sixty years old, of his mother's infrequent visits to the children's part of the house. 'My Mother used to come up sometimes,' he wrote as he remembered her presence in the nursery; then he added drily, 'and we Children were not much comforted.' [III, 331] Even Mrs Purcell's mother was upset by her daughter, and Edward once heard her say in exasperation, 'My dear, you are a very fine Woman, but a *bad Mother*.'[8]

Edward's father was by no means unfeeling, but he could hardly have filled the gap in his children's lives caused by their mother's long stays away from home. According to one who knew him for years, 'He could sit a horse well, but in ordinary affairs was unable to take care of himself, much less of others.'[9] He was so absentminded that on one occasion he went upstairs to change for dinner, and when he had removed the clothing he was wearing, he climbed into bed, where he was found sleeping hours later as his guests waited for him to reappear. He had few of his wife's artistic interests and none of her love for foreign languages, which Edward inherited. Most of Mr Purcell's friends were the Suffolk squires with whom he hunted, and it was only luck that one of them, Major Edward Moor of Great Bealings, took a fancy to the timid little boy and used to invite him on walks, where he would talk as if they were equals in age. Major Moor was compiling a dictionary of Suffolk folk speech and instilled a love of it in Edward, who was not yet seven.

Occasionally old Mr FitzGerald would come to Bredfield for shooting or to stay when he sailed, but he never succeeded in breaking through Edward's reserve, although he tried to do so by demonstrating the tricks of the parrots that accompanied him on his travels, or by lecturing to him on Napoleon. It was probably with his grandfather that Edward first went sailing at Aldeburgh on the cold North Sea that he learned to love. Swimming lessons there were less successful, and seventy years later he remembered his 'first terror at being ruthlessly ducked into the Wave that came like a devouring Monster under the awning of the Bathing Machine – a Machine whose Inside I hate to this Day'. [IV, 532] His boyhood fright at Aldeburgh kept him from learning to swim until long after he was grown.

With their mother absent in London and their father more interested in horses than children, Edward and his brothers and sisters were chiefly under the care of tutors and governesses, who taught them their duty without much sense that they needed more. Edward's sister Jane wrote that their 'early life was one of extreme discipline & entire obedience so that it prevented any outlet of thought or independent action in any of us'. She remembered Edward as a 'very delicate sensitive Child' who suffered particularly from the regime. It must have been a relief to him when at last he was released from the family schoolroom and sent to a private school in Woodbridge, where he stayed for a year or two.

His spiritual education was accomplished with as much difficulty as his more formal lessons. The parson of the parish, who was treated as if he were a private chaplain to the family, showed no awareness that his duties extended to the children. In any case, if he had noticed the unhappiness of Edward and his brothers and sisters, he would not have dared interfere, for he was the sort who 'used to lay his Hat on the Communion Table and gabble over the

Service, running down the pulpit stairs not to lose the opportunity of being invited to a good dinner at the Hall'. Edward's sister, who both asserted his heterodoxy and was at pains to deny it if anyone else made the same claim, put the blame on the parson's shoulders: 'a boy like my Brother Ed. whose questioning spirit followed him through life had little, or nothing to help him on in his spiritual life.'[10] It was perhaps unfair to ask more guidance of a clergyman who had taken to drink in sheer funk over the uncertainty of his own position.

FitzGerald was inclined to associate places with emotions he had known there, and as an adult he refused to go into Bredfield Hall, although he would walk in the gardens and peer in at the window of the room where he used to be beaten as a boy for his mild transgressions. 'Bredfield Hall', written when he was thirty, is not an accomplished poem but something of his submerged sadness at the memory of his life in the house comes through the jingle:

> Lo, an English mansion founded
>   In the elder James's reign,
> Quaint and stately, and surrounded
>   With a pastoral domain.
> With well-timbered lawn and gardens,
>   And with many a pleasant mead
> Skirted by the lofty coverts,
>   Where the hare and pheasant feed.
>
> *   *   *
>
> But all the sunshine of the year
> Could not make thy aspect glad
>   To one whose youth is buried here.
> In thine ancient rooms and gardens,
>   Buried – and his own no more
> Than the youth of those old owners,
>   Dead two centuries before.
>
> *   *   *
>
> Yet the secret worm ne'er ceases,
>   Nor the mouse behind the wall;
> Heart of oak will come to pieces,
>   And farewell to Bredfield Hall!

Today the park at Bredfield is desolate and overgrown, and

conifers mark the site of the house, which was torn down shortly after World War II.

In 1816 the Purcells joined the tidal wave of English sweeping over Paris immediately after Waterloo. They stayed two years, but it is not clear why they went in the first place; certainly not for the usual reason of their countrymen, flocking across the Channel to live well while saving money on the favourable exchange rate. In fact, their stay must have been very expensive, as they kept Bredfield on in their absence, to have a ready place for their temporary returns to England. Mrs Purcell was taken up by the English émigrés in Paris, but it is unlikely that she went there only to become part of their constricted little circle, which besides the aristocracy included a good many respectable but dull middle-class English assiduously reproducing the life in Clapham or Mortlake that they had left behind them, precisely the persons with whom she was most bored. It is more probable that she and her husband were attempting to make their marriage work by quitting both her London and Mr Purcell's Suffolk in order to live together in neutral surroundings. If so, the results left something to be desired.

At seven Edward was old enough to be deeply influenced by the strange environment and by the language that rapidly became almost as familiar to him as English. The first year the family lived in a house standing in a vineyard in what was still the rural setting of St-Germain-en-Laye. All the children shared a master in French and a dancing master, and the boys learned fencing from an old soldier. There were surely other lessons for them, but by the time Edward's sister got around to writing down her memories in 1883, they no longer seemed very important to her, as perhaps they did not at the time. Edward danced well, but nothing is recorded of his fencing.

At St Germain he loved to watch the restored Bourbon court, also newly come from England, as they swept by in state to hunt in the forest, portly old Louis XVIII in the lead with his Guard in blue and silver uniforms, followed by Monsieur his brother surrounded by his own Guard in green and gold. Once, in the spring of 1817, he heard them approaching down the avenues of flowering chestnuts and limes, preceded by the mellow sound of 'Tra, tra, tra' on the horns. 'And then Madame [of Angoulême] standing up in her Carriage, blear-eyed, drest in White with her waist at her neck –

standing up in the carriage at a corner of the wood to curtsey to the English assembled there – ', to which FitzGerald in old age added laconically, 'my Mother among them'. [III, 584]

In the summer the children and their father returned to Bredfield, and it was presumably during their absence that Mrs Purcell set out on the first of her Continental travels, accompanied by one of her bad-tempered King Charles spaniels. She explored France during the time they lived there, and in 1820 she visited Germany. On some of her later trips she was accompanied by her husband, but generally she seems to have travelled bravely in a train of three carriages with only feminine companions, guarded by a courier and a retinue of servants. When she was sixty-one in 1840 she went on a ten-month tour of France, Belgium, Germany, and Italy, the last of which she had not visited previously and which was the real point of the long trip.

During her 1840–1 tour she kept a journal several hundred pages long, in which she noted her impressions of the places she visited. There are long descriptions of works of art, more dutiful than original, although she obviously loved both painting and architecture; when she was uncertain of the validity of her own impressions, she copied her entries from a guide book. Occasionally she compared 'these divine *old* masters' unfavourably with those she knew in 'England! dear England!', for it was undeniable that 'no one beats our own "Landseer" in dogs.' Surprisingly, she was prim about artistic nudity: 'The famous "Torso" of Belvedere is I dare say justly celebrated but does not come within the premise of female criticism, as its details are principally anatomical.'

With the practised eye of the owner of thousands of acres, she commented shrewdly on the agricultural methods of the land through which she passed, and she lamented that so many peasant women spoiled their complexions by wearing hats that failed to shield them from the sun. She had special sympathy for Continental women of her own class, who were deprived of the protection of English laws governing marriage settlements; it made her shudder to consider what her own life might be if her husband were to control all her money. The ruined castles of the Rhine drew from her an anguished *cri de coeur* for 'the poor wives who inhabited them! What must have been the fate of one, united to a licentious, cruel and perhaps foolish man, vested with unlimited power over her fortunes, and her life, who wearied by that restraint which vice must always feel from the presence of virtue, chose the shortest method of throwing it off – The *Dungeon* will tell the rest.'

Except for a slight slackening of her observance of the Sabbath, nearly a year in the proximity of Roman Catholicism did little to shake her firm Anglican convictions: 'our noble Liturgy spoils one for all other modes of Prayer.' But even a woman of her staunch principles found it impossible to ignore the Papists while living in Rome. At first St Peter's was chiefly notable as the 'most agreeable promenade' in the city during the bad weather, but finally she attended services there. Her derisory reactions may be typical of widespread Protestant feelings, but they also show amusingly how sartorial matters became confused with spiritual principles. After one High Mass she wrote that the Pope wore a 'red petticoat' which they 'proceeded to *air*' by swinging to and fro 'a hot chafing dish' before he put over it a 'white and gold apron or rather pinafore'. She was even more critical of the standards of decoration in heathen churches: 'Surely, if Virgins, Saints and Martyrs are to be dressed, they ought at least to have well made gowns, and well dressed wigs.'

It was the royalty of the duchies and minor kingdoms she visited, and the titled travelling English, that brought out her awed enthusiasm. In Baden-Baden she mingled with 'princesses and Countesses Dukes and Princes without end', but she was perplexed at the indecencies of the waltz they danced and could not 'conceive how any man can permit his wife to be exposed to the familiarities of such a dance'. In Naples she was presented to the King and Queen, and when they later met at a ball she recorded every word of His Majesty's polite enquiries about the weather and her sight-seeing. She attended the English church in Rome and was rewarded for her assiduity by seeing the Duchess of Cambridge: 'it is pleasant to see these great ones brought [by] this reasonable Act of homage to the King of Kings to the level of our common humanity. Each time when I have seen her she has honored me with a very court-eous salutation.'.

Her too-persistent pursuit of 'great ones' seems like an attempt to make up for her failure to storm the fortress of London society at home, but she was not always successful. On leaving Rome she decided that it would have been a poor place to live for long: 'There is but one good street, The Corso, the rest of the City is dark dismal and dirty. Of the resident Society a stranger without very favourable introductions can know but little.'[11] What we know of her makes her sound like one of those women of consequence but ambiguous standing in the novels of her son's friend, Thackeray: restless, dissatisfied, unfulfilled, unable either to be content as wife and mother or to force her way into the heart of the society for which she longed. It is perhaps no wonder that occasionally she turned to imposing her will upon her own family.

In 1817, when the family had reassembled in France, they settled for their second year in Paris itself, in the rue d'Angoulême, in a house Robespierre was said to have occupied during the Terror. Edward and his brothers made up stories of all that had happened in the house and told them to their sisters, until they thought that 'the guillotine [was] hanging over our heads every night.' The almost morbid fascination he felt all his life with bloodshed and the workings of the criminal mind was already established, and for the first time he followed in the newspapers the course of a sensational murder trial. With his mother he attended the theatre, and he made frequent trips to the Louvre, which instilled in him at that tender age lifelong passions for drama and painting. And he fell in love with the city, 'all irregular and picturesque; with Shops, Hotels, Cafés, Theatres, etc. intermixed all along the Boulevards'. [III, 584] His apparent happiness in France shines through his father's remark that he kept the whole family in temper with his good humour and fun. 'His affections were deep but partial,' wrote his sister, Mrs Wilkinson, who felt that she had been excluded from them, 'old Friends, old Servants seemed part of him, but his special love was given to my sister Mrs Kerrich, he was her Friend, her Confidant.' Although he was a 'hearty laugher', there was a 'vein of sadness about him, a looking at things on the dark side which often opprest him and which only in his delicately constituted mind a *full* reception of the Truth would have soothed & eased'.[12] But Truth, which she equated with full acceptance of Christianity, was something he never found, in either France or England.

In the autumn of 1818 the French interlude ended with the death of Mrs Purcell's father, old Mr FitzGerald, so that she and the family had to return home.

What Mrs Purcell received at her father's death must have been an enormous sum, since it was regarded as the major part of her fortune, and she had already inherited between half and three-quarters of a million pounds. Whatever the exact amount, it was so large that it seemed reasonable for Mr Purcell to adopt his wife's maiden name as his own and to take the FitzGerald arms, even though he was a member of the family only on his mother's side. After this he and his entire family were known as FitzGerald, which simplifies reference for us, if not for him.

If any real rapprochement had been achieved by the FitzGeralds during their residence in France, it apparently vanished upon their return to England. Probably Mrs FitzGerald found it difficult to respect a husband who was not so wealthy or so imperious as she; with his assumption of her name, she returned the distaff to his hands and once more resumed her London life. The exact nature of their relations was quite unpredictable; on at least one occasion late in life they tried a formal separation, but at the time of Mr FitzGerald's death they were still attending parties together occasionally. Mrs FitzGerald appeared at family gatherings in the country increasingly rarely, and most often she spent her time in Portland Place or Brighton while her husband stayed in Suffolk.

Among the properties that Mrs FitzGerald inherited was the Irish family seat, Little Island, where she seems never to have lived for more than brief periods, although her eldest son spent a good bit of time and money on it when he eventually inherited. Boulge Hall, which had been bought for her and her husband when they were married, was still occupied by the inconveniently long-lived Mrs Short; it was a pleasant house, and one suspects that pique at being unable to use it was at the root of Mrs FitzGerald's dogged determination not to settle in one of her other country estates until she could have Boulge. Castle Irwell, Pendleton, near Manchester, was a small country house in spite of its name, not in good condition but nevertheless one that the family often used for short periods. Unfortunately, it was situated near a vein of coal, the attempted extraction of which was to bankrupt Mr FitzGerald. Since 1810 Mrs FitzGerald had owned the estate of Naseby Wooleys, Northamptonshire, which included in its three thousand acres a great deal of the battlefield of Naseby, the scene in the Civil War of the defeat of Charles I by Cromwell, who was somewhat mistily claimed by the family as an ancestor. Whatever the truth of the genealogy, the hallway at Naseby Wooleys had a wooden figure clad in what was known as Cromwell's armour, and his gold watch was kept in the house. Although it was in beautiful country that Edward FitzGerald loved, the house was considered remote, and his mother is said to have gone into it once, disliked it, and never returned. (It should probably also be recorded that among the conflicting family traditions about the house was one that it was her favourite among her properties.) She had also inherited a half-dozen other Northamptonshire manors, St Thomas' Priory in Staffordshire, and property in Middlesex. It was probably later that her husband bought Seaford Lodge in Sussex; it is probable that he also owned property in Leamington and in Kent.

By now the FitzGeralds were in possession of what seemed to others a disproportionate share of the habitable estates in the British Isles, but they continued to rent Bredfield for another eight years after returning to England, and it was from Bredfield, in the autumn of 1818 immediately after their grandfather's death, that the three sons were sent away for the first time, as boarders at the King Edward VI Grammar School in Bury St Edmunds.

Having his brothers with him made the transition easier for Edward than it might have been, but it was not difficult in any case, since he found the school thoroughly congenial. There was little at home for him to miss except his sister Eleanor, and the school was an exceptionally good one for the day. His brother John, who was six years senior to Edward, was in the sixth form, and Peter, two years older than Edward, was far from scholarly by nature, so that he was put in the first form with his younger brother.

When the FitzGeralds arrived at Bury, Dr Benjamin Heath Malkin had been Headmaster for seven years, and in that time he had already made the school one of the best in England and something of a rarity for its time, largely because of the unusual respect he paid to nascent signs of intellect in his pupils. He was a portly, handsome man in his late forties, active in spite of his lameness, which was engagingly said to have come of an Achilles tendon snapped by his exertions on the dance floor at a hunt ball. Discipline seemed to him a necessity rather than a pleasure, and he deliberately kept the rules of the school simple, since he had no wish to entrap the boys in violations of them. Greek and Latin were paramount, as in most other schools of the time, but of his own

41

III Peter, Edward and John [FitzGerald], from painting attr. Thomas
Lawrence.

volition Dr Malkin saw to it that there was an unusual amount of
English composition and study of literature. Predictably in a school
so dependent upon one personality, some boys felt the Headmaster
was capricious, both in the 'jawing' that he gave them and in his
favouritism among the pupils, but by his respect for them as his
own equals he kept the affection of nearly all. Like her husband,
Mrs Malkin brought energy and rare kindness to her dealings with
the sixty pupils. Years later FitzGerald used to burst out in praise
of her motherliness, quite unlike any he had known at home.

As new boys Edward and Peter shared a study but were very different in their intellectual capabilities. Edward was a scholar, first
in his form during his initial year; although his course thereafter
was erratic, he usually managed to stay in the upper half of the
form without ever again reaching the top. After a mistaken start in
third place in his first year, Peter quickly sank to his natural level at

the bottom of the form and remained there in comfort until he left school. Edward was too dreamy ever to be good at games, but Peter gave his love to the pastimes that he had learned with his father at Bredfield. Before leaving home he had begun driving a team, and at Bury he missed the horses until he conceived the idea of walking on his half-holidays some five or six miles to the high road, where he met the London coach, bribed its driver, and drove it recklessly into Bury at top speed, with its frightened occupants screaming behind him. When the passengers complained to Dr Malkin, he forbade Peter to drive the coach again. Nothing daunted, Peter changed his cap and gown for mourning, bribed the local undertaker, and drove a hearse and four horses at funerals. But his love of speed again overcame his caution, and once more complaints were made by grieving relatives to Dr Malkin, who said with characteristic calm, 'I don't see that I need interfere unless the passenger complained.'[13]

Among the small pleasures of Edward's schooldays were the times when he was visited by Major Edward Moor, who remembered his walks with the shy small boy at Bredfield and their conversations about Suffolk dialect. On his visits Major Moor would give 'his namesake' a seven-shilling piece, the only times in his life that FitzGerald ever saw such a coin.

Besides Peter, Edward had close companions in the new friends he made at school: William Bodham Donne, William Airy, James Spedding, and John Mitchell Kemble, whom Edward had presumably known before, since Kemble's parents were friends of Mrs FitzGerald and Edward would in old age reminisce about having played with Kemble's sister Fanny when they were small. Like Fitz-Gerald, all these Bury friends went on to Cambridge; all of them achieved at least mild distinction, and all of them remained his friends until death.

Of the diverse gifts with which FitzGerald was blessed, none was greater than his talent for friendship, which first had free play at Bury. But it was also noted there that his affection could be almost embarrassing in its intensity, and it was not dampened if the object of his ardour happened to be handsome. Not an unusual feeling for a young boy at a boarding school, but it was to become characteristic of his adult emotions. More than half a century later FitzGerald's estranged wife Lucy apparently wrote a curious little sketch of her husband, having watched from afar the intensity of his feelings for younger men who swam into the beating light of his attention and then sank into disappointment. If the account is actually her own, it is unusual in being the only recorded unkind judgement she ever made of him, and it is as near as anyone who knew him well came to speaking directly of his sexual inclinations: 'Touching his boyhood, the deduction may be ventured, not without a shade of certainty, that if among his school-fellows flourished any embryo Apollo he would have temporarily consti-tuted the youth his heart's idol. No doubt, in course of time, the transfigured urchin would give indubitable proof that he was but honest clay after all, and temporarily darken the universe for Fitz-Gerald.' This could hardly have been more direct in hinting at his feelings for such young men as 'Posh' Fletcher, the sailor who dominated so much of his life after the break-up of their marriage; and 'not without a shade of certainty' seems to indicate that she wanted it understood that she was completely aware of those feelings and perhaps that she had suffered because of them.

In writing of his remarkable ability at making and keeping friends, she shrewdly and not unkindly suggests how that talent tended to take the place of more usual relations with women when he was grown: 'Chief token of his disposition is found in the knowledge that his friendship was sought and acquired by several of the ablest and most sterling characters in the school, diverse in mood and talent among themselves but discovering a common ground of sympathy in him. In more than one case it was "a marriage of true minds", and the alliance thus begun was to endure throughout life.' Ordinarily there could be nothing more common-place than references to a 'marriage of true minds' and to an alliance that was 'to endure throughout life', but their tone here is perceptibly altered when we realize that they were probably written by the wife who failed to make a marriage of any kind with him, and whose alliance with him lasted at most a few weeks.[14]

Mrs FitzGerald's strictures, it must be remembered, were made in hindsight, and though they seem acutely perceptive about the mature FitzGerald, there is nothing to indicate that as a boy he ever recognized more than simple pleasure in the friendships that brightened the eight years he spent at Bury before setting out for Trinity College, Cambridge, in the autumn of 1826.

CHAPTER II

Cambridge

In 1825, a year before Edward FitzGerald went up to Cambridge, his family had moved from Bredfield after renting it for a quarter of a century, but once more they took a rented house as they waited for Boulge, rather than occupying one of their own numerous country residences. Wherstead Lodge stands two or three miles south of Ipswich, commanding extensive views of the broad estuary of the River Orwell; today it is prosaically enough the head office of the Eastern Electricity Board and disfigured by additions, but something of the rural atmosphere persists, largely because of the splendid outlook from the grounds, which were laid out by Humphry Repton. When the FitzGeralds lived there, it was still a simple square Georgian house of considerable size, built of light-coloured brick covered in creeper, the plainness of the exterior giving little hint of the elegance within, of large rooms, handsome domed stairway, and the fine collection of paintings by Canaletto, Hogarth, Kneller, Lely, and Reynolds, which were of such quality that connoisseurs made special expeditions to see them. The house belonged to Sir Robert Harland, whose family had spent £50,000 on refurbishing it at the end of the eighteenth century before proceeding to let it for nearly fifty years; the tenant immediately before the FitzGeralds was Lord Granville, who paid an annual rent of £1,000, presumably not far from what the FitzGeralds paid.

Bredfield had been set in closed-in country; Wherstead looked to wider horizons, some of which were metaphorical as well as literal. Of all the family houses in which he ever lived, this was the only one that Edward FitzGerald loved sufficiently to record his pleasure in it. Although he was never fond of towns, nearby Ipswich had a range of interest that Woodbridge had not offered.

There were excellent book shops, such as James Reed's, where he first read Scott, and greater ease of access from London meant that many of Mrs FitzGerald's artistic friends like Macready came for long visits. There was more variety of local acquaintances, too, including minor writers and painters as well as the hunting squires that Edward had been used to at Bredfield. The poetic circles of Ipswich were responsible for his first meeting in Wherstead one young woman with whom he was to fancy himself in love, and another whom he was to marry in misery, Lucy, daughter of Bernard Barton, the Quaker poet of Woodbridge, whom Edward had apparently not known while living at Bredfield. Even Mr Fitz-Gerald's interests broadened out from hunting and shooting to a new involvement in sailing, a sport that Edward enjoyed too. As an older man FitzGerald preferred rural seclusion to town life, but he became restive when he thought the escape lines from his isolation were being cut.

Liberation, first glimpsed at Wherstead, was fully revealed at Cambridge. The delightful sense of suddenly acquired maturity and freedom that any young man feels when he goes up to the university was intensified by FitzGerald's natural indolence, since he was no longer kept up to the mark as he had been at school in Bury. So long as he attended compulsory chapel, kept from public scandal, and made his tutor believe that he was doing a modicum of work, he was free to do what he liked, leaving the dread thought of examinations for another time, another year. At seventeen he was for the first time treated as a man not a boy, although he was perhaps not ready for such an assumption about his maturity.

In his day college rooms in Cambridge were considerably more expensive than lodgings in the town; besides, as several of his contemporaries found, the intimidating size of Trinity could make it too impersonal for a shy man. In his own case it was surely not lack of money but innate diffidence about making his way in college that led him to live in lodgings. His first rooms in October 1826 were with a Mrs Perry at 19 King's Parade, and he found so little complaint with them that he stayed for more than three years until he had received his degree. Mrs Perry's was a small, steep house whose ground floor is now occupied by a shop. FitzGerald's sitting room, reached by a stair almost like a ladder, looked out on King's College chapel and the Senate House; on the floor above was his bedroom with the same agreeable prospect. His apartments had the pleasantly faded, old-fashioned atmosphere of most under-graduate lodgings, and twenty years later he said that in the interval not so much as a print on the walls had changed.

There was nothing unusual in FitzGerald's light-hearted attitude to his studies, for the subsequent careers of most undergraduates were unaffected by their academic standing, and for many even a degree was not prerequisite to success. The majority of those who worked hard at their studies either intended to be ordained or wanted to become Fellows of a college; in practice that usually meant the same group. There was never any question of Fitz-Gerald's being diligent enough to justify his expecting a fellowship, and nothing could have been further from his mind than Holy Orders, since the remnants of orthodox faith from his boyhood had nearly disappeared. Besides, he knew that he would never need a profession to earn a living.

Despite his indolence, FitzGerald got on well with his tutor, Connop Thirlwall, who, he said, 'took a little fancy to me, I think'. Although he admired the senior members of the college whom he got to know, like many undergraduates he felt some unexamined scorn for the figures of authority whom he had not met. He decided that Christopher Wordsworth, the Master of Trinity, to whom he had probably never even spoken, was 'pompous and priggish', in which he was 'like all Wordsworths', this last a reference to the Master's brother William, whose popular stock was not high in Trinity. FitzGerald, who knew little of his works at this time, gave the poet the nickname of 'The Daddy', in mockery of the over-earnestness he claimed to find in Wordsworth's poetry. The Master often drawled out his responses in chapel, so in imitation FitzGerald referred to him as the 'Mēēserable Sinner', and inevitably his brother became the 'Mēēserable Poet'. [III, 656]

One of the least winning features of FitzGerald's lively person-ality and quick wit at striking out a phrase was that he was often reluctant to let go of a joke. To the end of his days he continued using his nickname for Wordsworth and boasting of having invented it, long after the fun had worn out of it, so that it sounded tedious and bitter to his friends. Even after he had learned to admire Wordsworth's poetry, he still felt compelled to repeat his banter about it. There is good evidence, too, that such close friends as Spedding and Tennyson grew irritable after years of being made fun of, feeling with some justice that the apparently good-humoured joking covered an unconscious, unacknowledged resentment of their achievements.

The course of study, or tripos, that FitzGerald and most under-graduates read was divided into natural philosophy, which was primarily mathematical; theology and moral philosophy, which was largely concerned with the proofs of Christianity; and Greek and Latin literature. And of these burdens mathematics was the greatest, for the majority of undergraduates the most common reason for their needing private crammers, and the usual direct cause of their leaving Cambridge without a degree. FitzGerald's contemporary, Alfred Tennyson, for example, was so convinced of the impossibility of mastering mathematics that he simply gave up studying it, believing that it was better to read classics, write poetry, and then leave the university without ever attempting to sit its examinations. FitzGerald and his friends used to have long joint study sessions in the vain hope of coming to grips with the subject. One of Thackeray's delightful drawings of Trinity undergraduates shows a group of his puzzled friends grappling with 'Conic Sections', which gave him the title for the sketch. Among the others sits FitzGerald, his down-turned mouth indicating that he is no happier than his fellows, but his rapt, far-away expression suggest-ing that he has long since given up thinking of ellipses and parabolas.(See plate IV.)

He was not lazy about subjects that interested him, and he read deeply in the classics and in English and French literature, but the two latter were no help in his prescribed studies. He was never philosophical by nature, politics had little interest unless they touched him personally, and the startling changes in scientific knowledge that were taking place when he was a young man passed him by. His enthusiasms were for poetry, novels, foreign languages, the theatre, painting, perhaps music above all; it is a pity that 'amateur' has acquired pejorative associations, for it accu-rately conveys the true love of the arts that inspired him.

He performed well on both piano and organ, 'but *his taste not perfect*', as one of his more fastidious friends pro-nounced.[1] Another friend, with whom he became intimate after leaving Cambridge, remembered how he 'very often arranged

IV FitzGerald at Trinity, from drawing 'Conic Sections' by Thackeray.

concerted pieces for us to sing, in four parts, he being tenor. He sang very accurately but had not a good voice.' [I, 415] He had some small skill at composition but unusual ability at arranging and transcribing the works of others. It is a disposition of talents reminiscent of his great gift for translation that resulted in *The Rubáiyát of Omar Khayyám*, completely overshadowing a slender aptitude as an original poet.

At Cambridge he took part as pianist in the frequent concerts of the Camus Society, which gave amateur performances in college rooms, the instrumentalists varying from ten to twenty, the exact number not often known before they turned up to play. Nor was the standard of performance more predictable, although the 'hautboys' were said to be excellent and the cellos of exceptional quality. Handel was the patron saint of the society, and in his honour each programme began with one of his works. It was probably the only organized society to which FitzGerald belonged in his life, and it epitomized his love of sociable music-making, informality, and good fellowship.

FitzGerald was far from naïf musically, and he had a surprising catholicity of taste for his day, including an unusual knowledge of English madrigals, of Purcell, Handel, Haydn, and of Mozart, whom he revered as the greatest of geniuses long before such an evaluation was accepted by contemporaries. Old emotions stirred by harmony and melody interested him far more than novelty or even originality, and though he admired the grandeur of Beethoven, only *Fidelio* touched him deeply. In later life he became enthusiastic about Bellini, Rossini, and Meyerbeer, and we find with a start that before his death he was listening to Wagner's music and attending an early performance of *Carmen*, which he disliked not because it was too modern but because he found it hackneyed and unmelodious. Twice friends sketched his characteristic appearance at the keyboard: John Allen drew him as he sat bolt upright at a small old-fashioned piano, either at the Camus or in his Cambridge rooms, and Charles Keene recorded how he looked at the end of his life, hunched over the Minima organ in his Woodbridge house, playing from memories of seventy years. (See frontispiece and plate XVIII, p. 286.)

Little evidence remains of FitzGerald's first year at Trinity; two years later Thackeray described him as 'a very good fellow but of very retired habits', and it is improbable that he had been any less reclusive at the beginning of his university career. Living at Mrs Perry's kept him from the embarrassment his shyness would have imposed if he had lived in college, but it also prevented his getting to know his contemporaries as quickly as he might have done.

Two of his schoolfellows had already been in residence for a year when he arrived in Cambridge. William Donne, to whom he had been close at Bury, was the warmest, gentlest companion he could have asked for. Donne came of an old-fashioned Norfolk family, and he had inherited some of the uncompromising intellectual and spiritual honesty associated with his home county. Beneath his modest wit and humour was a self-sufficient stability that kept him from ever needing to prove himself in the eyes of others. After keeping ten terms, he left Cambridge without a degree, refusing to subscribe to the Thirty-Nine Articles. He went on to attain a mild fame as literary critic, and in 1852 was appointed Librarian of the London Library. When they had both gone down from Cambridge, FitzGerald and Donne became even closer, largely through mutual delight in their warm and amusing correspondence. But they were separated as undergraduates because Donne had gone up to Gonville and Caius rather than Trinity, where most of Fitz-Gerald's other friends were.

At Bury FitzGerald had been more intimate with Donne than with his good friend, John Mitchell Kemble, a man so different from Donne that it was a marvel they were so close. Kemble, son of the famous actor Charles Kemble and brother of Fanny Kemble, was a flamboyantly handsome man of mercurial brilliance and scant common sense. His family had made the London theatre their world; 'Jackie' Kemble turned the world into his own theatre, playing out his dozens of enthusiasms with histrionic flair, as often as not forgetting them when they had served his purpose. Improbably, he intended to take Holy Orders, and when that plan was reasonably abandoned, he even more improbably became a first-rate historian and philologist whose distinguished career was cut short by his death in 1857. Kemble's melodramatic self-regard made him a difficult friend, and though he was in Trinity, he had already made his own mark in the college by the time FitzGerald arrived, and their school friendship never ripened so much as Fitz-Gerald hoped. He was almost pathologically averse to the appearance of seeking intimacy with a man who was in any way his superior, and the mere fact of their seniority at Cambridge was explanation enough for his not pressing his friendship with Donne and Kemble while he was an undergraduate.

Probably FitzGerald led a fairly solitary life until 1827, when he was joined in Trinity by a friend from Bury, James Spedding, who was the first of the three men to whom FitzGerald was closest as an undergraduate. Spedding was the son of a wealthy landowner in Cumberland, at 19 already so dispassionate and mature in judgement that his friends referred to him as 'the Pope'. He was a born scholar and planned to become a Fellow of Trinity, an expectation in which he was eventually disappointed, although he went on to devote his life to the rehabilitation of the reputation of Francis Bacon, editing his works and writing his biography, a labour of some forty years that FitzGerald finally said left Bacon appearing more infamous and guilty than before. It was an opinion which most of Spedding's friends shared. Even as an undergraduate Spedding had the slightly unnerving ability to switch at a moment's notice from fun with his friends to solitary intellectual consideration; the detached judgement which they so admired was connected with a final reserve that kept him from the freest intimacy that his warm affection always seemed to promise. And for all his quirky unconventionality, he had an almost Puritanical sense of man's duty (probably heightened by his friends' disbelief in the worth of his own Baconian studies) that made him seem to disapprove of FitzGerald's life as a wasted one, so that they saw little of each other in later years, although their affection never waned. There was, however, also a great deal of prankishness in his nature, tolerance, and enormous humour: 'plenty of *the Boy* in him,' said FitzGerald, using his greatest compliment for another man. During his second year in Trinity FitzGerald found Spedding the centre of his attention, and he never failed in his gratitude for that time.

Spedding was particularly useful to FitzGerald in helping him overcome his shyness and in bringing out his drollery and good fun, aspects of his character that silently disappeared when he was uneasy with other persons. He had seen too much of his mother and her world ever to be in awe of money or social position, but intelligence, charm, ease, or good looks in another brought out his feelings of inferiority, making him seem stiff, even haughty. With Spedding he could laugh in the sure knowledge that everything he did was looked at with an affectionate eye.

Donne, Kemble, and Spedding had one achievement in common that in the small world of Cambridge divided them sharply from FitzGerald: they were all members of the Cambridge Conversazione Society, better known then and now as the Apostles. If it was not the most exclusive club in Cambridge, that truth had been hidden from the members, who pretended to think of themselves as the most élite group in the grandest college of the only university in the world worth considering. Their joking only partially concealed a real feeling of superiority that outsiders had no trouble in sensing.

As the official name of the Society suggests, the Apostles were formed for the group reading of essays and the discussion of matters that they felt were inadequately considered in university lectures and examinations; only religion and party politics were excluded topics, and even those were not always possible to avoid. Probably more important than the intellectual aims of the Society was the chance it gave a dozen undergraduates to feel part of a real community within a university that seemed increasingly impersonal. They had their own slang, they tried to see each of the other Apostles at least once a day, above all they provided unstated affection for each other. (It should be noted, however, that the affection probably did not include the homosexuality that has become popularly associated with a few of the Apostles in our own century, following revelations about the Bloomsbury group and about members of the Society who have been recruited by foreign powers for espionage.)

Theoretically, the membership of the Apostles was a secret, but it was moderately well-known to the rest of the university. Most of them came from Trinity, and they were chosen for a carefully undefined combination of intelligence, personality, and manner. There were usually about a dozen members, and they kept their numbers down by electing only men who were known personally to each of the other members and unanimously approved. A few men such as Alfred Tennyson and Arthur Hallam were so widely admired in the university that their election probably cut some corners, but in theory new members were selected only after an intense scrutiny that must have been even more unnerving because of the pretence that it was not taking place. If FitzGerald was ever considered for election, which seems improbable, he would not have shown up well in the elaborately casual visits made to prospective members by Apostles who had not yet met them. Had he been elected, he would not have contributed a great deal to the formal discussions of the group, but no one could have given more affection or been more grateful to receive it.

In fact, he benefited considerably from the Apostles, since as an intimate of Donne, Kemble, and Spedding he was automatically accepted by the other members, so that a list of his friends made while he was at Cambridge or soon after would probably include more Apostles than others: men like W. H. Thompson, Douglas Heath, Richard Monckton Milnes, Stephen Spring Rice, W. F. Pollock, and Alfred Tennyson. It would be easy to overestimate the feelings of exclusion that he may have felt at not being a member of the Society himself, but he must have been comforted by forming deep and lasting friendships in his last year with two outstanding men who had also never been invited to become Apostles: John Allen and W. M. Thackeray.[2]

Allen was a clergyman's son who had been brought up to believe that anything he enjoyed smacked of the devil, and since he had a decided love of the world and the flesh, he was in an almost constant state of contrition. In a series of diaries written when he was an undergraduate, and now in Trinity Library, he catalogued in a precise small hand his innocent backsliding, but a modern reader often feels that his peccadilloes are remembered with as much nostalgia as repentance, and that quiet amusement at himself threatens his resolutions to reform his sinful nature. 'Wicked, wicked me' is a constant refrain, but something suspiciously like unrecognized regret at lost opportunities seems to sigh through his protestation that at least he has never been 'guilty of the crimes of Drunkenness or Adultery'.

FitzGerald presented Allen with a difficult moral dilemma, since he was clearly a good and lovable man but was deficient in the Christian belief that Allen thought was prerequisite to happiness. The very circumstances of their first meeting presented a problem: Allen knew that their intimacy, 'the bright remembrance of which I shall look back on with delight till the day of my death', dated from a breakfast party he had attended against his conscience, since it was on a Sunday. Worst of all, FitzGerald was often slothful, and indolence was the sin that Allen most feared.

Drink, the theatre, rich food, inattention during chapel, cards: each represented irresistible temptation to Allen. All were forsworn, all proved too tempting to resist for long. 'O what a wicked fickle character am I!' he would write in remorse. Like most diarists he occasionally ran out of steam, and that too became a matter for self-reproach: 'I have been for several months very careless & neglectful of my Diary, but with God's help I intend to be so no more.' But even with divine aid and the more extreme measure of an alarm clock, he was unable to get out of bed for morning chapel. Usually he tried to be 'Up at 8', and on one triumphant occasion he was 'Up before 8', which quickly became 'Up soon after 8', degenerated into 'Up late' and settled into 'Up pretty well soon after 10'. In despair he wrote, 'Oh, if I could get up in the morning and amend my life!' In his sketch book he once exultantly drew the tip of FitzGerald's nightcap and his nose, all that he could see on the singular occasion when he struggled out of bed to make an early call on his friend and found that FitzGerald was even sleepier than he. On the supposed sins of his dear 'Johnny Allen' FitzGerald cast an amused eye, and he listened patiently to Allen's attempts to turn his thoughts to orthodox devotion. Although he would not accept such exhortation from others, FitzGerald tried not to upset Allen's faith, but a few of the diary entries suggest that he was not above pulling Allen's leg by making his own doubts sound more heretical than they were.

In spite of Allen's odd unworldliness he was a splendid companion. Naturally, he was much busier than his friend, since he was working hard in the hope of furthering his career after ordination – FitzGerald complained that he was often 'wrapped up in old books and Theology' – but there was time for some of the mild revelry his diary records, and FitzGerald was usually to be found with him. They took many of their meals together, they went to breakfast parties and wine parties, they took part in the endless round of calling on acquaintances that was customary, they walked or rowed to Chesterton to play bowls and drink ale, they sang and smoked too much, and they talked. As Allen's boast about not being guilty of drunkenness or adultery suggests, they had little taste for grosser dissipations, and they avoided the sense-less fighting with bargees and the frequenting of brothels at Castle End and Barnwell to which many of their contemporaries were addicted. It was primarily the presence of Allen that awakened FitzGerald to the pleasures of undergraduate life, and from him he learned to respect religion, since Allen was walking proof that piety had no necessary connection with sanctimony.

After he had gone down from Cambridge, FitzGerald used to return there regularly to visit his friends who had not yet taken their degrees, chief among them Allen, and when they were separated, the two kept up a considerable correspondence, more impetuously affectionate on FitzGerald's side than Allen's. 'I have such love of you, and of myself, that once every week, at least, I feel spurred on by a sort of gathering up of feelings, to vent myself in a letter upon you,' wrote FitzGerald, 'but if once I hear you say that it makes your conscience thus uneasy till you answer, I shall give it up. Upon my word I tell you, that I do not in the least require it. You, who do not love writing, cannot think that any one else does: but I am sorry to say that I have a very young-lady-like partiality to writing to those that I love: but I find it hard work to those I care not for.' [I, 121] The warmth of the letters naturally diminished after Allen's marriage in 1834, and though it continued regularly for some years after that, their friendship inevitably slackened as Allen became more immersed in his clerical career and FitzGerald retired deeper into Suffolk. After Allen was appointed to a Shrop-shire living they saw little of each other and their correspondence became scarcely more than a gesture to their joint memory of youth.

In the Michaelmas term of 1829, his last in Cambridge, Fitz-Gerald began special tuition with William Williams of Corpus Christi, in the hope of learning enough mathematics to pass his examinations the following January. In Williams's rooms Fitz-Gerald for the first time met William Makepeace Thackeray, another Trinity man, then beginning his third term. That summer Williams had gone as Thackeray's tutor to Paris, where his pupil learned little mathematics but absorbed a good deal of less theor-etical knowledge.

Paris had spoiled Thackeray for the more formal aspects of uni-versity life, and he welcomed a new companion. In the few weeks that remained of FitzGerald's undergraduate days, the two men became such friends that at the end of his life Thackeray said that of all the men he had ever known he was fondest of FitzGerald. One of their closest bonds was a shared sense of the ridiculous, and together they poked fun at their studies, teased their friends, sang extravagant songs, slipped off to London to smoke and drink chocolate and go to the theatre, and even talked uneasily of their religious doubts.

Thackeray was also a friend of Allen, different though their behaviour was, and their intimacy may have grown because the tastes that Thackeray indulged were not so different from those that Allen worked hard to suppress. With his memory of Paris still strong, Thackeray was beginning the careless pleasures that worried his friends. In France he had discovered his passion for gaming and by the time he returned to England, according to his biographer, he was already a confirmed gambler. He had seen enough of the demi-monde to excite his easily aroused sexual feelings, and it did not take him long to fill the gap in his experience indicated by his statement of innocence at the time he met Fitz-Gerald: 'Quand notre amitié a commencé, je n'avais pas encore appris à aimer une femme.'[3] FitzGerald never shared his love of gambling, however, and he did not have Thackeray's inflammable sexual make-up; indeed, there is no absolute proof that he had any physical relations in his entire life.

Though they represented little temptation to him, FitzGerald was not censorious about his friends' sexual adventures, and Thackeray could talk frankly of his dissipations as he could not to Allen. Thackeray loved 'to talk and write bawdy to congenial company',[4] which included FitzGerald. After his friend's death FitzGerald felt compelled to censor the letters he had received, before returning them to Annie Thackeray. To intimate male friends FitzGerald himself occasionally used mildly obscene language, which was more often scatalogical than sexual; James Spedding's sisters destroyed most of the letters he had received from FitzGerald because they were shocked by passages 'intended solely for masculine eyes'. [I, 249, n.1]

On one important matter Thackeray and FitzGerald disagreed. As always, FitzGerald despised ostentatious or extravagant living of the sort represented by his mother, while Thackeray was already developing the fascinated, ambivalent attitude to such behaviour that created the tone of so much of his fiction. In his own life he was beginning to behave as prodigally as if he had great worldly expectations, while at the same time he saw clearly the folly of such conduct in others. It was no accident that of all FitzGerald's friends only Thackeray came to know Mrs FitzGerald well, was a frequent dinner guest in Portland Place, and even received embarrassingly expensive gifts from her. There is no evidence that she was the original of any particular Thackerayan character, but he could hardly have seen a better exemplification of what he found alternately intensely attractive and deeply meretricious in London society.

FitzGerald always remembered his undergraduate days with pleasure, but he would have enjoyed them even more if he had made the acquaintance of Allen and Thackeray earlier. One of his most noticeable traits was his inability to be happy unless he had a male friend, occasionally two as at the end of his Cambridge career, to occupy the centre of his attention and affection. 'Johnny' Allen, 'Willie' Thackeray, William Browne, Edward Cowell, 'Posh' Fletcher: the story of his friendships with them is almost the narrative of his life. He had many other good friends who included Donne, Spedding, Alfred and Frederick Tennyson, W. H. Thompson, Carlyle, Bernard Barton, George Crabbe, W. F. Pollock, Frederick Spalding, Aldis Wright, and Charles Keene, but he was never as emotionally involved with any of them as he was with the small group of whom Allen and Thackeray were the first. 'Being alone,' he wrote after leaving Cambridge, 'one's thoughts and feelings, from want of communication, become heaped up and clotted together, as it were: and so lie like undigested food heavy upon the mind: but with a friend one *tosseth* them about, so that the air gets between them, and keeps them fresh and sweet.' [I,133] On another occasion he told Allen, 'I am an idle fellow, of a very ladylike turn of sentiment: and my friendships are more like loves, I think.' [I, 153]

Probably those last few weeks of the Michaelmas term in 1829 were more unadulterated fun than FitzGerald had in any other comparable period of his life. When he and Thackeray were helpless with laughter or when 'Old Thack' called him 'Teddibus' or 'Neddikens', it was hard to remember that ahead, just as the

New Year was beginning, lay the end of his undergraduate career and of all that fun, or that he was totally unprepared for even the comparatively mild rigours of the examinations for a simple pass degree. Thackeray was no help: although he had not yet announced the fact, he had no intention of ever taking either examinations or degree, and in the meantime he laughed at study, professing that he had once met a few reading men, 'who are very nice fellows, only they smell a little of the shop'.[5]

At last FitzGerald took fright, and instead of returning to Wherstead for the holidays, he remained in Cambridge over Christmas, working as hard as he knew how. His equanimity began to fray under the strain, and Allen recorded in his diary that 'his temper is much soured by approach of degree', although it was still wonderfully improved by generous doses of Allen's port with biscuits and cheese. Without much hope he began his six days of examinations on 15 January 1830. Mathematics went better than he had feared, but he was sure he had done badly in theology and moral philosophy, particularly in dealing with Paley's *Evidences of Christianity*, which was a notorious sticking-point for generations of Cambridge men, and which provided a nearly insuperable barrier for FitzGerald, who had to be master of it without believing a word.

When examinations were over, FitzGerald was plunged in gloom for two days, waiting for the results and fearing the worst. On the night they were to be posted, he dined with a group of sympathetic friends and then played whist. At last, after staying themselves with still more food, they all trooped out at 1 a.m. and found that FitzGerald had been ranked 106th in the pass degrees. 'All delighted,' Allen recorded joyfully. 'Walked out Trumpington Road making a great noise and very happy.'

Mrs Perry's lodgings had proved more of a home for FitzGerald than any of his family's numerous houses, but when the Trumpington Road had settled again to its nocturnal silence, he had to face leaving Cambridge forever. His leave-taking would have been easier if he had had prospects of anything that was even remotely as exciting as what Arthur Hallam had called 'this college-studded marsh'. His parents would have liked being certain of his future, but he saw no reason to take employment, for which he would probably be unfitted in any case. He had been receiving an allowance of £300 at Cambridge, and it was unlikely that his mother would stop that; it was not princely but it was as much as most professional men made in a year, and he could easily live on it, since he had small taste for expensive dissipation. So far he did not even know where he was going to live; his Cambridge lodgings had given him a predilection for small rooms whose cosiness allowed him to keep all his most precious belongings within easy reach of an armchair, and there was little chance of finding something of the sort in any of the FitzGerald mansions. Above all, Cambridge had given him a family of beloved friends, and even his brother Peter and his sister Eleanor could not substitute for them. Besides, he would hardly ever see those two favourite relatives, since Peter had joined the Army and, following her marriage to a Norfolk squire, Eleanor had moved to Geldestone, just over the borders of the neighbouring county. If he had had the ordering of Utopia, FitzGerald would surely have seen to it that it resembled one of the more rackety Oxford or Cambridge colleges, peopled with lively young men devoted equally to artistic pursuits, intellectual enquiry, and the horseplay of sheer animal spirits. His love of Cambridge never left him, and he had trouble leaving Cambridge.

FitzGerald had too self-conscious a fear of seeming sentimental to prolong his departure by more than a few days. He made the rounds of his friends for the last time and packed his belongings, in his preoccupation forgetting to put in his hairbrush, a pair of pumps, and his supply of cigars. Then on 26 February, his last day in Cambridge, he spent a long time with Allen, who wrote that night that he had 'talked when alone with Fitzgerald [sic] on serious subjects & begged him to think about religion, promised me he would'. In parting Allen gave him a copy of 'Jeremy Taylor's holy living & dying – pray God that it might be of service to him'. Typically, in return for Allen's concern over his salvation Fitz-Gerald 'brought to my rooms the print of the Girl at the Well'. At this remove it is hard to know whether FitzGerald was gently teasing Allen by the exchange, or merely giving him an artefact that seemed as valuable to him as Taylor's gorgeous exhortations appeared to Allen. The following morning Allen made his noblest effort for FitzGerald by leaving his bed early: 'Got up between 8 & 9 went & bid FitzGerald good-bye – both of us melancholy – .'

Cambridge

The first surviving letter that appears in the collected edition of FitzGerald's correspondence was written two days after he left Cambridge. It is not totally unfeeling to be thankful that he was lonely so much of his life, for out of that seclusion came his finest legacy to English literature, the long series of thousands of letters by which he kept in touch with the world. Friendship, gaiety, love of literary and visual art in nearly every form, music, sensitivity to the changing seasons of Suffolk, the hard work of writing and translation, loving gossip about his acquaintance: all these inform his wonderful correspondence, in which only occasionally is the surface clouded by a shadow of the melancholy and loneliness that were such a basic part of his life.

CHAPTER III

Thackeray, Tennyson
and Browne

Only two days after leaving Cambridge FitzGerald was in trouble. His mother had taken the occasion to make clear to him the duties of a youngest son. The details of her demands are not certain, but they appear to have been for increased attendance on her in London in place of his father, now that he no longer had the excuse of Cambridge and preoccupation with his studies. In a rare assertion of his own will against hers, Edward also wanted the conclusion of his university career to be a symbolic event, but for him its meaning was that of independence, and he apparently refused to fall in with Mrs FitzGerald's request. Understandably, he preferred to announce his stand by letter rather than in person. Instead of going to her London house or to Wherstead when he left Cambridge, he headed straight for Geldestone Hall, Norfolk, the home of his sister Eleanor, who was now the wife of John Kerrich, squire of that village.

In his correspondence there are occasional grumbles when Fitz-Gerald felt that he was too dominated by his mother, but this is the only recorded instance of open rebellion. Resistance to her was useless, a truth long since discovered by her husband, who on this occasion could only meekly support her, particularly since it was his absence that made another escort necessary. 'I do not know how long I may remain here,' Edward wrote to Allen from Geldestone. 'I have of course decided nothing of what I shall do: though my Father has decided something for me in reducing my allowance from £300 to £200. This wretched policy to induce me to succumb to my Mother defeats its own end: for it shows to what a stretch he is put to. I must certainly betake myself to France and live on what I have.' [I, 79]

More practical heads than FitzGerald's soon prevailed upon him to end his singular resistance. Allen initially advised against quarrelling with his mother, and John Kerrich completed the persuasion. 'I always felt', Edward told Allen, 'that my letter was written more from a hope of utility, than from a sense of duty: therefore, all the good that can be done has been done, and it is only left to apologize for the manner of doing it. This, you will say, is rather a Paley-like doctrine: and rather betokening that I committed the crime with a view to repent of it. But this is not the case: for I thought not of the duty at the time, but only of the advantage.' [I, 80]

Despite the disclaimer, he had surely not been so deceived as to think he had a chance of worsting his mother, but his brief spurt of defiance was necessary for his own self-respect. He then composed a letter of apology to her, accepting her demands; in his diary Allen recorded that he 'had a letter from Fitzgerald saying he was reconciled to his Mother thank God for it'. A year later Edward was behaving as if the whole short-lived incident had never occurred: 'I have been ever wishing to get into the country,' he told Allen, 'but find that I am very useful to my Mother: and as I wish to do all that may be good, I do not leave town: nor shall, till July.' [I, 96] At her nod he would dutifully travel half-way across England to accompany her to the opera or theatre, or act as extra man at dinner, or take his unmarried sisters around the country. His mother's triumph was nearly complete, and she had everything she could want from him except respect; his love for her was too deeply engrained to be destroyed.

On only one matter Edward seems to have dug in his heels until he won. Rather than stay in 39 Portland Place with her when he was in London, he insisted thenceforth on rooms of his own, most often not far away in Charlotte Street, where the shabbiness of his surroundings amused his friends. No doubt his lodgings were chosen as at least an unconscious protest against the grandeur of his mother's house. It was a curiously unreal existence for him, leaving his seedy rooms to go to Portland Place, then returning to their squalor after a dinner eaten off gold plate. It might have been his salvation, of a sort Allen would not have meant by the word, if he had succeeded in the one flare of rebellion of which we know, even if he had thereby lost a large part of his income.

In return for his acquiescence Mrs FitzGerald apparently increased his allowance to a sum more befitting a man who had completed his university career and lived in his own lodgings (see p. 91). If she had planned it deliberately, there was scarcely a better way to ensure his future compliance with her way of life.

FitzGerald never made the move to France that he had threatened, but he did go there for a long holiday after the formality of taking his degree at Cambridge on 23 February 1830. He set out for Paris by himself, apparently with no close contacts in the city except a maiden aunt, his father's sister, who fortunately turned out to be kind and hospitable.

Because he was lonely for Allen and Thackeray he fell into bad spirits, spending too much time on 'long and whining' letters back to England, to which he decided to return at once. To his incredulous pleasure Thackeray suddenly appeared from Cambridge at the beginning of April, and miraculously Paris was all it should have been. Together they visited the Louvre, which was transformed by Thackeray's company. FitzGerald wrote home of his delight in the pictures, and of the statues of the 'lovely and very modest Venus' and a 'very majestic Demosthenes'. [I, 82–3]

Their fun was compounded by the knowledge that Thackeray had no business being in Paris. In Cambridge he had received a windfall of £20 and determined at once to go to see FitzGerald and perhaps to indulge himself in some more disreputable pleasures. As he was preparing to leave for the Channel boat, his tutor, William Whewell, asked where he intended to spend his holiday, to which Thackeray replied with glib inventiveness, 'With my friend Slingsby, in Huntingdonshire.'

FitzGerald seemed even better company than usual because he was not inclined to press Christianity on Thackeray, as Allen had been doing the past term. Only a few days after FitzGerald's departure for Geldestone, Allen wrote in his diary that 'when Thackeray came in, we had some serious conversation when I affected him to tears he went away with a determination tomorrow to lead a new life. Prayed for him Fitzgerald & myself afterwards in tears.' Even though Thackeray had characteristically postponed his reformation until 'tomorrow', it was a relief to feel that FitzGerald had no designs on his soul or his behaviour. In Paris Fitz himself had been considering religion again without arriving at a firm conclusion. 'I have not got on with Jeremy Taylor,' he wrote to Allen, 'as I don't like it much. . . . I much more like the general, and artless, commands of our Saviour.' [I, 80]

With the freedom of decorum induced by being on foreign soil, the two young men wandered the boulevards, ate well at 'two francs a head', smoked far too much, had plenty to drink, and stopped to sing unselfconsciously to the accompaniment of barrel-organs turned by street musicians. As usual, Thackeray overspent his purse, and FitzGerald had to lend him more.

After spending some three weeks with FitzGerald Thackeray left again as unexpectedly as he had appeared. His empty pocket was probably the cause of his sudden departure, but there is some tenuous evidence that he had contracted a venereal disease that made it necessary to return to London. The matter would be irrelevant in a life of FitzGerald were it not that it probably shows something of his easy tolerance of a kind of conduct far more raffish than any of his own.

With Thackeray gone Paris once more lost its glitter; 'it will empty at the first of May,' wrote FitzGerald [I, 82], and he considered spending the rest of his time in the French countryside. Instead he stayed on in the city tending his aunt, who had been hurt in a fall, announcing that he would be there for the remainder of the summer. Soon even his strong sense of duty could not overcome his loneliness for his friends, so that on 18 May, less than a month after Thackeray had departed so hastily, he was happily installed at Mrs Perry's in his old rooms, seeing his Trinity intimates.[1] The familiar rounds of calls began again, and on 22 May Allen and Fitz had a 'Mackaral' supper with W. H. Thompson. 'Pleasant evening but too much Metaphysics' was Allen's verdict. But he could not have too much of Fitz, and after the latter had set off for Southampton for the summer, Allen wrote in his diary: 'There are some bright spots in every one's life which not only are most sweet to look back on, but affect us for the remainder of it, when we think not of them, so as to make us perceptibly happier & perhaps better. I have many such, my Intercourse with most dear Fitzgerald is not one of the least brilliant.'

For two or three years thereafter FitzGerald was to suffer more from his 'Blue Devils' (or, at least, to mention them more often) than at any other period. At this remove it is easy to see that a good many of his recurrent moods of depression were due to not knowing what the future held. Closely linked to this was his lack of religious certainty, which seemed even more miserable in contrast to Allen's faith. 'I was heavy at soul to think that such fine talents as his were frittered away because he was in error,' Allen wrote after a long day spent in delightful talk of *The Tempest*. 'Oh that dear FitzGerald's heart might be turned.'

It took FitzGerald a long time to settle finally on a lightly disbelieving tolerance of Christianity, and the process was painful: 'I may truly say that I improve every day in works, if not in belief and words. I still vacillate like a fool between belief and disbelief, sometimes one, sometimes the other for I have no strength of mind, and very little perception.' [I, 88] By the end of 1830, however, he was beginning to be slightly defensive about his scepticism: 'I am not the simple minded man I was when a Freshman,' he announced.[2] At last he temporarily cut off discussion of the subject with Allen: 'I am afraid there will ever be a great gulph between us.... I wish that the not being happy without the prospect of Heaven were a proof of Religion: but alas! 'tis no more so, than a beggar's not being happy without a penny in his pocket is a proof that there soon will be a penny in his pocket: it will make him happy to believe so, but the penny is as far off as ever.' [I, 130–1]

There is not the slightest evidence that he ever tried to unsettle the faith of any of his friends and relatives. Indeed, most of his family genuinely thought that he was a believer at heart in spite of never going to church in the latter part of his life. But he would never willingly have caused them unhappiness by making his doubts overt. Several close friends were clergymen, and with them he maintained a quiet mutual respect for each other's views on religion. He had considerable admiration for Christ and for Christianity, even if he felt that it was not for him. From his letters it is apparent that his deepest belief, on which he tried to dwell as little as possible, was in an immensity of indifferent or inimical universe dwarfing a human life with only too finite beginning and end. It was the source of his immediate rapport with the beliefs that he recognized in the *Rubáiyát* and thought that he perceived in the Greek tragedians. It was not an easy doctrine to hold, and at times he obviously found it inadequate, but he learned to bear whatever pain it brought without complaint. What he could no longer

66

believe existed in a deity he increasingly sought in his friends.

In November 1830 Edward was sent off to his family's estate at Naseby Wooleys in Northamptonshire to act as his father's deputy in the management of the land. Although the London season had begun, he was not required there by Mrs FitzGerald, since his father was in the capital when Parliament was sitting, and could act as her escort. When Parliament was not in session Mr Fitz-Gerald would go to Pendleton, near Manchester, where he had begun the disastrous mining enterprise that was to end in his bankruptcy. It is not certain what duties Edward undertook at Naseby, since most of the crops were already harvested and it was too late for the collection of rents. Presumably he was intended to get the feel of the land, for it was the first time he had been asked to oversee any of the sources of his family's income. He was meant to work with his elder brother, the heir to the family fortunes, but John had not turned up. Nor had the regular agent for the estate; on his arrival Edward discovered that he had 'decamped with something above £5000 of my dad in his pocket. Pleasant this, to hear of a November morning'. [I, 92] It was an accurate omen of Mr FitzGerald's inability to control his money, for only two years later he was to lose still more when another agent at Pendleton absconded with the funds of the mine.

Edward probably had little more business sense than his father, but he loved the 'noble country' and its 'primitive inhabitants'. Instead of staying in the family house he had rooms with Charles Watcham, who acted as butler when the family was in residence and lived on one of the estate farms at other times. FitzGerald was content with bucolic pleasures, 'to dine with the Carpenter, a Mr. Ringrose, and to hear his daughter play on the piano-forte'. He reported that the tenants of the estate were dazzled with his new blue surtout, and 'at Church its effect is truly delightful.' [I, 92] It was typical of the amused pleasure he always took in the simplicities of rustic company.

Much of his leisure was spent wandering over the high fields on which the battle of Naseby had taken place, imagining the spots where the fighting was bloodiest, looking with fascination at the places where turnips grew best because, according to local tradition, they were the communal graves of the casualties. On a hilltop about a mile from the centre of the battle ground

FitzGerald's parents had erected an obelisk to commemorate the action, somewhat complacently recording on the base that it had been paid for by 'the Lord and Lady of the Manor'. Edward referred to the monument as the 'pillow', and in the same spirit Thackeray wrote of the victor of the field as Oliver Crummles. In his enthusiasm FitzGerald sought out local traditions concerning the battle from the blacksmith, who turned out to be an authority on it, and from the gardener John Linnet 'whose daughter Sarah is weak in the head and "can't abear Cromwell"'. To Allen he wrote, 'I am quite the king here, I promise you.' [I, 92]

But his kingdom was not Cambridge, nor were his subjects comparable to his Trinity friends. After a month in Northamptonshire, FitzGerald raced back to his rooms at Mrs Perry's, which he kept permanently rented, so that he could be at home there whenever he wished. The only sorrow was that 'Old Thack' had not returned to Trinity that autumn and now was in chambers in the Middle Temple reading law. As they had done so many times before, Allen and FitzGerald made mulled wine, left cards for their friends, prepared apple-pie beds for those who were unlucky enough to be out when they called, or simply sat quietly together and read. Their conversation frequently turned to religion and to FitzGerald's difficulty in believing in miracles; perhaps with mischievous intent he bought as a Christmas present for Allen a volume of Hume's *Essays and Treatises on Several Subjects*, in which he wrote: 'Incredulity is only Credulity saying NO instead of Yes.'[3]

To FitzGerald Allen appeared somehow different, less simple of manner than he had been, and the whole change seemed symbolized by their joint call to leave cards for Arthur Hallam, a new friend of Allen's, for Hallam represented a stratum of undergraduate society considerably smarter than Allen was used to move in. A few days later, as FitzGerald was making an omelette for supper at Allen's, Hallam returned the call, and though FitzGerald liked him, Hallam still seemed an unlikely friend for Allen. Only a week before Fitz's arrival Allen had run into William Wordsworth, and he reported that recently he had met two Apostles, Alfred Tennyson and Robert Tennant. It was too much for FitzGerald, who, as soon as he left Cambridge, wrote to Allen: 'You are now such a heterogeneous sort of animal that I scarcely know how to talk to you.... you are a little bitten with Unions, and

Quinquagints [a debating society], and Tennysons, and Tennants, and aren't half so much "*a whole*" as you used to be.' [I, 94] It was a curious reversal of roles, with FitzGerald scolding Allen for worldliness, but it showed both his honest unhappiness that one he loved might be thought of as a social climber and his slight jealousy at his friend's success in the little world of Cambridge.

Of social climbers he saw enough in his mother's house in London. It was a relief to escape Portland Place to be with his own friends after helping entertain his parents' guests. 'Will you come up to London?' he wrote to Allen, whom he forgave with far more alacrity than he censured him. 'I have lodgings apart from my home where I breakfast, etc. Herein can you be well lodged and boarded. I should be glad to get your acquaintance for my family, but we are different from other people, and I never have introduced any of my friends to my Father or Mother.' [I, 94]

Most of the spring of 1831 FitzGerald was dancing attendance on his mother in London, with an occasional excursion to see his father in Seaford or Naseby, or a visit to his old Cambridge coach, Williams, who was now a curate near Alresford. When Mrs Fitz-Gerald needed 'a gentleman at Brighton', he accompanied her to the resort he soon grew to hate. She rented houses there for years; her son disliked 'the roaring unsophisticated ocean at one side', although he reserved his full scorn for its 'four miles length of idle, useless, ornamental population on the other'. [I, 469–70]

Edward had always scribbled verses, but at Naseby the previous autumn he apparently thought seriously for the first time of being a poet, even though he seems not to have believed that he had any special talent. His sudden enthusiasm may have owed something to the publication in the summer of 1830 of Tennyson's *Poems, Chiefly Lyrical*. The two men had not yet met, but FitzGerald was very much aware of the tall young Lincolnshire poet, who was particularly conspicuous in Cambridge as being one of three handsome, eccentric brothers who were all becoming known for their poetry. He had often seen Tennyson in Trinity and its environs, and most of his friends were well acquainted with the poet, who for a brief period had been an Apostle. One of the most curious – and most enduring – of FitzGerald's peculiarities was his inability to recognize that his gifted friends (at least three of them must be counted literary geniuses) had any natural endowments beyond those of the common run of men. He was far from conceited about his own talents, but rather endearingly it simply never occurred to him that if he tried he might not produce work as distinguished as theirs. All his life he felt perfectly free to rewrite novels or poems that he loved, no matter who the author, smoothing out whatever he did not like, and he casually gave uninvited advice to Thackeray, Tennyson, and Carlyle about improvement of their works. Tennyson's poems had been circulating for a long time among his friends before they were published in 1830, so that FitzGerald had probably seen some of them in manuscript, and he certainly read them soon after publication. No doubt it was in part unconscious emulation of Tennyson that led him to begin filling foolscap with verses during the long evenings in Naseby when he was not listening to the estate carpenter's daughter performing on the pianoforte.

Unlike most young writers FitzGerald was lucky enough to have his first serious poem published by the first editor to whom it was submitted: actually, by the first two editors who saw it. He sent off 'The Meadows in Spring' to the *Athenaeum* early in 1831, assuming with youthful impatience that it would appear almost immediately in the literary weekly. When he heard nothing, he assumed equally quickly that it had been rejected without so much as a note to tell him so. Then, on 9 July, it appeared in the columns of the weekly, and the editor wrote: 'The writer must not imagine that the delay in [its] appearance was occasioned by any doubt; but the pressure of temporary matters – and poetry itself is sometimes temporary, and contributors touchy.' [I, 102]

Unfortunately, before its publication FitzGerald had once more sent off the apparently rejected poem, this time to a literary miscellany, *The Year Book*, whose editor William Hone accepted it and got it into print so promptly that it appeared in his miscellany two months before it came out in the *Athenaeum*. It was Charles Lamb who first spotted that Hone had 'been hoaxed with some exquisite poetry', since it was thought that he had written the anonymous lines himself. He disclaimed the authorship but added in words that pleased FitzGerald when he finally read them: ''Tis a poem I envy.' [I, 102]

'Tis a sad sight
  To see the year dying;
When autumn's last wind
  Sets the yellow wood sighing
    Sighing, oh sighing!

When such a time cometh,
  I do retire
Into an old room,
  Beside a bright fire;
    Oh! pile a bright fire!

And there I sit
  Reading old things
Of knights and ladies,
  While the wind sings:
    Oh! drearily sings!

      *   *   *

Thus then live I
  Till, breaking the gloom
Of winter, the bold sun
  Is with me in the room!
    Shining, shining!

Then the clouds part,
  Swallows soaring between:
The spring is awake,
  And the meadows are green, –

I jump up like mad;
  Break the old pipe in twain;
And away to the meadows,
  The meadows again!

In his letter to Hone that accompanied the poem FitzGerald accurately put his finger on what is best and worst about both this particular poem and much of his other original verse. 'These verses are in the old style; rather homely in expression; but I honestly profess to stick more to the simplicity of the old poets than the moderns, and to love the philosophical good humour of our old writers more than the sickly melancholy of the Byronian wits. If my verses be not good, they are good-humoured, and that is some-

71

thing.' [I, 98] Homely, good-humoured, and simple they certainly are, but they lack intellectual content and prosodic assurance. The truth is that at twenty-two FitzGerald as yet had little original thought to give weight to his verse, and the paucity of integrated ideas and organization is shown by the slack connections between the thirteen stanzas, most of which begin with 'and', 'but', 'then', 'or', or 'when', so that their order often seems arbitrary. Fitz-Gerald's talents in 1831 were still better suited to comic or occasional verse than to lyrics, however homely and good-humoured. It would not be worth commenting on the fact if the poem were not so exemplary of the quality of his poetry when he tried to work independently of the ideas of other men, ideas which could totally transform his works into confident, flexible lyricism.

At the time FitzGerald continued secretly to write verse, most of which has disappeared, but a greater burden of his creativity went into a long series of letters, 'a red-hot correspondence' he exchanged with Thackeray in the 'immortal summer of foolscap', 1831. Each letter was written in snatches over seven days until it was closed on the weekend and dispatched. Of all these letters only one of FitzGerald's has survived, an impromptu that runs to well over 3,000 words, obviously the product of his need to be with his friend. The range of subjects in the letter is as wide as one would expect from the jottings of a week: Paley and miracles, theatre-going, Pope's poetry, Shakespeare, Cowper, Courtly Love, Hume's essays, among others, all discussed in a spectrum of moods. Running through the whole letter is FitzGerald's desperate and nearly unacknowledged need of friendship.

'Now, Thackeray, I lay you ten thousand pounds that you will be thoroughly disappointed when we come together – our letters have been so warm, that we shall expect each minute to contain a sentence like those in our letters. But in letters we are not always together: there are no blue devilish moments: one of us isn't kept waiting for the other: and above all in letters there is Expec-tation!... Do not think I speak thus in a light hearted way about the tenacity of our friendship, but with a very serious heart anxious lest we should disappoint each other, and so lessen our love a little. I hate this subject and to the devil with it.' For fear he might become too earnest Fitz then had a glass of port in thankfulness for Thackeray's companionship and sent him a versified tribute as part of the letter. What had seemed hackneyed in 'The Meadows in Spring' is here converted into playfulness:

> I cared not for life: for true friend I had none
> I had heard 'twas a blessing not under the sun:
> Some figures called friends, hollow, proud, or cold-hearted
> Came to me like shadows – like shadows departed:
> But a day came that turned all my sorrow to glee
> When first I saw Willy, and Willy saw me!
>
> *   *   *
>
> We may both get so old that our senses expire
> And leave us to doze half-alive by the fire:
> Age may chill the warm heart which I think so divine,
> But what warmth it has, Willy, shall ever be thine!
> And if our speech goes, we must pass the long hours
> When the Earth is laid bare with a Winter like ours,
> Till Death finds us waiting him patiently still,
> Willy looking at me, and I looking at Will!

Near the end of the letter, in words that suddenly flash out of the surrounding banter, he wrote, 'I see few people I care about, and so, oh Willy, be constant to me.' [I, 103–11]

FitzGerald's movements for a few years after leaving Cambridge suggest that in return for attendance on his mother half the year he was given freedom for another six months, which he divided roughly between Cambridge, where he aimed to stay two or three times each year, periods corresponding when possible with the university terms; London, for shorter stays to see those friends with whom he had been unable to spend time while escorting his mother; and Geldestone, which for the next thirty years he treated as his real family home, rather than one of his parents' residences, which he visited rarely.

The first few years he went to Geldestone it was primarily a refuge for him, the one place where he could always arrive unannounced and be sure of an unquestioning welcome, his own room ready for him, and the freedom to live as he liked while there and leave when he wanted to. Then, from the mid-1840s he tried to be a prop to his sister as her husband sank into black depression, leaving her to rear the children and manage their business affairs to the best of her ability. After she died in 1863 FitzGerald felt her absence so keenly that he stopped going to Geldestone altogether, in spite of his love of his nieces and nephews and his sorrow for his brother-in-law.

In the 1830s, however, he could not have managed his life without the knowledge that he was always welcome at the pretty eighteenth-century Hall at Geldestone. It was a substantial residence but so unpretentious as to give the impression of being only a superior farm set near the road in modest grounds that hardly merited the description of park. Without advance warning to the Kerriches he would drop off the four o'clock Norwich coach, walk across the long grass to the house, bypassing the door, step in at one of the floor-length windows of the music room, sit down at the piano, and play a few bars of Handel announcing his arrival.

Whatever had been bothering him, Geldestone seemed the perfect restorative, and his letters are full of the idyllic life there. He loved his sister deeply and felt great affection for his brother-in-law until Kerrich's mental troubles were reflected in what FitzGerald thought was unkindness to Eleanor. The eight daughters and two sons presented something of a financial problem to their parents, particularly after Kerrich lost most of his family money by investing in his father-in-law's mining venture. FitzGerald quietly helped the family during the last forty years of his life and left the bulk of his estate to the children.

He used to wake at five at Geldestone, in order not to miss the morning, throw open his window over the wide valley of the River Waveney, then lie reading in bed and waiting for the bells of Beccles church. 'Morning, noon, and night we look at the Barometer, and make predictions about the weather. When will Jupiter piss thro' his sieve? as Aristophanes says. The wheat begins to look yellow; the clover layers are beginning to blossom, before they have grown to any height; and the grass won't grow: stock therefore will be very cheap, because of the great want of keep. That is poetry.' [I, 248]

After breakfast FitzGerald would often walk to one of the pretty neighbouring villages and sketch. One spring he wrote of lying flat all morning on a garden bench reading Tacitus to the sound of a nightingale, with 'some red anemones eyeing the sun manfully not far off'. [I, 224] Luncheon was simple, Cambridge cream cheese on one occasion, and at Geldestone he began his experiments in vegetarianism. Non-meat eating would be a better description, since he

74

disliked green vegetables and often subsisted on bread and fruit, although he complained that after leaving off beef, his life had 'become of an even grey paper character'. [I, 287] At the end of his life he ate little but bread and butter with tea. 'The great secret of all is the not eating meat. To that the world must come, I am sure.' [I, 336] But he was not doctrinaire: he gave guests meat or fowl if no fresh fish was available or would quietly eat meat himself rather than cause his hosts embarrassment by refusing it. For a long period he scarcely drank wine at all. In any case he was probably not a great gourmet; smelts and port was one menu he served a guest, and before he gave up meat he praised a dinner that makes modern readers think more of gastritis than gastronomy: 'Boiled leg of pork, parmesan cheese, and a glass of port, maketh a dinner for a prince.' [I, 107] Thackeray once suggested to his mother that she invite FitzGerald for dinner: 'you needn't mind the expense for he only eats potatoes & drinks water.'[4] But anything simpler than the splendid dinners at Portland Place would have won Fitz's approval.

It was the custom at Geldestone on Sundays to 'dine children and all at one o'clock: and go to afternoon church, and a great tea at six – then a pipe (except for the young ladies) – a stroll – a bit of supper – and to bed'. [I, 325] FitzGerald missed the presence of the children on weekdays when they were not at table. We get a glimpse of those long Norfolk evenings in one letter to W. F. Pollock: 'It must be very nearly half-past 9 I am sure: ring the bell for the tea-things to be removed – pray turn the lamp – at 10 the married people go to bed: I sit up till 12, sometimes diverging into the kitchen, where I smoke amid the fumes of cold mutton that has formed (I suppose) the maids' supper.' [I, 248]

After luncheon FitzGerald would often ride, an exercise seldom mentioned anywhere but at Geldestone, spud up weeds from the garden, or cut dead blossoms off the roses before going indoors to begin another letter. 'I sit down to write to you,' he told Allen, 'my sister winding red worsted from the back of a chair, and the most delightful little girl in the world chattering incessantly. So runs the world away.' [I, 224] Another time he told a friend, 'I live in a house full of jolly children: and the day passes in eating, drinking, swinging, riding, driving, talking and doing nonsense: the intervals being filled with idleness.' [I, 278]

For if FitzGerald loved his sister Eleanor more than all others in his family, his favourite group of relatives was her children, one of whom seemed to be born nearly every year. They were brought up well and simply, and their parents' necessary economy contrived to make them less spoiled than other children of their age and class, as content with small treats as large. FitzGerald was the perfection of 'Uncle Edward': loving, playful, generous, and unshockable. Several times he mentioned his excursions with 'a covey of children with bonnets on' to a great gravel pit in the wood, where he joined them in scrambling up and down the sides of the hole until they were all filthy, since on Saturdays 'they may dirty stockings and frocks as much as they please.' [I, 242, 525] With all the family pride that a childless man feels, he would invite friends for a slightly helter-skelter stay at Geldestone. 'I know you are somewhat shy of strangers,' he wrote to W. B. Donne: 'but you need be in no fear here: for we are homely people; and don't put ourselves out of the way: and so if you can put up with dining off a joint of meat at half past one with us and the Children, and can stand an occasional din of the same Children romping in the passage, I think you have no excuse at all.' [I, 154]

Geldestone seemed like Eden to him, but it was noticeable that he could leave whenever he had had enough of scraped knees and childish voices in the passage. He was wise enough to know that even Paradise may at last have its *longueurs*. FitzGerald was not afraid of involvement, but the fact that he could be so eloquent about the happy lives of others at the very time that he seldom tore off the insulation that protected him from the world may indicate something of the cast of mind of a man who stood one step away from direct experience most of his life, even to the extent of being much more talented at translation than at original poetry.

In 1857 he wrote in praise of the breeding, simplicity, and charity of his Kerrich nieces to Allen's sister-in-law, then added sadly, 'There is however some melancholy in the Blood of some of them – but none that mars any happiness but their own: and that but so slightly as one should expect when there was no Fault, and no Remorse, to embitter it!' [II, 296] In mentioning their tainted blood he was probably referring to their heritage from their father, but he knew that it also came from his own side of the family.

FitzGerald's elder brother John had been strange all his life, sufficiently so at Cambridge to warrant special attention for eccentricity in a city where some might have thought he would pass for average. His sister Andalusia, five years Edward's senior, suffered badly from melancholia, and Mrs FitzGerald had occasionally to ask Edward to switch his attendance from herself to his sister. The condition of 'Lusia' was enough to make Edward worry about his own sanity. In 1832 he wrote to Allen, 'Last week I was unhappy and in low spirits on account of the same turmoil in my head that I had once at Seaford. For that I had the satisfaction of finding a cause, smoking: but for this I have none, except the notion that it may be a defect in my reason or head, which is what annoys me. Living close by my sister who has this malady pronounced exaggerates my fears: which I hope are groundless.... The other night when I lay in bed feeling my head get warmer and warmer I felt that if I should pray to some protector for relief, I should be relieved: but I have not yet learned the certainty of there being any.' [I, 119]

'November weather breeds Blue Devils,' he was told by a friend, adding that a French proverb says, 'In October, de Englishman shoot de pheasant: in November he shoot himself.' This, he feared, might be his own case, 'so away with November, as soon as may be'. [I, 122] Only too frequently he had a 'blue Devil' night with 'no God, no sleep'. Once, on the coach from Leicester to Cambridge, looking at the rich landscape 'full of promise' and feeling 'like an Angel', he suddenly found the tears running from his eyes: 'I could not tell why.' [I, 134] The dread that his own melancholy might at any moment turn into something like Lusia's profound depression was enough to explain his hesitation at becoming too involved with life and founding a family of his own. The fear of going mad, had he known it, was far from uncommon among his acquaintance and was shared by others such as Arthur Hallam and Alfred Tennyson.

FitzGerald's meeting with Tennyson, the first in many years of close but uneasy friendship, took place at the end of 1831 in Cambridge. FitzGerald had intended to spend the entire Michaelmas term in Mrs Perry's rooms, but a summons from his mother to Brighton interrupted his plans. On his return to Cambridge from the seaside he passed through London, where he dawdled for three weeks, staying with Thackeray and recreating something of their

Paris sojourn. Together they went to theatres and museums, bought pictures, and saw so many old friends that Cambridge no longer seemed immediately compelling. 'I dont think my room will ever appear comfortable again,'[5] Thackeray wrote in affectionate regret after Fitz had finally set off for Cambridge, before deciding to follow him there later that month.

Once he was in Cambridge it was everything that FitzGerald remembered, although he found that names, even speech, were mysteriously altered in the brief time he had been away. Arthur Hallam noticed the same phenomenon only three months after he went down from the university: 'New customs, new topics, new slang phrases have come into vogue since *my* day which was but yesterday.'[6] FitzGerald was pleased to do a round of calls with Allen and meet new friends. On 7 December Allen wrote in his diary: '... walked about then dined with FitzGerald at 5, Mazzinghi & Sansum there, went to Garden's to tea, the 2 Tennysons Hallam & Tennant there.'

Alfred Tennyson was seldom very forthcoming with strangers, and it is improbable that he and FitzGerald talked much on this their first meeting, but both he and his brother Frederick were to be among those whom FitzGerald most loved. Like his younger brother, Frederick was tall and handsome, but he was the only one of the Tennysons with fair colouring, so that he and Alfred looked very different. He had a wild temper that could seem almost insane, but he was also affectionate, highly intelligent, and so sympathetic that it was he, of all FitzGerald's correspondents, who drew the most sparkling letters from Fitz's pen.

FitzGerald had often noticed Alfred Tennyson before this in Trinity and in the Cambridge streets, looking, as Fitz remembered, 'something like the Hyperion shorn of his Beams in Keats' Poem: with a Pipe in his mouth'. [IV, 272] On closer inspection Tennyson may have seemed a bit less god-like, since he was often negligent about washing, but there was no disguising the sensuous mouth, chiselled nose, and distinguished bearing that made him so startlingly good-looking. Carlyle called him 'One of the finest looking men in the world. A great shock of rough dusty-dark hair; bright-laughing hazel eyes; massive aquiline face, most massive yet most delicate, of sallow brown complexion, almost Indian-looking'.[7]

FitzGerald never forgot this first meeting and mentioned it in passing many times in the decades the two men were friends. As his future wife was to notice, FitzGerald often responded to good looks in other men, but his response to Tennyson was probably less physical attraction than envy that one man should be so triply blessed, with intelligence, poetic genius, and the appearance of a god.

For Tennyson the meeting was obviously less memorable, but it is only fair to say that he hardly ever recalled much about initial impressions, and anyway FitzGerald's appearance was far less striking than his own. Fitz was nearly as tall as Tennyson, and probably almost as heavy (by 1842 he weighed fourteen stone), but he had little of the poet's great strength and muscularity or the bold, almost arrogant, presence that made Tennyson so startling to meet. Fitz's face was soft and round, with highly arched eyebrows that gave him a perpetually startled appearance when he was young. His long, straight nose was joined to an unusually fleshy and vulnerable mouth by an upper lip hardly distinguished from the septum, and his chin was deeply cleft. His appearance would have seemed little but pleasant and sensitive had it not been for bright blue eyes that flashed incongruously and occasionally imperiously from a face nearly as dark as Tennyson's own. Only three photographs were ever taken of FitzGerald, all at the same sitting, after he was middle-aged, but both they and the drawings of him that remain give the impression of extraordinary, almost disturbing mobility of countenance.

Not long after meeting Tennyson, FitzGerald wrote to Allen to tell him of how he had dreamed of one of Tennyson's poems on the journey from Cambridge to London: 'when I came up on the mail, and fell a-dozing in the morning, the sights of the pages in crimson and the funerals which the Lady of Shalott saw and wove, floated before me: really, the poem has taken lodging in my poor head.' [I, 112–13]

'What *passions* our friendships were,' Thackeray remembered of this time. The slightest signs of cooling were enough to make any of the set from Cambridge feel melodramatically that all intimacy was gone. 'What a short lived friendship ours has been,' Thackeray wrote of his acquaintance with FitzGerald in the spring of 1832; 'The charm of it wore off with him sooner than with me but I am afraid now we are little more than acquaintances, keeping up from old habits the form of friendship by letter – .'[8] What slight he imagined is no longer discoverable, but in an attempt to heal the fancied breach he invited FitzGerald to accompany him to Paris and Italy. Fitz chose instead to go to Wales to be with Allen. It was to be one of the most momentous decisions he ever made, and he was to remember vignettes of the Welsh stay until his death.

On going to Wales FitzGerald sailed from Bristol to Tenby, which he intended to make the centre of his holiday, after a brief visit to Milton a few miles away to spend some days with Allen at Freestone Hall, the home of Allen's cousin James. On the steam packet from Bristol FitzGerald and a sixteen-year-old boy had struck up an enjoyable conversation. William Kenworthy Browne was a conventionally handsome boy with passions that would have bored FitzGerald intolerably had they been expressed by his own family. Browne had little interest in music, and he seldom read a book that was not required of him, but he loved hunting, shooting and fishing. He had vague aspirations to the Army, and it had occurred to him that it might be pleasant to be a country Member of Parliament. He sounds, in short, very like what Mr FitzGerald must have been as a boy. What Browne lacked in intellectual spark, he made up for by good manners and attractively spontaneous naïveté. Apparently he was travelling alone, and no doubt his independence appealed to FitzGerald.

After staying with Allen, FitzGerald returned to Tenby, where he had taken lodgings in Rees's boarding house in Back Street, reserving two rooms overlooking the sea and a row of fishermen's huts, in the hope that Allen or another of his friends would occupy the second of them and eat 'bachelor's fare, for as long as he will'. [I, 116] Allen never arrived, but FitzGerald was not lonely without him, since young Browne was staying in the same house. They spent the remainder of the holiday together.

Browne's home was in Bedford, where his father had been alderman, then mayor. His family was prosperous and was making its way upward socially, trying to shake off its background in trade, which in the future was to be an embarrassment to Browne's wife. There was at least a pretension to gentility in the family; Browne's father had added the final 'e' to the name, and they were well on their way to the hyphen in their surname in the following century. Mr Browne had also assumed the arms of a sixteenth-century Warden of the Merchant Taylors' Company, from whom he claimed descent, and during the 1840s he became involved in litigation over shares in the Bridgewater Navigation Company, which his mother's family had bought, and for which he claimed a settlement of £100,000 was still due to them. His case was never concluded. FitzGerald did not take Mr Browne's claims seriously, either to fortune or to lineage, and he spoke of the family as rising from the 'trading classes'. But both Browne's youth and his prob-ably plebeian origins were attractive to FitzGerald, who liked nothing better than being teacher-cum-surrogate father to the young men he befriended. In return William Browne gave the affec-tion and unquestioning respect that FitzGerald expected of those he helped. In spite of the seven-year difference in their ages, the friendship was close from the first. Six years later FitzGerald told Allen: 'You and Browne (though in rather different ways) have cer-tainly made me more happy than any men living. Sometimes I behave very ill to him, and am much ashamed of myself.' [I, 215] Nearly all the letters that passed between Browne and FitzGerald in the next quarter of a century have disappeared, but there is nothing to indicate that Browne's response to FitzGerald's ill-treatment (if it was not imaginary) was ever anything but good-tempered and forgiving.

FitzGerald's deep belief that his own happiness could never last long found expression in fear that the contentment Browne brought him would vanish. 'He has shot at rooks and rabbits and trained horses and dogs: and I – have looked at him: and well I may while I can, for his like is not to be seen.... his very perfection of nature somehow forebodes a short continuance: and as dramatists are said to prematurely kill such characters as they find it difficult to sustain, so it is that Nature cannot or will not carry on her finest creations through the five acts. Indeed, there is something anomal-ous and perhaps insupportable in the appearance of one perfect character in a world of imperfection and inconsistency.' [I, 225–6]

On the anniversaries of the day when he and Browne met, Fitz-Gerald used innocently to write of his own good fortune to his friends, probably to their embarrassment. Letters still survive from the tenth, twentieth and twenty-fifth anniversaries, in which every detail of Tenby is remembered, both the golden hours on the rocks overlooking the sea and the rainy day 'when one of those poor starved Players was drowned on the Sands, and was carried past our Windows after Dinner; I often remember the dull Trot of Men up the windy Street.' [II, 345] For twenty-five years FitzGerald recalled vividly his first sight of Browne in the boarding house, 'with a little *chalk* on the edge of his Cheek from a touch of the Billiard Table Cue'. [II, 296] Half a century after their meeting he was still repeating the 'stray verses applicable to one I loved':

> Heav'n would answer all your wishes,
> > Were it much as Earth is here;
> Flowing Rivers full of Fishes,
> > And good Hunting half the Year. [IV, 264–5]

As a piece of music or remembered scent may drown others in nostalgia, so the name of Tenby itself could summon up Browne for FitzGerald for the rest of his days, and after his friend's death he could never bear to return there.

CHAPTER IV

Mirehouse and Boulge Cottage

'When I shall be in town, I cannot say: nor do I know whither I shall go when I leave this place,' wrote FitzGerald from Geldestone. 'It seems an absurd thing that a man who has all the world before him doesn't know where to go: but this is really the case with me.' [I, 153] More than a desire to know where to spend the next few weeks drove him. Behind his awareness of being faintly ludicrous in his indecision lay a real fear that there were too many possibilities for him, all of them tempting, none of them compelling, and that he might consequently end only as a collection of fragments not a whole man. He dreaded having no fixed home, no definite purpose in living, not even the necessity to earn a livelihood, and the longer he was out of Cambridge the more pressing became his need for a central core to his life. Allen, who knew his problem but probably had little understanding of its causes, continued to hold out the promise of religion, which as usual seemed attractive to FitzGerald when all else was hopeless. 'I assure you, a slender pretence will make me throw myself upon Christianity,' he wrote to Allen. 'I have always told you that I knew a religion to be necessary for men.' [I, 121] But as always he was finally unable to embrace it.

For a time he continued to hope to be a poet, and in 1832 and thereafter his letters contained snatches of what he had been writing. Of the stanzas of one poem he said that 'there is a sort of reasoning in them, which requires proper order, as much as a proposition of Euclid.' [I, 127] The accompanying verses hardly bear out any claim of relentless logic, but his statement suggests that he at least recognized his own difficulties with organization.

That he was thinking seriously about poetry is also shown by his growingly shrewd remarks about his wide and somewhat unorganized reading, which are among the delights of his correspondence. When he re-read Shakespeare's sonnets, he found that he had 'had but half an idea of him, Demigod as he seemed before, till I read them carefully.... I have truly been lapped in these Sonnets for some time: they seem all stuck about my heart, like the ballads that used to be on the walls of London.' [I, 122] In 1833 he told Donne of having 'bought a little pamphlet which is very difficult to be got, called The Songs of Innocence, written and adorned with drawings by W. Blake (if you know his name) who was quite mad, but of a madness that was really the elements of great genius ill-sorted: in fact, a genius *with a screw loose*, as we used to say'. [I, 140] Of the opening of Tennyson's 'Dream of Fair Women' he wrote, 'This is in his best style: no fretful epithet, nor a word too much.' [I, 128]

FitzGerald read little criticism except that written by his friends, and his own literary judgements were remarkably uninfluenced by others. What he had to say was unconventional, often eccentric, but it was pithy. The obverse of this freshness in judging poems and novels was the tenacity with which he held to his judgements; once he had announced he did not like the works of a writer, he seemed thereafter to read them only for confirmation of his prejudices. He often felt more admiration than he allowed himself to express, but he wrote and spoke as if he thoroughly disliked the poetry of Wordsworth, both Brownings, Rossetti, Swinburne, and nearly all of Tennyson's later works.

Much as he loved music, it is unlikely that he ever believed he would become a serious composer, but in the doldrums of the 1830s he tried his hand at settings of several pieces of favourite poetry, with results sufficiently pleasing to encourage his dabbling in composition for the rest of his life. Some of his other diversions were as assorted as sprees of theatre-going with Spedding and learning to swim in the Waveney near Geldestone, defeating at last the fear of water induced by the bathing machine at Aldeburgh when he was a boy.

Constant movement, even greater than that required by his mother, was a way of preventing himself from thinking of the future. It kept his body in motion but only prolonged his mental turmoil. His temporary addresses were many: Geldestone, Wherstead, London, Naseby, Mrs Perry's Cambridge rooms, Castle

Irwell near Manchester ('a funny little castle, like a needle box', he wrote disparagingly to Allen in fear it sounded too grand), and Bedford, where he made his first visit two years after meeting William Browne at Tenby. 'I think I must go there as I have promised very deeply: and he has put off other engagements to serve me,' he told Allen. [I, 146]

When he first knew Bedford, he dismissed it as a dull county town, but it grew more beautiful in his eyes as it was associated with Browne, until at last he decided that even the River Ouse lingered 'in the pleasant fields of Bedfordshire, being in no hurry to enter the more barren fens of Lincolnshire'. [I, 230] A few years after his first visit, on another stay with the Brownes in Cauldwell House on the edge of the town, he already loved the 'garden on one side skirted by the public road, which again is skirted by a row of such Poplars as only the Ouse knows how to rear – and pleasantly they rustle now – and the room in which I write is quite cool and opens into a greenhouse which opens into said garden: and it's all deuced pleasant.' [I, 230] But it was affection not the beauty of nature that coloured the landscape for him.

The first four years after taking his degree he returned annually to Cambridge, usually staying at Mrs Perry's for a term or two. When he was there he could blot out the future and revert to the careless life of an undergraduate. Kemble, who had been away in Germany, returned to Cambridge and wrote early in 1832 that 'Ned FitzGerald and I have struck up a very great friendship and he turns out to be a very fine fellow.' On another of Fitz's stays there, Kemble said that 'James Spedding and E. FitzGerald have set up their tent among us this term, and are delightful additions to our set.'[1] Rather ominously FitzGerald spoke of his 'circle' as if intending to spend the rest of his life with his old friends recapturing the flavour of earlier days, and he joined a group to read Shakespeare: 'it is good so far as that men may meet together pleasantly once a week, under his noble name. We are also to have a dinner on his birthday.' [I, 135] Throwing off his future worries allowed him to revel innocently in the pleasures he loved: 'Last night I smoked for the first time,' he wrote to Allen of one visit, 'and came home merry, and played the Harmonious Blacksmith out of pure remembrance of you.' [I, 131] A few months later he was writing of the beauty of the chestnut trees on the Backs: 'I have been laughing out

of measure of late: by which learn that I am in good case.' [I, 136]
But each year fewer of his contemporaries came back to Cambridge, and after 1834 he returned only occasionally, as if aware of
something faintly unbecoming in trying to hold on to the habits of
youth.

As FitzGerald watched his old friends slipping into careers and
matrimony, he clung more tightly to those who seemed disinclined
to form relationships that would separate them from him.
Spedding, for example, with whom he had been so intimate at Bury
St Edmunds and again during Fitz's second year at Cambridge,
seemed to be having nearly as much trouble as FitzGerald in
finding his feet. His inclination was to a quiet scholarly career, pre-
ferably as Fellow of Trinity, although he had already failed twice to
win a fellowship. The religious doubts he shared with FitzGerald
prevented him from taking Holy Orders, and an art course in
London had left him with an ability at quick sketching and the
knowledge that he really had little serious artistic talent. As he tried
to think of an alternative career he stayed at home in Mirehouse, a
Cumberland estate on the banks of Lake Bassenthwaite where his
father, a Whig squire, farmed the land and raised cattle. It is clear
that there was friction between Spedding and his father over his
future, and it was partly the chance to ease the tension that made
Spedding invite FitzGerald for a stay of a few weeks in April 1835.

The second guest at Mirehouse was another Cambridge contemporary who was also at sea about his future: Alfred Tennyson. Not
that he was in any doubt about his intentions, for he had not
wavered since he was five in his determination to become a poet.
He had had a mild success with his 1830 *Poems, Chiefly Lyrical*
and the 1832 *Poems*, but so far there was little public awareness
that a great poet had arrived. In 1835 he was still living uneasily in
Somersby, in the Lincolnshire rectory his family continued to
occupy after the death of his father, the incumbent of the parish.
He was constantly short of money, and to finance the trip to Mirehouse he sold for £15 the gold Chancellor's Medal he had won at
Cambridge for his poem 'Timbuctoo'.

FitzGerald and Tennyson took to each other instantly on this
their first opportunity for close acquaintance, and they spent a
good bit of time alone together when Spedding was needed by his
father. The weather that spring was the worst that the Lake

V 'Alfred Tennyson, taken by James Spedding as A. T. sat in a
Cumberland shed waiting for the rain to cease, 183[5]'.

Country could provide, and only between squalls of freezing rain could they take the dogs for walks or climb the neighbouring fells. Much of the time the three young men spent in the big library at Mirehouse, where Tennyson sat reading with his feet on the fender, his cloak drawn up around his neck.

Naturally, their most constant subject of conversation was poetry, and Tennyson often read aloud in a deep-chested voice that Fitz compared to the 'sound of a far Sea, or of a Pine-wood'. He preferred his own reading to that of Fitz or Spedding, the latter of whom Tennyson insisted sounded 'as if Bees were about his mouth'. Although he read from the little red manuscript book that held the poems he was currently writing, and from Keats and Milton, Tennyson's favourite to read was Wordsworth, whom he referred to as that 'dear old fellow'.

Indeed, Wordsworth was an unseen presence at Mirehouse. He had been a schoolfellow of Mr Spedding, who is believed to have helped him financially on at least one occasion, and James Spedding had spent some time with him at Trinity, then renewed his acquaintance with the old poet after he had left Cambridge to come to live at Mirehouse. Tennyson deeply admired Wordsworth and thought of him as the greatest of living poets. Outside the hall door of the house a great sheet of daffodils spread down to the lake, several hundred yards away, a living reminder of the poet, who lived in Rydal Mount, some twenty miles to the south.

Since Cambridge FitzGerald had read a great deal more of Wordsworth's poetry than he had known when he carelessly dubbed him 'The Daddy', and he had come quietly to respect both man and works. 'I have been poring over Wordsworth lately,' he wrote at the end of 1832: 'which has had much effect in bettering my Blue Devils: for his philosophy does not abjure melancholy, but puts a pleasant countenance upon it, and connects it with humanity. It is very well, if the sensibility that makes us fearful of ourselves is diverted to become a cause of sympathy and interest with Nature and mankind: and this I think Wordsworth tends to do.' [I, 127] But at Mirehouse the almost undiluted admiration of the poet by Tennyson and Spedding stuck in FitzGerald's throat, and he returned to his old banter about him; it patently annoyed Tennyson, but as he often did when playfully excited, FitzGerald continued long after the fun was gone for the others. On one famous occasion he was speaking of the husband of his sister Jane and mentioned that he was 'a Mr Wilkinson, a clergyman'; it was probably Tennyson who said, 'Why, Fitz, that's a verse, and a very bad one, too,' but it was FitzGerald who decided that it was typical of Wordsworth's blank verse.

After a fortnight at Mirehouse Spedding and his guests left for Ambleside, where they moved into a comfortable inn for a week to scull on Lake Windermere and walk in the mountains. Just after they had settled in, Spedding was called back to Mirehouse, leaving Fitz and Tennyson alone. FitzGerald, who had been feeling odd man out because of his lack of interest in politics and because of his difference of opinion about Wordsworth, found it much easier to be alone with Tennyson, whose amusing 'little humours and grumpinesses' were only the externals of a mind that Fitz profoundly revered. Without Spedding, Tennyson was much more willing to talk nonsense and to tell Fitz unaffectedly about the poetry he was writing, including the 'Morte d'Arthur', which currently occupied him.

As always, FitzGerald responded impulsively to a gesture of friendliness from someone he admired, welcoming Tennyson as an intimate. At Ambleside, in a silent gesture of remorse for having annoyed him, he bought at the local bookseller's a copy of Wordsworth's recently published *Yarrow Revisited* and gave it to his new friend with an inscription recording his affection.

A short distance from their inn lived Wordsworth himself, and when Spedding came back to Ambleside, he tried to get Tennyson to go with him to meet the older poet. Tennyson wavered, then decided not to go. Two days later FitzGerald left the Lakes, and Tennyson went back to Mirehouse with Spedding. The trip and the beginning of his friendship with Tennyson were so engraved on FitzGerald's memory that he still thought of them in detail when he was well over seventy. 'W[ordsworth] was then at his home,' he wrote in 1881: 'but Tennyson would not go to visit him: and of course I did not: nor even saw him.' [IV, 414]

What FitzGerald did not know was that after his departure Spedding convinced Tennyson that he ought to visit Rydal, where their names were recorded in the visitors' book under May 1835. Tennyson, who had previously been hesitant, was apparently at last persuaded to go because FitzGerald would not be there and could not joke about Wordsworth after their call. Once they had gone to Rydal Tennyson and Spedding could not tell FitzGerald or any of his friends that they had done so, for fear he would be hurt if he realized that they had waited until he left the Lakes.[2]

The whole affair would hardly matter in an account of Fitz-Gerald's life if it did not indicate how easily his flippant manner could unintentionally alienate others, and how it could involve them in an inconvenient web of falsehood. As FitzGerald's letters indicate, he did not even believe the banter in which he had engaged at Wordsworth's expense, but the nuisance he caused was real enough.

'I will say no more of Tennyson than that the more I have seen of him, the more cause I have to think him great,' Fitz wrote when he had left Ambleside, happily unaware of the trouble he had been. 'I must however say, further, that I felt what Charles Lamb describes, a sense of depression at times from the overshadowing of a so much more lofty intellect than my own ... I could not be mistaken in the universality of his mind; and perhaps I have received some benefit in the now more distinct consciousness of my dwarfish-ness.' [I, 162–3]

It was the beginning of half a century of friendship, but they were not untroubled years, for FitzGerald could be an awkward friend, however loving. The sense of inferiority he said he felt in the Lake District often caused him to express himself assertively, and the more famous Tennyson became, the more FitzGerald seemed to feel that his own self-respect demanded that he tell the poet what he did not like about his works. It was not behaviour calculated to make relations easy with anyone; with the thin-skinned Tennyson it constantly threatened the end of their friendship. Had he been reproached for tactlessness, FitzGerald would surely have been genuinely surprised that his frankness was not recognized as the very mark of affection.

In 1835 there was still nothing but purest good-will on both sides. FitzGerald, who hated to be caught red-handed in an act of generosity, particularly one involving money, at last screwed up his courage to offer help to Tennyson, characteristically making light of the whole matter:

Dear Tennyson, though I am no Rothschild, my wants are fewer than my monies: and I have usually some ten or twelve pounds sitting very loosely in my breeches pocket – To what doth this tend? – Marry, to this – I have heard you sometimes say you are bound by the want of such a sum: and I vow to the Lord that I could not have a greater pleasure than transferring it to you on such occasions. I should not dare to say such a thing to a small man: but you are not a small man assuredly: and even if you do not make use of my offer, you will not be offended, but put it to the right account. It is very difficult to persuade people in this world that one can part with a Bank note without a pang – It is one of the most simple things I have ever done to talk thus to you, I believe: but here is an end: and be charitable to me – [3]

The offer of 'ten or twelve pounds' was of course not meant literally as an upper limit for Tennyson; rather, it was a deliberate understatement to spare him embarrassment, for what evidence remains suggests that the amounts involved were considerably more than that. In 1844 Carlyle repeated to FitzGerald Tennyson's remark that 'you were a man from whom one could take money', and long afterwards he told Charles Eliot Norton that 'for many years in Tennyson's poor days' FitzGerald gave him £300 out of an annual income of £800; the truth of the matter probably lies somewhere between Carlyle's habitual hyperbole and FitzGerald's usual understatement.

It is difficult to be specific about the income of either FitzGerald or Tennyson, since each of them tended to speak as if he had less money than in fact he had: FitzGerald out of embarrassed modesty, Tennyson out of a slightly selfish desire to foster the belief that he was a poor man. After his reconciliation with his mother in 1830 Fitz's undergraduate allowance of £300 must have been increased considerably, since we know that by 1848, when his father went bankrupt, he had capital of at least £10,000, which suggests that Carlyle's estimate of £800 p.a. was not far wrong.

In 1835, shortly after FitzGerald's offer to him, Tennyson inherited £6,000 from his grandfather's estate, so it is unlikely that he would have accepted more than trifling sums from Fitz at that period. But by 1840 he had begun investing his capital unwisely, and three years later he was virtually penniless. If FitzGerald did give him £300 annually, it was presumably between 1843 and

1845, in the latter of which Tennyson received £2,000 from an insurance policy on the life of the man who had swindled him out of his inheritance; 1845 was also the year when Tennyson was granted a Civil List pension of £200, so that even he could see that he was no longer in real need.[4]

Whatever the exact sums involved, it seems clear that FitzGerald helped Tennyson financially over a decade, with fairly large sums for perhaps two years. Three hundred pounds was the annual amount he eventually allowed his estranged wife after their separation, and though the claims of a wife would seem greater than those of a friend, FitzGerald undoubtedly felt far more affection for Tennyson than he did for the woman he married, so that it was not out of character for him to give them equal allowances.

For all his clinging to his bachelor friends, Fitz could not find much comfort about his own future in the undecided Spedding and the impoverished Tennyson. What was painfully apparent was that they, like himself, were alone and often lonely as well, for there was no one person who specifically needed them. Donne had been married since 1830 and Allen since 1834, and both seemed considerably happier than either of his companions at Mirehouse. Thackeray, who had inherited a comfortable competence, had already rid himself of a good portion of it and by 1835 was in Paris, busily disencumbering himself of the rest as he fell tumultuously in love with Isabella Shawe. Happiness appeared more probable if one were in love or, failing that, at least married, or part of a family.

The point was made even clearer two months after FitzGerald left Mirehouse, for he found himself improbably cheered by being part of the family that usually pleased him least: his own. When he returned to Wherstead he found the entire gathering there except his mother, who habitually avoided such occasions. Part of the reason for the convocation of relatives was that his brother John's wife was dying, in spite of which she remained cheerful and composed, as did 'all my brothers and sisters, with their wives, husbands, and children: sitting at different occupations, or wandering about the grounds and gardens, discoursing each their separate concerns, but all united into one whole.... it is like scenes of a play.' [I, 167–8]

Among the guests at Wherstead was the daughter of a neighbouring clergyman, Elizabeth Charlesworth, a friend of 'Lusia' and Isabella FitzGerald. She was twenty-three, Fitz's junior by three years, plain, 'healthy, and stout, and a good walker ... and can jump over stiles with the nimblest modesty that ever was seen'. [I, 179] She was also noticeably pious and wrote poetry that was no worse than that produced by others in the local artistic set, who tended to make Wherstead their centre. She particularly liked sitting in the library there listening to the FitzGerald sisters play the new music that Edward had brought from London or Cambridge. There is no hard evidence that Fitz paid her any attention until he began to feel some slight envy of his married friends.

In July 1835 Mr FitzGerald announced that they were leaving Wherstead and that the family was going to inhabit Boulge Hall at last, after waiting thirty-four years for the death of the previous tenant, Mrs Short, and the end of her life interest in the property. Boulge, according to Edward, had 'no great merit' and most of his brothers and sisters were married by then, so that its original purpose as family home scarcely applied. Certainly it was improbable that he would ever feel that his own spiritual home was there. Moving from a house he liked to one that he thought ugly and undistinguished also meant leaving behind the bookshops and music of Ipswich, the sense of being near the sea, and the friends made by the family in their ten years at Wherstead, including Elizabeth Charlesworth. As Donne and Allen wrote of their contentment as husbands and fathers and Thackeray sent news of his rhapsodic progress toward matrimony, Fitz felt that the time had come to make such a move himself. Much might be gained and little lost. 'He has some of the inconveniences of marriage even in his state of innocence,' was Donne's opinion, 'and among them I should reckon not the least that of accompanying Mrs. FitzGerald (his Mother) the round of the theatres.'[5]

It was not the first time that FitzGerald had mentioned the possibility of marriage. The previous year he had wondered whether he 'should marry, and have a small house and garden here in Suffolk; and so forth. I am sadly in want of a home in the Country, and have often thoughts of advertising for room in some family, where there was cheerful society.' [I, 156] The lack of a young woman to marry and the unimpassioned quality of his reflections indicate how little serious he had been.

In the letter announcing the impending move to Boulge

FitzGerald tried to whip up enthusiasm about marriage to Elizabeth Charlesworth to match Thackeray's passionate longing for Isabella Shawe, and succeeded only in sounding like a well-read young man who knew from novels what he should be feeling – and was not:

And now, my dear Boy, do you be very sensible, and tell me one thing – think of it in your bed, and over your cigar, and for a whole week, and then send me word directly – shall I marry? I vow to the Lord that I am upon the brink of saying 'Miss — do you think you could marry me?' to a plain, sensible, girl, without a farthing! There now you have it.... I have at last come to a conclusion in morals, which is this: that to certain persons of a doubting temper, and who search after much perfection, it is better to do a thing slap dash at once, and then conform them-selves to it. I have always been very unmanly in my strivings to get things all compact and in good train. But to the question again. An't I in a bad way? Do you not see that I am far gone? I should be as poor as a rat, and live in a windy tenement in these parts, giving tea to acquaintances. I should lose all my bachelor trips to London and Cambridge, I should no more, oh never more! – have the merry chance of rattling over to see thee, old Will, in Paris, or at Constantinople, at my will – I should be tied down – these are to be thought of: but then I get a settled home, a good companion, and the other usual pro's that desperate people talk of. Now write me word quickly: lest the deed be done! To be sure, there is one thing: I think it is extremely probable that the girl wouldn't have me: for her parents are very strict in religion, and look upon me as something of a Pagan. When I think of it, I know what your decision will be – NO! How you would hate to stay with me and my spouse, dining off a mutton chop, and a draught of sour, thin, beer, in a clay-cold country. You would despair – you would forsake me. If I know anything of myself, no wife would ever turn me against you: besides, I think no person that I should like would be apt to dislike you: for I must have a woman of some humour lurking about her somewhere: humour half hidden under modesty. But enough of these things.... [I, 172–3]

Thackeray's reply has disappeared, but since he understood his friend so well, he almost certainly accepted FitzGerald's covert invitation to discourage him from marriage. Encouragement, even a strong push, was what Fitz required if ever he were to propose. He had told Allen about Elizabeth Charlesworth for a long time before he hesitantly asked his advice on marriage, in February 1836, some seven months after he had first broached the matter to Thackeray, seven months in which his emotions had become no more ardent, however much he might ginger up his expression of them:

> I have just returned from a dance round my room to the tune of Sir Roger de Coverley.... Now you must know that there has been staying here for a fortnight the young damsel I have often told you about: and I like her more than ever. She has shewn sense and clearsightedness in some matters that have made me wonder: judging by the rest of the world. Yet have I not committed myself – no, my Johnny, I am still a true Bachelor. What do you think of me? You would like this woman very much, I am sure. She is very pious, but very rational.... Item, eats very little meat – humph! – drinks no wine – understands good house-keeping – understands children (ill-omened consolation!) – ay, there's the rub. Should I dance round my room to the tune of Sir Roger de Coverley if I were married, and had seven children? Answer me that. [I, 178–9]

The letter is closed by 'your very affectionate Bachelor'.

FitzGerald's friends were no more convinced than he was that he ought to marry. A full eight months after he had written to Allen, he revived the subject with Donne, but any pretence at urgency had long since disappeared: 'I am ashamed of living in such Epicurean ease: and really think I ought to marry, or open a book at a Banker's, that I may not be more happy than my fellows. Seriously, I do not mean to speak disrespectfully of marriage, etc., but I only mean that it must bring some cares, and anxieties.' [I, 184] Donne could hardly take such a remark seriously, and he laconically recorded: 'I advise him however to let well alone.'[6]

Even the younger generation at Geldestone, in whom he usually delighted, became 'a room full of chattering Children' when he considered the melancholy prospect of paternity. [I, 186] In the summer of 1837 he settled into his own house, and after that no more was heard of marriage with Miss Charlesworth except a rather chilling prank he mentioned to Thackeray a few months later, which calls into question his sincerity in everything he had said before of her and of matrimony: 'I have just written to … Browne a long and circumstantial account of my proposing to a young Lady: I think he must be taken in: and I look forward with pleasure to the letter of congratulation that he will write.' [I, 209] His conduct on this occasion anticipates in part the perplexing mixture of compassion and apparent callousness that he displayed a dozen years later upon actually becoming engaged. Probably Elizabeth Charlesworth never knew that he considered proposing to her, but FitzGerald's ineptness with women may have made her attach more significance to his good manners than he intended, much as Lucy Barton was to do. Certainly, his letters betray no hint of understanding either what Miss Charlesworth might feel or, even more puzzlingly, how his seemingly insensitive joke would strike Browne or Thackeray.

FitzGerald's attitude to the marriages of his friends was probably predictable. At first his innate distrust of women would make him fear that old friendships were necessarily cut off by the new relationship; 'Come, I don't believe that your marriage shall make any great difference in you, after all,' he told Allen to conceal his trepidation. [I, 149] Before Allen's marriage in 1834 FitzGerald wrote to him as 'Dear my Johnny'; then, during the period when he was not sure whether the wedding had taken place, he addressed 'My dear Allen'; two months later he called him 'Dear Allen'. Until he was certain how a new wife might feel about him, he would sometimes inappropriately invite her husband to come to stay with him alone, but once he was sure he was accepted, he could relax into the status of family intimate, fond of both husband and wife.

He was not always successful with his friends' wives. Isabella Thackeray, for instance, although she was grateful to him, worried that he wasted her husband's time; but she was of course mentally unstable, so perhaps her reaction was not typical. When the Thackerays were married in 1836 Fitz sent them a handsome gift of money, which prompted Thackeray to reply that he was 'so used to these kinds of obligations, that I don't say a word more.... I intend with your money to buy chairs and tables, to decorate this chamber.' Three years later his wife wrote that she was 'half cross with Fitz and his tail.... They seem as if they could not breathe without William, and thats all very well but they forget they have 300 or 400 a year to take life easy upon, and though we may have *double* that yet it must be earned. I must say that I believe Fitz would give W. his last shillg and often thinks of what he can do that is obliging to me. I believe he has as much to suffer in other respects as any one. One sister mad and the second that he dearly loves dying of a complaint of the lungs. Then he has to grieve over the selfishness and utter heartlessness of his Mother, who does not seem to care if her children live or die[.] I wish I was rich sometimes but if with riches comes such a love of the world as to make one forgetful of the ties of nature may I ever remain as I am.'[7]

Presumably Mrs FitzGerald's lack of concern for Lusia and Isabella prompted Isabella Thackeray's remarks. 'A man must in one way or another be married in this world,' wrote Donne of Fitz, 'and *he* is married to two sisters, who make him their gentleman usher 'usque ad aras', but there he leaves them, for he puts them into their pew, bows to the clergyman, and marches out.'[8] When the family moved from Wherstead, Edward went with them to care for his sisters, once more taking over duties that properly belonged to his parents.

FitzGerald never learned to like it, but Boulge was a handsome and spacious Queen Anne house with extensive gardens and a dignified old park full of mature oaks. 'Doesn't this name express heavy clay?' [I, 267] he asked in exasperation at the house, and another time he complained to Frederick Tennyson that 'Day follows day with unvaried movement: there is the same level meadow with geese upon it always lying before my eyes: the same pollard oaks: with now and then the butcher or the washerwoman trundling by in their carts. As you have lived in Lincolnshire I will not further describe Suffolk.' [I, 272] But his reactions to places were more often occasioned by his emotions at the time than by objective observations.

Even in the midst of his disgust with Boulge he could not deny his deep affection for the countryside. 'I love the country more than London,' he wrote to Allen, 'and I often think that when you have got a living somewhere ... out of London, I should feel strange there ever after. I do not suppose that I shall henceforward make many new acquaintances in town, as I am not in the way to do so; but try and wrap myself round with the domestic affections of brothers and sisters and nephews and nieces, and live a quiet life in the country. I am looking out for a horse.' [I, 189–90]

By February 1837 he had found a solution to the problem of how to keep an eye on his sisters without having to share a house with the rest of his family when they came to Boulge. A lady companion was brought to live with his sisters, and he took over what he called 'a small Cottage of my Father's close to the Lawn gates, where I shall fit up a room most probably. The garden I have already begun to work in.' [I, 192] His new quarters had originally been built by the long-lived Mrs Short, who was unable to live amicably with her husband and had erected the one-storey cottage with 'mouse-coloured' thatch to which she retired when they were quarrelling. After Colonel Short's death she moved back into the Hall and let the cottage for short periods. The various tenancies had reduced an already badly built little house to a state of damp disrepair. FitzGerald patched up the worst parts only, since he intended to stay but briefly. Initially he remained in the cottage from early spring until driven out by cold weather, using it, he said, as a place 'where I have my books, a barrel of beer which I tap myself ... and an old woman to do for me'. [I, 255] Once he was installed, his mother demanded less of him as escort in London and Brighton. For a few years he managed the farms at Boulge in place of his father and became improbably interested in 'books about compost' and in the supervision of hedging and ditching.

As he became fonder of living by himself, he improved the cottage minimally for year-round occupancy, fitting up the two front rooms for his own use and the rest for his housekeeper, Mrs Faiers, and her husband, who worked on the estate. But it never became really comfortable, and even after improving it, he described his home as 'a hut with walls as thin as a sixpence: windows that don't shut: a clay soil safe beneath my feet: a thatch perforated by lascivious sparrows over my head'. [I, 423] The summer refuge he took over in 1837 became his only home for more than fifteen years, until his brother John and his family moved into the Hall after Mr FitzGerald's death. Of all the family houses in which he had camped out for nearly thirty years, this was the first with which he felt personally identified. Had he been owner, not tenant, he would have spent the rest of his life there.

To the right of the front door was FitzGerald's study, and across

VI Boulge Cottage, watercolour by E. J. Moor.

the corridor his bedroom, both papered in a 'still green' chosen as an unobtrusive background to his paintings; little of it can have been visible in the study, however, for most of the walls were covered with shelves holding FitzGerald's books (bought for their contents not their bindings or even their rarity, so that his collection was a constant disappointment to bookish friends). Stacked around both rooms were more paintings for which there was no hanging space. A bust of Shakespeare stood in a study recess, and in one corner was a small square piano on which he would resolve his feelings at any hour of the day by pounding out one of Handel's great choruses. Since he kept few clothes and was un-interested in caring for them after he had bought them from expensive tailors, he had no wardrobe; both rooms were littered with boots and hats, as well as music, walking sticks, scarves, and the books he was reading. All of them could be brusquely shoved aside when he threw himself prone on the floor in order to cut up a painting he had just bought, to make it fit a frame he already owned, or when he decided to repaint a section of one that seemed to him lacking in interest.

Another occupant might have felt that the park of Boulge and its gardens were enough, but FitzGerald immediately began surrounding his house with traditional cottage flowers, chosen primarily for brilliant colours. He particularly delighted in spring blossom: anemones, wallflowers, irises, poppies, and the scarlet of early geraniums. The borders of his little garden served to distinguish the limits of his own domain from that of the rest of the family.

Mrs Faiers's culinary abilities were not taxed by FitzGerald's usual menu of bread and fruit with tea, and he seldom asked more of her, as much because he hated bothering servants as because his tastes were so unimaginative. 'And now I am going to get some potatoes and what else my old woman can give me' [I, 663] was a typical response to her talents. However, when he began having guests in the cottage to whom he wanted to give more usual fare, the household was apt to fall apart. Once, when expecting neighbours for dinner, he had to write asking them to bring oysters and cheese with them from Woodbridge: 'I have a fowl hanging up; and if my Father's cook arrive, as I think she will, tonight, she shall handsel her skill on my fowl. For I doubt Mrs. Faier's powers of Bread-sauce – I doubt she would produce a sort of dumpling.' [I, 515] But his 'old woman' loved it when FitzGerald entertained, and she was quite unaware of any failure as a cook. Years after he had left Boulge Cottage she came to see FitzGerald and sat asking about the 'Gentlemen whom she used to see at my Cottage. I find that one of her Glories is that, *once*, she and I entertained six Divines one Evening at that same Cottage (she is not certain if not *seven*).' [II, 469]

In this, his first attempt to make his own world, FitzGerald was patently drawing on his memories of Cambridge and his lodgings with Mrs Perry, recreating the ease with which he could reach out for a book or a sheet of music, putting up with inadequate service in order to save his 'old woman' from having to exert herself. What was unlike Cambridge, however, and what made Boulge only a pale imitation, was that he lacked a circle of like-minded friends, and so he set about the patient assembly of such a group. It was not the solution to loneliness that every man would have sought, but it suited him well.

100

Boulge itself was a hamlet of eight houses and some twenty inhabitants besides those at the Hall. When FitzGerald first went there, it was comparatively isolated, reached by fly from Woodbridge a mile or two away, where the coach from London put down visitors. After the railway reached Ipswich in 1846 it was much more accessible. In telling one guest 'the means to get to Ipswich', FitzGerald outlined the choices: 'A steamboat will bring you for five shillings (a very pretty sail) from the Custom House to Ipswich, the Orwell steamer; going twice a week, and heard of directly in the fishy latitudes of London Bridge. Or, a railroad brings you for the same sum: if you will travel third class, which I sometimes do in fine weather. I should recommend *that*; the time being so short, so certain: and no eating and drinking by the way, as must be in a steamer. At Ipswich, I pick you up with the washerwoman's pony and take you to Woodbridge.' [I, 562]

One of his earliest friends at Boulge was the Reverend George Crabbe, son of the East Anglian poet and vicar of Bredfield, who had come to his parish the year before the FitzGeralds arrived at Boulge. In spite of his admirable biography of his father, Crabbe was no lover of poetry, a topic about which he and Fitz often argued. There was more than a touch of Parson Adams about both his appearance and his temperament. A great Wellingtonian nose, clothes as careless and soiled as FitzGerald's own, and a big muscular body that became terrifyingly uncontrolled when he lost his temper gave him a frightening demeanour. At heart he was as tender and compassionate, even sentimental, as he was fierce of bearing, and his wrath was usually reserved for cruelty or lack of consideration, although his inability to see that another might reasonably differ from him on matters of theology or morals often made him find transgression where there was none. He was so improvident with his limited finances that his daughters had to empty his pockets before he left the house, to keep him from giving every penny to the poor, and he was so preoccupied with the salvation of his flock that it did not occur to him that he was unusual in praying aloud for them by name, 'including Mary Ann Cuthbert', whose sexual morals were in need of special Providence. In his wrath over the ravage of the countryside he once said of a landowner who had felled some oaks that he had 'scandalously misused the globe'.

101

In the quarter-century of their friendship, FitzGerald used to walk a mile across the fields to Bredfield so often that it became in spirit an extension of Boulge Cottage for him. Usually he would arrive after the Crabbes' evening meal, sing glees with the family, then retire to the vicar's study, which Fitz named the 'Cobblery', to smoke and argue the hours away until so late that frequently he spent the night rather than follow the dark path back to Boulge.

Friends, who easily recognized how deep their affection was, would sometimes have to intervene to make peace between the two men. FitzGerald was often untypically apologetic when he wanted to avert Crabbe's anger, although he could usually regard it with equanimity and even laugh at it. Once, when Crabbe had attacked him 'most furiously on the old score of *Pride*, on which the man is distracted', FitzGerald noted with slightly tight-lipped amusement that 'I am dropped out of his Category of Heroes for ever! he shall always be right glad to see me, he says: but he never can be disappointed in me again! How much the best footing is this to be upon with all one's friends.' [I, 541] Another time, after a long explanation of why Crabbe should not take disagreement on theology as a personal attack, Fitz concluded the account of his own blamelessness: 'I hope, therefore, to have a civil letter from you, and a reception of no common elegance when I ring at the door of Bredfield parsonage again.' [I, 654]

In spite of his protestations FitzGerald himself was not always easy to get along with. Crabbe's son, who succeeded his father in Fitz's affections, remembered his first impression of him as 'proud and very punctilious ... always like a grave middle-aged man: never seemed very happy or light-hearted, though his conversation was most amusing sometimes'. [I, 414–15] One of Crabbe's daughters found him 'a man one stood in awe of with all one's liking for him', and she remembered that if the children were sent into the garden to tell him that luncheon was ready, 'he was sure not to come if called, though he wd. come, if not called', and if the family had 'provided vegetables *specially* for him, his favourite food he wd. then eat meat'.[9] Whatever the differences between Crabbe and FitzGerald, however, there was never any real question of their sincere affection and shared respect.

It is probably because their voluminous correspondence has not survived that Thomas Churchyard seems far less intimate with

VII FitzGerald as young man, watercolour by Thackeray.

FitzGerald than Crabbe was, although at one time they were clearly very close. Like most of FitzGerald's literary and artistic circle around Woodbridge, Churchyard was some years his senior: eleven years in his case, twenty-four in Crabbe's. He was a lawyer who had fallen out of love with the law and flagrantly gave so much time to an illicit union with painting that he nearly forgot his first vocation. The story is told that one client had been cooling his heels in Churchyard's waiting room for a long time while the solicitor hid himself behind a closed door to finish a picture. At last the client sent a clerk to enquire whether he was going to see Churchyard or whether he ought to consult another solicitor, to which the answer was returned: 'Mr. Churchyard says to go to Hell – you'll find lots of attorneys there.' [I, 29]

Improbably, Churchyard developed into a prolific painter of considerable talent, although he had not taken seriously to art until mature years. His Suffolk landscapes are now recognized as charming examples of the East Anglian school of painting, in which he counted himself the disciple of 'Old' Crome. His portraits are less successful, but to them and to his watercolours we owe a good bit of our knowledge of what Woodbridge and its inhabitants looked like in the middle of the last century. His pictures are now sought after, but while he was alive, they were either given to friends or sold for a few shillings, which put considerable strain on his slender earnings from the law, since he had a large family to support; at his death his unmarried daughters would have been left in penury if FitzGerald had not helped them financially.

Churchyard and FitzGerald constantly talked about painting, and Churchyard advised the younger man about some of his purchases of pictures, not always to his advantage. They bought for each other and occasionally traded what they already owned. It was the prospect of talking them over with Churchyard on his return to Boulge that often animated FitzGerald in his search for pictures when he was in London. Besides his love of painting, Churchyard had a great interest in poetry, and he became an important member of FitzGerald's little group of Woodbridge friends.*

---

*Probably Churchyard painted FitzGerald's portrait at least once, but it is not certain that any example has survived. The painting that changed hands at Sotheby's on 6 July 1983, lot 245, as the record of such a sitting does indeed

The third of the Suffolk cronies whom Fitz saw a great deal of in the 1840s was Bernard Barton, 'the Quaker Poet', so called not only for his religious persuasion but also, according to his friends, because there were no other Quakers who could be counted as poets. Like Churchyard he loved the art he pursued as an amateur far more than he did his more conventional vocation, which was the humble one of clerk in Alexander's bank in Woodbridge. Unlike Churchyard, however, he had small talent for the muse he pursued so vigorously, but he never realized that sad truth, for he often considered giving up his job in order to write poetry full-time, although Byron, Lamb, and Southey (with all of whom he corresponded) were at one in discouraging him from doing so.

Opinions of Barton's poetry range from the scathing to the fore-bearing, but perhaps the most succinct is that of A. C. Benson, who said that it was 'only remarkable for its firm grasp of the obvious'.[10] It was often written at a jog-trot, and even Barton recognized ruefully how slipshod he was: 'I am just such a Poet as my Neighbour Tom Churchyard is an artist – he will dash you off slight & careless sketches by the dozen, or score, but for touching, re-touching or finishing – that is quite another affair – and has to wait – if it ever be done at all.'[11] After Barton's death FitzGerald had no hesitation about altering his poetry drastically before publishing it for the benefit of Barton's daughter. In a newspaper notice of his death FitzGerald said of the nine volumes that had survived Barton, 'Thousands have read his books with innocent pleasure: none will ever take them up and be worse for doing so.'[12]

Barton's family had once been well-to-do but came down in the world. Before his move to the Woodbridge bank in 1806, he had been a private tutor in a Liverpool family and an unsuccessful busi-nessman. It was said that he was unable to balance his own accounts, but apparently that was not held a disqualification for working in a bank. The descent of his fortunes had done nothing to spoil his sweetness, cultivation, good humour, and charm, but there is some evidence that it was a sore disappointment to his only child, Lucy, at whose birth his wife had died.

Although he remained a faithful Quaker, Barton was far from

---

resemble Churchyard's work, but the subject seems so old (many years older than FitzGerald looked in photographs taken eight years after Churchyard's death) that it is difficult to be sure of the identification. (See plate XII, p 236.)

representing the gloomier reaches of his persuasion, and other Woodbridge Quakers were said to distrust him because he had 'Mr' on his brass doorplate, wore embroidered waistcoats, bought pictures, wrote poetry, and was the most genial of hosts, serving liberal gin and water to his frequent guests. Only at FitzGerald's constant pipes and cigars did he draw the line, insisting that tobacco smelled remarkably like guano. The Bartons lived in the centre of Woodbridge, and when Fitz was spending a long evening in the town, he often stayed overnight with them.

Barton's daughter Lucy, who was a year or two FitzGerald's senior, had acted as her father's devoted housekeeper and jealous guardian since her teens. On one occasion she was so incensed at a bad review of his works that she was with difficulty dissuaded from going directly to London to box the ears of the critic. Barton's salary was not enough to maintain them in the style she felt their ancestry deserved, but she was so efficient at cutting financial corners that they seldom seemed short of money. Most of her friends were far wealthier than she, among them FitzGerald's sister Isabella, who used to invite her to Wherstead and Boulge. Her conversion to Anglicanism when she was a young girl may have been motivated in part by the hope of rising a rung on the social ladder, but if so she was none the less devout in her new religion and energetic in spreading it by writing Bible stories for children and teaching Bible classes, where she was known as a stern disciplinarian.

Nature had not compensated for her lack of money with physical beauty. She was tall, raw-boned, so heavy-featured as to look somewhat masculine, and she walked with a determined stride that made local children shout 'Step-a-yard!' at her on the street. Her voice was deep, with a drawl that sounded affected.

The admirable aspect of Lucy Barton was that the disadvantages that would have made most young women bitter had left her open and singularly good-natured, although letters from Charles Lamb to her father suggest that she had some kind of breakdown in 1829.[13] In 1835, when the FitzGeralds went to Boulge, she was in her late twenties, settled into energetic spinsterhood with neither rancour nor expectations. FitzGerald was punctilious about paying his respects to her, and the first surviving letter he wrote to her father concludes politely 'with kind remembrances to Miss

Barton'. It was scarcely surprising if she felt a special interest in the well-to-do bachelor, now that he was the companion of her own father and often in their house.

The last habitual member of FitzGerald's circle at Boulge was Francis Capper Brooke of Ufford Place, a wealthy landowner whose real love was for his library, said to be one of the finest private collections in England. Brooke was the only one of Fitz-Gerald's neighbourhood friends who came from his own social class, since by now Fitz studiously avoided the kind of acquaintance his parents made. In the country he was not expected to escort his mother, as he was in town, and he peremptorily turned down social invitations from the local gentry, saying that of all abominations a formal dinner party was the worst.

Brooke did not share Fitz's disdain of social distinctions, and he is said to have ignored Barton's broad hints about how much he would like to visit the library at Ufford, since neither bank clerks nor Quakers, however bookish, were normally among his guests. Brooke frequently invited FitzGerald, however, and gave him the run of his library, even though he was slightly put out by his guest's negligent clothes and occasional absentmindedness. Fitz liked to tease Brooke, who was something of a dandy and repaired time's ravages to his face with the help of cosmetics. Once FitzGerald said, 'Brooke! You should be ashamed of yourself!' 'Why?' asked Brooke. '*Because*, you falsify your years! You've no business to look so young.' The friend who liked to tell the story added, 'Poor Man, he did look young, but his youth was used to *come off terribly* – on his *hat lining*, & pocket handkerchief when hot!'[14]

When Brooke was well over seventy he was still disingenuous about his age, and FitzGerald wrote that 'Brooke is, as you say, so wonderful an Elder, that he *may* have fought at Waterloo when six years old.' [IV, 266] Brooke occasionally joined Crabbe, Churchyard, and Barton at Boulge Cottage, but there is no record of his entertaining the group at Ufford.

FitzGerald's little circle at Boulge was almost like a rebirth on a small scale of a Cambridge undergraduate society, but he was in no danger of confusing the two. He called it 'the faded tapestry of country town life: London jokes worn threadbare; third rate accomplishments infinitely prized; scandal removed from Dukes and Duchesses to the Parson, the Banker, the Commissioner of Excise, and the Attorney'. [I, 562]

In 1843 he wrote that 'On Saturday I give supper to B. Barton and Churchyard.... We are the chief Wits of Woodbridge. And one man has said that he envies our conversations! So we flatter each other in the country.' [I, 412] It would seem impossible to miss the echo of longing for wider society that lies behind his joking but disparaging words, but most writers on FitzGerald have apparently been taken in by the phrase 'Wits of Woodbridge', perhaps even by the capital letter, and have treated the group as if it were a formal society, not a casual, fluid group of friends who met to stave off the intellectual boredom of country life and to poke gentle fun at any pretensions about the level of their conversation. It is true, however, that a few locals of Woodbridge also missed the joking and believed that FitzGerald and his friends thought of themselves as intellectually exclusive, which occasioned some slight resentment.

Barton was sufficiently amused and pleased by the group to speak in mock grandiloquence of each of their suppers as a 'symposium'. His account of one of them is probably a fair indication of the intellectual heights of such occasions:

Tom Churchyard drove me over last night to a Symposium given by Edw FitzGerald to us two, and old Crabbe – lots of palaver, smoking, and laughing – my head swims yet with the fumes, and odours of the baccy and my sides are sore with laughing – Edward was in one of his drollest cues [sic] and did the honors of his cottage with such gravity of humor that we roar'd again. It was the oddest melange! [Tea] Porter, Ale, Wine, Brandy Cigars – Cold Lamb, [Sallad], Cucumber – Bread & cheese – no precise line of demarcation between tea – and Supper – It was one continuous *spread* something coming on fresh every ten minutes – till we wonder'd whence they came, and where they could be put. Gentlemen! the resources of this cottage are [exhaustless] – shouted our Host – Mrs Faiers! the [Sallad] there! the Cucumber here – Oil at that corner Vinegar & Pepper yonder – there put the jug of Cream & that glass of butter in the middle – push those wine & brandy bottles close together – Certes it was rare fun – We kept not up our Orgies to a late hour, tho', as our

Clerical friend had his duty for to-day to think of – We were all at home I guess about ten....[15]

It was from evenings like this at Boulge that the popular Fitz-Gerald legend dates, of the whimsical and usually amiable countryman with peculiar clothes and even stranger manners, hospital to a fault with his cronies but generally unsocial, regardless of convention and rank but quite capable of snubbing anyone who seemed to him to be pushing: certainly not a bumpkin but not fitting easily into the pattern of a gentleman either. Much of the tradition is true, but subsequent generations have emphasized the lovable eccentricity without bothering with what lay behind it: either the paralysing loneliness or the long hours of quiet literary labour that helped keep his life on an even keel.

CHAPTER V

Browne's Marriage

Even having Boulge Cottage was not enough to curb FitzGerald's wandering, and when he set out on one of his aimless trips, news of him came from all over England; suddenly in 1837 there was a fixed centre to his roaming, but it was emotional not geographical. 'He is leading his usual philosophic life in London,' wrote Donne in May of that year, 'ie taking every thing easily and making the most of whatever comes in his way, which if not philosophy is something quite as good.' In London he had for the first time a companion wherever he went. 'Some time since not being an angler himself, and not particularly affecting the company of rivers and standing pools, he nevertheless struck up an acquaintance with one who occupied himself by such waters: and this amphibious friend proves, from his account, to be one of the most agreeable acquaintances possible. He has had him in London, introducing him probably to the Paddington canal & Serpentine, and pointing him out to the humane society as a person that should be looked after.'[1]

FitzGerald and William Browne had kept in touch in the intervening years since their stay together in Tenby in the summer of 1833, and FitzGerald had stayed at least once in Bedfordshire with the Browne family. Everything he learned about Browne made him more fond of him. The wholehearted joy of FitzGerald's affections when they fastened on one person made it impossible for him not to tell everyone he knew about the friend. His letters are full of Browne, extolling his unspoiled simplicity, his intelligence that had been untainted by a university education, and his singular abilities at hunting, shooting and fishing. Not qualities, of course, that Fitz-Gerald was in the habit of praising, and some of his friends like Donne were gently — possibly knowingly — amused at his boyish enthusiasm.

110

VIII William Browne as young man.

FitzGerald liked to introduce Browne to those he loved, but he kept him from his family, in particular his mother, who would probably have been more puzzled by Browne's background than by his being only twenty-one. Browne was not a success with all Fitz's friends either. Frederick Tennyson 'despised' him, and Thackeray, although he did not spell out the reasons, plainly did not like him, referring to him as 'Little Browne' until FitzGerald protested. 'You don't know what a good boy he is,' he complained. 'I suppose there are more such than I am aware of: I fancy that the better virtues and characteristics of Englishmen have slipped away from the aristocracy, and settled among the trading classes apart from London, who are yet unspoiled.' [I, 209] From remaining evidence it is difficult to be sure who saw Browne more clearly, Thackeray or FitzGerald. Fitz was certainly not unbiased. 'Truth is the ticket,' he once wrote of portraiture, 'but those who like strongly, in this as in other cases, love to be a little blind.... One fancies that no face can be too delicate and handsome to be the depository of a noble spirit.' [I, 570–1] As in portraits, so in friendship.

On at least one occasion FitzGerald took a rather harder look at Browne than usual and characterized him in what appears to be a balanced fashion: 'Has very good abilities; a smooth-mannered person; more surface than depth; quite a man of the world; fond of argument, but not ill-tempered; careful, thoughtful for others, and a good contriver; gentlemanly; would not do a mean thing.'[2] Much what Browne seems to be in accounts by others than FitzGerald.

In the early summer of 1838 FitzGerald went again to stay with the Brownes. 'I am much in love with Bedfordshire,' he told Barton, as usual confusing topography and persons. [I, 213] He stayed briefly, then returned to London, where he went the rounds of the picture galleries, knowing all the while that what he really wanted to see were the 'pretty villages and vales' of the Ouse. After three weeks he left London and went back to Bedfordshire and Browne for July and August.

FitzGerald's description of one of his holidays, that in 1840, is typical of half a dozen years. 'We have been staying at an Inn by the side of the river Ouse: he fishes, etc. I do nothing as usual.' In truth he spent most of his time sitting quietly by Browne, 'best of good fellows, and absolutely wanting in nothing that may become a man', either reading or making accomplished amateur water-colour sketches. After a year or two, FitzGerald kept his own horse in Bedford, so that he and Browne could ride together, although his letters scarcely mention his being mounted elsewhere, except at Geldestone. Occasionally he would even take a gun with his friend. 'A little riding, driving, eating, drinking, etc. (not forgetting smoke) fill up the day.' [I, 258] The major artistic tastes that Fitz-Gerald and Browne shared were for painting and architecture. From Bedford they made excursions to Boughton, the Duke of Buccleuch's house, to see his Raphaels, and to Woburn Abbey for the Duke of Bedford's great collection of Canalettos; at both places they loved the pictures and found the houses too grand for their taste.

It is hard for modern readers to understand, but FitzGerald probably never directly faced the emotions that the younger man stirred in him. As he told Allen, he would try without success to concentrate on other pursuits, such as the pages of Pindar: 'But while I have Browne at my side I do not read much: he being very much better than any books in my opinion.' His letters to Allen never overtly mention the depth of his feelings for Browne, but they often reveal his lack of ease about the friendship. The mention of having Browne at his side sends him in the next sentence into a pleasurable but disturbing vision of the future; all his concern, however, is expressed for an idleness that was typical of those long days beside the Ouse: 'I have some new plans and anticipations floating in my head about all of which I should very much like to talk with you. I wish you would tell me if you think I do wrong in leading such an idle self-seeking life. Sometimes I am frightened at finding myself in such a state. I wish you would say something about this.' [I, 216] It is almost impossible to miss the plea for approval of a life that he found both delightful and profoundly unsettling, and the plea is directed to the friend whose moral rectitude he most respected.

Surely more than sloth lay behind his worry, which was so often brought out by being with Browne: 'in half an hour I shall seek my Piscator, and we shall go to a Village two miles off and fish, and have tea in a pot-house, and so walk home. For all which idle ease I think I must be damned. I begin to have dreadful suspicions that this fruitless way of life is not looked upon with satisfaction by the open eyes above. One really ought to dip for a little misery: perhaps however all this ease is only intended to turn sour by and bye, and so to poison one by the very nature of self-indulgence. Perhaps again as idleness is so very great a trial of virtue, the idle man who keeps himself tolerably chaste, etc., may deserve the highest reward; the more idle, the more deserving.' [I, 230] It is hard not to believe that the key to his unconscious lies in the single word 'chaste', which seems so out of place here and probably points to other unacknowledged feelings.

When at last he left Bedfordshire, it was to join his sisters dutifully in Lowestoft, but he could not bear doing so alone:

> I have been spending a very pleasant time; but the worst of it is that the happier I am with Browne the sorrier I am to leave him. To put off this most evil day I have brought him out of Bedfordshire here: and here we are together in a pleasant lodging looking out upon the sea, teaching a great black dog to fetch and carry, playing with our neighbour's children, doing the first five propositions of Euclid (which *I* am teaching him!), shooting gulls on the shore, going out in boats, etc. All this must have an end: and as usual my pleasure in his stay is proportionably darkened by the anticipation of his going, and go he must in a very few days. Well, Carlyle told us that we are not to expect to be so happy. [I, 215]

Together FitzGerald and Browne drove 'about in a gig as happy as needs be', visiting old Suffolk manor houses. Of Helmingham, the moated Tudor hall of the Tollemaches, Fitz said that such 'an old Squire's gable-ended house is much more English and aristocratic to my mind' than the grandeurs of either Boughton or Woburn. [I, 216] Before he went home, Browne gave the black retriever they had been training to Fitz, who named him Bletsoe in memory of the prettiest of the Bedfordshire villages in which they had fished that summer, and of its inn, 'the cleanest, the sweetest, the civillest, the quietest, the liveliest, and the cheapest that ever was built or conducted'. [I, 257] Not, to tell the truth, that he needed the dog to remind him.

For a number of years they tried to spend at least two holidays together, one of which was often taken in London. 'I have been more idle than usual for the last fortnight, having had my Venator, W. Browne, with me,' Fitz wrote typically in the spring of 1839. Often the fear of Browne's death overwhelmed him, and he worried neurotically about his health. When he looked at him it seemed that Browne's like was not to be seen, but 'Perhaps also he will not be long to be looked at; for there are signs of decay about him.' [I, 225] When Browne actually did die young, FitzGerald was too sensible to believe that in the past he had foreseen the event, but his sorrow was deepened by having for so long been silently conscious of Browne's mortality.

After a period with Browne it was difficult for him to adjust to living alone again, and separation seemed like an anticipation of death. In the summer of 1839 he wrote when he returned to Boulge, of having been 'lounging in the country, lying on the banks of the Ouse, smoking, eating copious teas (prefaced with beer) in the country pot-houses, and have come mourning here: finding an empty house when I expected a full one, and no river Ouse, and no jolly boy to whistle the time away with. Such are the little disasters and miseries under which I labour: quite enough, however, to make one wish to kill oneself at times.' [I, 231]

He did not, of course, commit suicide, and within a month or two he was off to Ireland to stay with his uncle Peter Purcell, taking Browne with him for what is the only recorded meeting between any of FitzGerald's family and his friend. From his uncle Purcell's house, Halverstown, in County Kildare, he wrote to Barton: 'We were all going on here as merrily as possible till this day week, when my Piscator got an order from his Father to go home directly. So go he would the day after. I wanted to go also: but they would have me stay here ten days more.' [I, 235]

There is little indication of what Browne's parents thought of his friendship with FitzGerald, unless the unexpected demand to return from Ireland be counted. FitzGerald regularly stayed with the Brownes, and he entertained Mr Browne at least once in London, occasionally bought pictures for him, and was asked to catalogue those the family already owned. Not very telling one way or another, but it seems to indicate his acceptance at Cauldwell House. If the Brownes disapproved of FitzGerald in any way, it was probably because he was not a model of the industry they hoped for in their son. They wanted William to become a gentleman, not to follow his family in trade, but like all parents with ambitions for their children, they often felt that he was growing away from them.

For different reasons FitzGerald also had mutually conflicting wishes for Browne. He liked to think of him as a boy not a man, one who still was in need of social and intellectual guidance; it is significant that in writing to Thackeray, he called Browne a 'good boy' when he was already twenty-one. It might have been pleasant to keep him frozen perpetually at that stage of development, but FitzGerald knew that the fulfilment of his own wishes would have been harmful for the younger man.

Browne had no particular aptitude for the professions or even for earning his own living; when his father suggested possible occupations, FitzGerald disapproved, particularly if they would remove him from Bedford. Browne was devout, with slight High Church leanings if we are to trust the biographical hints in Fitz-Gerald's essay, *Euphranor*, but when there was a suggestion of his taking Holy Orders, FitzGerald thought it 'a pity he should be spoiled', although his reaction probably reflects his attitude to the Church as much as his belief that it was unsuitable for Browne. When, in 1840, Browne was setting out for Carlisle as Surveyor of Taxes, FitzGerald blamed his own disappointment on Mr Browne: 'Poor fellow, he leaves his old home because his screw of a father won't do anything for him, and cannot be grateful enough that he has begotten a Gentleman. He would have him live on a shilling a day.' The beloved long lazy fishing trips would stop when William left Bedfordshire. 'Hang me if I couldn't cry, and spit in the face of old Browne at the same time. I will marry or go hang. It is wrong to talk in this way: but really the old gentleman has

> Like a base Indian thrown a pearl away
> Richer than all his tribe.

For is not the heart of a Gentleman (N.B. not an Esquire) better than the whole Art of Skinning Flints as practised from the earliest ages.' [I, 262]

FitzGerald never flagged in his devotion to Browne, but now he had to recognize that the fresh-faced boy of sixteen he had met in 1832 was a grown man. They continued to meet, and FitzGerald frequently stayed at Bedford after Browne's return from Carlisle, but the old relationship was changing. In 1842 Fitz wrote of being with the 'whiskered man', who had become a 'man of business, of town-politics, and more intent on the first of September than on anything else in the world'. He concluded resignedly, 'I see very little of him.' [I, 336] In silent recognition of the change, he sold the horse he had kept stabled at Bedford.

At the back of FitzGerald's emotions was always the sad knowledge of the difference in their ages. 'N.B. I am growing bald,' he wrote when he was thirty-one, at what seemed to him the onset of middle age. Nor did a 'red face and fourteen stone weight' help to retard the passing of whatever small physical attraction he had ever possessed. Eight years had gone by since first he became acquainted with Browne at Tenby, but they had passed so quickly that his recollection of the summer was as fresh as if only a day or two had intervened: 'I remember a ravine on the horn of the bay opposite the town where the sea rushes up. . . . I can walk there as in a dream.' [I, 255]

As one recent writer on the Victorians has suggested, 'Freud has enlightened us; but he has also changed the nature of experience', and in particular he has made it perilous 'to describe the pleasures of friendship in the vigorous and enthusiastic language that came naturally to our ancestors'.[3] It is impossible to be precise about FitzGerald's feelings for Browne, but any name except love would surely falsify them. What is in question is not the nature of his affections but how aware FitzGerald was of their source. Certainly our own day overemphasizes sexuality as the cause of behaviour and emotion, but conversely many Victorians managed what seems to us the difficult balancing act of believing that love between men which had no overt physical consequences was therefore untouched by physical motivation.

Since FitzGerald was intelligent and highly self-conscious, and since his feelings about both men and women were so often couched in physical terms (although not obviously sexual ones), we have to swallow our own natural predispositions if we are to accept that he was literally unaware of the nature of his responses to several of the men who were so important in his life. But he was adept at glossing over what he hated to acknowledge in his own nature, and only the unconscious import of his language tells us what he felt he had to hide from himself and others. After the

117

failure of his marriage, for example, he refused to admit that anything but his own middle-aged rigidity of habit made it imposs-ible to live with his wife, but the physical terms in which he spoke of the marriage is a truer index to the real causes of its failure than the reason he consciously advanced. Usually there was a good deal more going on between the lines when he wrote of his young men friends than he realized.

On the other hand it would be foolish to ignore the spontaneity and freedom with which he so often spoke of his attraction to Thackeray and Allen, then to Browne, and later to Posh Fletcher. Only the most innocent and unself-conscious love could permit itself to be spoken of in such rhapsodic terms without embarrass-ment. At least FitzGerald was not embarrassed, although some of the friends in whom he confided may have been. It is most improb-able that he ever faced up to the nature of his feelings for other men until his friendship with Posh Fletcher began to wane some time around 1872. Half of what makes FitzGerald so attractive to us today is his essential innocence, but in this matter it was an inno-cence so long preserved that it had lost its bloom and become more like naïveté.

In the increasingly long periods when he could no longer be with Browne, FitzGerald found it hard to settle in either country or town, always longing for the place he had left and despising his current whereabouts. When he returned to Boulge from London and his 'usual pottering about in the midland counties of England', there was nothing but 'the same faces – the same fields – the same thoughts recurring at the same turns of road'. [I, 455] In the country 'one hears no music, and sees no pictures, and so one will have nothing to write about.' There was only reading, with 'a Thucy-dides to feed on: like a whole Parmesan'. [I, 303] But when he was in London he would buy himself bunches of flowers to remind himself of Suffolk and swear that he could be forever content with a rural life, with no more excitements than 'handing out my eldest nieces to waltz, etc., at the County Balls' or receiving an invitation to lecture at the Ipswich Mechanics' Institution on 'any subject except controversial Divinity, and party Politics'.

The longer he stayed in London the greater his discontent with it, and he used his letters as almost tactile substitutes for Boulge. 'In this big London all full of intellect and pleasure and business I feel pleasure in dipping down into the country, and rubbing my hand over the cool dew upon the pastures, as it were. I know very few people here: and care for fewer; I believe I should like to live in a small house just outside a pleasant English town all the days of my life, making myself useful in a humble way, reading my books, and playing a rubber of whist at night.' [I, 308] It is perhaps important to remember that he was writing here to Barton in Woodbridge, and like every good letter-writer he had an instinctive sense of what his correspondents wanted to hear: what he claimed to miss was precisely the life that Barton habitually led. This was neither flattery nor hypocrisy but a sensitive awareness of the moods of others, making for a shimmering protean shift of observation from letter to letter, which lent spontaneity to his correspondence.

Nor was it strictly true that his acquaintance in London was small, for he had plenty of friends there who had only to show him a glimmer of affection to have it returned fourfold. His acquaintance with Alfred Tennyson, begun at Mirehouse, flourished in London in spite of rough spots and abrasions. In 1837 the Tennyson family had moved to Essex, so that it was easier for Alfred to come to town, although he felt so short of money that he constantly begged a bed from his Cambridge friends installed there. During the late 1830s and 1840s he often descended on Fitz-Gerald in his London lodgings. 'We have had Alfred Tennyson here,' FitzGerald wrote of one such visit in 1838; 'very droll, and very wayward: and much sitting up of nights till two and three in the morning with pipes in our mouths: at which good hour we would get Alfred to give us some of his magic music, which he does between growling and smoking; and so to bed. All this has not cured my Influenza as you may imagine: but these hours shall be remembered long after the Influenza is forgotten.' [I, 211]

When FitzGerald returned in the evening to his rooms, he would sometimes find that Tennyson had made his bed on a sofa uninvited; when he was awake he would work on the poems in the 'large Butcher's Account book' [I, 239] in which he kept record of them. FitzGerald was probably half-serious when he once stipulated that Tennyson might come to stay if it were for a short time only: 'Poor fellow: he is quite magnanimous, and noble natured, with no meanness or vanity or affectation of any kind whatsoever – but very perverse.' [I, 246] Tennyson was becoming more

119

neurotic and hypochondriacal, and FitzGerald, with the superb assurance of an indolent man who had never earned a penny in his
life, told him that his only cure lay in disciplined work and that he
ought to take up employment rather than drifting aimlessly from
friend to friend, believing that composing poetry was sufficient
occupation.

Without approving in the least of Tennyson's life, Fitz was none
the less sympathetic and generous when he saw the poet approaching financial disaster. The whole Tennyson family had been taken
in by an engaging and plausible rogue, Dr Matthew Allen, an old
friend of Carlyle, who ran a private lunatic asylum in Essex near
the Tennyson home. At the end of 1840 Tennyson first gave part
of his small inheritance to Allen, who had begun a company for
the production of 'Pyroglyphs', a kind of mass-produced wood
carving, which he was sure would make his own fortune and that
of his investors. In spite of the warnings of FitzGerald and most of
his other friends, Tennyson continued giving money to Allen
through 1841 and 1842, before he realized that all of his inheritance would soon be lost. At last in 1843 Allen admitted that his
company had come to financial ruin, and it was presumably then
that FitzGerald first gave Tennyson £300 annually to keep him
from serious penury and supported him during the next two years.

Tennyson was so upset by the whole Allen affair that he had a
bad breakdown at the end of 1843 and had to become a patient in a
series of 'hydropaths'. The rigours of the water cure, FitzGerald
thought, 'would do him good if he gave it fair chance – but he
smokes, and drinks a bottle of a wine a day'. [I, 479] Early in 1845
Allen died, and Tennyson benefited from an insurance policy on
his life. 'Apollo certainly did this,' wrote FitzGerald: 'shooting one
of his swift arrows at the heart of the Doctor; whose perfectly
heartless conduct upset A.T.'s nerves in the first instance.' [I, 474]
After Peel had granted Tennyson a pension, FitzGerald no longer
needed to help him.

Lending money is seldom the best way to ensure friendship.
Tennyson's misery and FitzGerald's generosity had brought them
closer together, but Tennyson had been made to feel dependent, a
state he could hardly bear, and FitzGerald unthinkingly assumed
that his own help had made him so intimate with Tennyson that it
was permissible for him to criticize his poetry without invitation.

He was much too sensitive to believe that his money had bought him an especial place in Tennyson's heart, but he found it difficult to understand that 'old Alfred' might need badly to reassert his emotional independence once he no longer relied financially on FitzGerald.

Tennyson's eldest brother Frederick was far more hot-headed than Alfred, truculent, and ready to resort to physical violence to make a point, but he and FitzGerald had an almost perfect friendship. They met shortly before Frederick inherited enough money to move to Italy, wrote to each other constantly – and saw each other seldom. Frederick Tennyson, more than any of FitzGerald's other friends, shared his passion for music, and he loved painting and poetry, the last of which he wrote so well that he might have made his name by it if he had not been financially independent, lazy, and reluctant to compete with his brother. Of all FitzGerald's letters those to Frederick Tennyson came nearest perfection, for they are unhurried and expansive, written at length, with an unbuttoned confidence that little explanation need be made to the recipient: more often records of Fitz's reading and attitudes than of his activities. 'You like to hear of men and manners,' he wrote to Tennyson.

Fitz's letters to Frederick Tennyson give a surprisingly detailed view of the state of English music in the middle of the century, as recorded by a sensitive and devoted amateur. His love of the art was so deep that he felt the absence of a piano as perhaps the only flaw in the Eden of Bedford, and it is typical of his willingness to try anything new that to remedy the deficiency he turned temporarily to the accordion: 'It is a nice thing to carry about with one. I never tried it till the other day; it is easy enough. One day I shall buy one.' [I, 333]

In his choice of composers he was essentially conservative without being reactionary. 'I grow every day more and more to love only the old God save the King style: the common chords, those truisms of music, like other truisms so little understood in the full.' [I, 333] Emotion and expression were more important to him than experiment, but he could easily understand that they might not be enough for a composer, as he told Frederick Tennyson: 'Mozart, I agree with you, is the most universal musical genius: Beethoven has been too analytical and erudite: but his inspiration is nevertheless true. . . . I think that he was, strictly speaking, more

121

of a thinker than a musician. A great genius he was somehow.... He tried to think in music: almost to reason in music: whereas perhaps we should be contented with *feeling* in it. It can never speak very definitely.' [I, 317–18] But he could not really deny Beethoven and said that he wished he might 'hear Fidelio once a week'. He was quite willing to welcome new composers and called Mendelssohn 'by far our best writer now, [who] in some measure combines Beethoven and Handel'. [I, 333]

His deepest love was kept for Handel, although he never wholly accepted the *Messiah*, because he preferred theatrical music to oratorio. In 1842 he sent to Frederick Tennyson, in Naples, a description of attending Macready's revival of *Acis and Galatea* at the Drury Lane Theatre, which not only recreates the evening with breathtaking immediacy but also shows how his love of music, theatre, and painting all combined in the performance:

You enter Drury Lane at a quarter to seven: the pit is already nearly full: but you find a seat, and a very pleasant one. Box doors open and shut: ladies take off their shawls and seat themselves: gentlemen twist their side curls: the musicians come up from under the stage one by one: 'tis just upon seven: Macready is very punctual: Mr. T. Cooke is in his place with his Marshal's baton in his hand: he lifts it up: and off they set with old Handel's noble overture. As it is playing, the red velvet curtain (which Macready has substituted, not wisely, for the old green one) draws apart: and you see a rich drop scene, all festooned and arabesqued with River Gods, Nymphs, and their emblems: and in the centre a delightful, large, good copy of Poussin's great landscape (of which I used to have a print in my rooms) where the Cyclops is seen seated on a mountain, looking over the sea shore. The overture ends, the drop scene rises, and there is the seashore, a long curling bay: the sea heaving under the moon, and breaking upon the beach, and rolling the surf down – the stage! This is really capitally done. But enough of description. The choruses were well sung, well acted, well dressed, and well grouped: and the whole thing creditable and pleasant. Do you know the music? It is of Handel's best: and as classical as any man who wore a full-bottomed wig could write. I think Handel never gets out of his wig: that is, out of his age: his Hallelujah chorus is a chorus not of angels, but of well-fed earthly choristers, ranged tier above tier in a Gothic cathedral, with princes for audience, and their military trumpets flourishing over the full volume of the organ. Handel's gods are like Homer's, and his sublime never reaches beyond the region of the clouds. Therefore I think that his great marches, triumphal pieces, and Coronation Anthems, are his finest works. [I, 303–4]

From his early days in the 1820s and 1830s with his mother at the Italian Opera House FitzGerald retained his belief that the singers of his youth, particularly the great Giuditta Pasta, were the finest the world had known. When Jenny Lind became the sensation of London in 1847 and 1848, he refused to 'go into hot crowds' to hear her, even though Spedding had completely lost his usual calm over her singing: 'Night after night is that bald head seen in particular position in the Opera house, in a stall; the miserable man has forgot Bacon and philosophy, and goes after strange women.' At last Fitz heard the 'redoubtable' Jenny Lind and said that even comparing her to Pasta was ridiculous. 'I cannot endure that she should clutch more money on the strength of her good character than the Italian whores ever stand out for.' [I, 604, 605, 586]

It is surely Romantic nonsense to talk of the 'music' of poetry and prose, as if they had more than very tenuous connections with Mozart and Beethoven, but it is hard not to sense in FitzGerald's attention and sensitivity to music a likeness to the care he took over the aural quality of his letters and translations.

During the early 1840s FitzGerald was clearly in good financial condition, as his gifts to Tennyson suggest, and he spent freely on pictures in London. He haunted auction rooms and sorted through the dusty back rooms of dealers, often coming up with great masterpieces that sold for only a few pounds and maintained their authenticity at least until he had a second, colder look on their arrival in Boulge. In 1841 he reported 'walking about in the wet to my favourite pawn brokers. Nothing very bad to be got just now. A sketch by Constable – £3 – quite genuine – and not a bit the better for that.' [I, 277] He did, however, buy two other Constables in 1842, for a few pounds, one of which sold at his death for 100 guineas.

The names of the painters whose works he bought for a song make the mouth water: Bassano, Velasquez, Gainsborough, and Titian are some occurring casually among his purchases. His methods of attribution were convincing to him if not to others: 'The picture must be an original of somebody's: and if not of Gainsborough's – whose?' [I, 292] Some of the attributions were suspect within a short time of purchase; others lasted his lifetime. One Titian that hung on his walls until his death was sold with his effects, then disappeared from sight; he left another Titian, which he considered his best picture, to the Fitzwilliam Museum, where it has since hung as the work of Ippolito Scarsella. [I, 294, n.1]

Even in Norwich he had no trouble in finding a Giorgione, then in an uncharacteristically early burst of doubt about his purchase, he called it 'either by Giorgione, or a Flemish copyist. But as I am not particular, I call it Giorgione.' [I, 406]

The extravagance with which he provided his pictures with superb pedigrees was a measure of his light-hearted enthusiasm, but he accepted with wry amusement the almost inevitable failure of his guesses and immediately set about plotting how he could sell the pictures again. He bought one large Opie, 'The Fruit Girl', in a flash of enthusiasm, and when closer examination revealed that it had been damaged by heat, he cut it down to a smaller panel and, 'as it has suffered during the late operation', he borrowed palette and brushes of a friend 'and lay upon the floor two hours patching over and renovating'. The result was such an improvement that he had it reframed and varnished: 'I hope some fool will be surprised into giving £4 for it, as I did. I have selected an advantageous position for it in a dealer's shop, just under a rich window that excludes the light.' [I, 306, 309] He tried to sell it to Browne's father, but even he was not fooled, and FitzGerald had to pass the results of his patching in the window of a dealer for many months after.

Frequently he bought for Barton or Churchyard, who had no chance to go to London auctions. For Barton he bought at £3.10 'a huge naked woman – a copy of Raffaelle – as large as life down to the knees – which you will allow is quite enough of her.... such exhibitions are not fit for Quakers' eyes. I have sent her to [Samuel] Laurence's house to preserve my reputation. He is a married man.' [I, 298]

By 1842 the initial fun of buying had begun to wear off, and he resolved on reform: 'After this year however I think I shall bid complete adieu to picture-*hunting*: only taking what comes in my way. There is a great difference between these two things: both in the expense of time, thought, and money. Who can sit down to Plato while his brains are roaming to Holborn, Christie's, Phillips's, etc.?' [I, 313] Of course he no more kept his resolve than he did most others, and to the end of his life he took pleasure in trying to outguess the artistic experts, seldom with more than limited success. Realistically, he wrote that 'the pride of making a good purchase and shewing one's taste: all that contributes to health and long life.' [I, 306] What more could he ask?

Inevitably, when he had been in London with his literary friends and when he had been considering problems of aesthetics (a word he despised as a pretentious Germanic neologism), he was led to reconsider his own poetic talents. So far, he realized painfully, he had little drive to write, only a shallow facility. 'I know that I could write volume after volume as well as others of the mob of gentlemen who write with ease: but I think unless a man can do better, he had best not do at all; I have not the strong inward call, nor cruel-sweet pangs of parturition, that prove the birth of anything bigger than a mouse.' His shrewdness about his own abilities suggests that he took poetry seriously in ways that he never did his efforts as musician or painter. 'I am a man of taste, of whom there are hundreds born every year,' he wrote in 1842, but he knew that his own comfortable circumstances allowed him to remain little more than a dilettante. What he had apparently never considered was the possibility of translation, the verbal equivalent of the rearrangement of other men's art that he had so often attempted with paintings.

It is improbable that his great outburst of poetic translation in the next two decades sprang from thin air, and there is some evidence in his letters that he was constantly and secretly writing verse that he destroyed without letting anyone else see it. 'As to an occasional copy of verses, there are few men who have leisure to read, and are possessed of any music in their souls, who are not capable of versifying on some ten or twelve occasions during their natural lives: at a proper conjunction of the stars. There is no harm in taking advantage of such occasions.' [I, 308]

One reason why FitzGerald remained diffident about his poetry was that he was constantly thrown in London into the company of men whom he knew in his heart to be infinitely his superiors as writers: Thackeray and Tennyson, of course, but also Carlyle and, on one occasion, Dickens. He was taken to Devonshire Terrace in April 1843 by Tennyson and Thackeray, whom Dickens had invited to spend the greater part of the day. The four men took a carriage drive together before dinner. FitzGerald was surprised at how small their host was, but he found him 'unaffected and hospitable. You would never remark him for appearance. A certain acute cut of the upper eyelid is all I can find to denote his powers'. [I, 389] After dinner they drank mulled claret and played a round game of cards. It was probably Dickens's courtesy to his Suffolk guest that turned the conversation to the poetry of Crabbe. Fitz-Gerald, whose admiration of his host's novels amounted almost to adoration, was somewhat embarrassed by Dickens's crimson waistcoat and worried, as he often did about men who had risen too rapidly from humble beginnings, that 'Dickens is a *Snob.*' He none the less recognized his honesty, concluded that he 'did not love Humbugs', and was 'a very noble fellow as well as a very wonderful one'.

FitzGerald's friendship with Carlyle dated from 1842, when he was taken to Chelsea by their mutual acquaintance Samuel Laurence, the portrait painter, with whom Fitz spent much time in galleries, and whom he commissioned to paint several of his friends, including Allen, Browne, Tennyson, Thackeray, Barton, and – years later – 'Posh' Fletcher. Laurence had already made four portraits of Carlyle and was on his way to recording many of the Victorian literary aristocracy. Before meeting Carlyle, FitzGerald had been unimpressed by his writings, largely because of his 'mystical language'. The French Revolution treated in German style by a Scotsman was too much for him: 'There is no repose, nor equable movement in it.' [I, 211] In person Carlyle was a different matter, and they took to each other at once, although Jane Carlyle remained unimpressed by Fitz for some years.

Curiously enough, Carlyle had that very summer made a trip to Naseby to inspect the scene of the battle in preparation for his work on Cromwell, actually walking over much of the land owned by the FitzGeralds. In conversation Fitz discovered that Carlyle and his companion, Thomas Arnold of Rugby, had mistaken the commemorative obelisk raised by Mr and Mrs FitzGerald on the highest point of the land for the actual centre of the battlefield. Carlyle, certain as always of his facts, was reluctant to believe him, and FitzGerald volunteered to re-examine the terrain when he went to Naseby two days later.

Pacing out the battlefield, sketching it in watercolours, and questioning the tenants about their knowledge of the graves on the land were considerably more amusing than collecting quarterly rents for his father, and FitzGerald threw himself with enthusiasm into sending Carlyle all the relevant information in a series of letters from Naseby, hoping thereby to keep him from making 'a mad mess of Cromwell and his Times'.

From Chelsea Carlyle peppered FitzGerald with requests. 'Were it not a most legitimate task for the Proprietor of Naseby, a man of scholarship, intelligence and leisure, to make himself completely acquainted with the true state of all details connected with Naseby Battle and its localities?' [I, 348] What interested Carlyle most were the anecdotes preserved in the neighbourhood, the vignettes and relics of the battle, all of which could be used as fodder for his vivid, metaphoric style.

FitzGerald found that his best fellow explorers were two farmers, 'one a very solid fellow, who talks like the justices in Shakespeare... the other a Scotchman full of intelligence, who proposed the flesh-soil for manure for turnips'. [I, 352] Together they opened part of one grave and found 'the remains of seven or eight poor chaps in this space.... They lay east and west alternately – as they pack fish.... One skeleton lay across the rest, jammed in it seemed.' [I, 357]

All the charnel horrors of the grave were described in great detail to Carlyle, and from it Fitz extracted a few souvenirs before closing it again. Carlyle's letters show that he got more than he had bargained for; in particular he was horrified by the teeth and bones that FitzGerald sent to Chelsea: 'To think that this grinder chewed its breakfast on the 14th of June 1645, and had no more eating to do in the world, or services further there – till now, to lie in my drawer, and be a horror!... I want no more bones, shin or other.' [I, 361–2] He was particularly haunted by the description of the skeleton lying across the others, and he wrote that 'one figure, by the strange position of the bones, gave us the hideous notion of its having been thrown in before death!' [I, 345] The single word 'us' is an indication of the way that he tended to appropriate the efforts of FitzGerald. Fitz in turn took some delight in shocking Carlyle, whose own style was designed to shock others with the horrors of war.

A few years later Fitz acted as intermediary between Carlyle and William Squire of Yarmouth, who offered some spurious Cromwell letters to Carlyle. All his help established his friendship with Carlyle, whom he often visited in Chelsea, entertained once in Suffolk, and to whom he wrote until the older man's death.

As FitzGerald judged the natural beauty of a particular place by his happiness there, so houses were often blamed for despondency. When Browne became too busy for endless Bedfordshire rambles with him, he discovered for the first time that his cottage was too damp for his health and that he needed to move to 'some permanent abode' where 'some friend is to be found'. A small cathedral town or a country market town, such as Ipswich, Woodbridge, Beccles, or Bungay would be suitable, but 'Bedford is better than all,' he decided, without specifying why that would be so. 'Give me some account of the house you spoke of at Bedford,' he asked of Browne in April 1843.

Nothing came of his enquiries, and the following spring, on Good Friday 1844, he received news that confirmed the worst of his fears and put all thought of moving to Bedford out of the question. Browne, he wrote, was 'in train to be married to a rich woman. When I heard that they could not have less than five hundred a year, I gave up all further interest in the matter: for I could not wish a reasonable couple more. W.B. may be spoilt if he grows rich: that is the only thing could spoil him. This time ten years I first went to ride and fish with him about the river Ouse – he was then 18 – quick to love and quick to fight – full of confidence, generosity, and the glorious spirit of Youth.' Somewhat incoherently, he told Barton: 'I ... hope he mayn't be defiled with the filthy pitch.... I repent in ashes for reviling the Daddy [Wordsworth] who wrote that Sonnet against Damned Riches.' [I, 430] A month later he was more composed if not more resigned when he told Frederick Tennyson of the approaching marriage: 'I am not thinking of moving from here just yet.... I hope to retain my

128

acquaintance with him, however, in spite of a wife's hatred of the particular friend.' [I, 442]

Elizabeth Elliott, whom Browne married on 30 July 1844, was the daughter of Robert Elliott of Goldington, near Bedford, who had been High Sheriff of the county. Among his properties were two large houses across Goldington Green from each other, and into one of them, Goldington Hall, Browne and his wife were to move on their marriage. It was a good match for Browne financially and socially, but apparently their joint income was not enough for a big house, a family, and the stable that Browne maintained. A few years later when the Brownes moved across the green into Goldington Bury, FitzGerald lent £6,500 to his friend, which was a small fortune in those days, nearly enough to earn income as large as FitzGerald thought Mrs Browne brought to the marriage. In return he took a mortgage on their house and thirty-six acres, valued at £8,500.

In time FitzGerald became reconciled to the marriage and to the thought of Mrs Browne, who had once been equated with 'filthy pitch' for her 'Damned Riches'. He described her as a 'very good, quiet, unaffected, sensible, little woman'. It suited his modest ideas of society that they lived 'with very little company; and seem to desire none'. A year and a half after their marriage he accepted his first invitation to Goldington, where he was pleased to find that much of their furniture came from the Streatham house of Mrs Piozzi, the friend of Samuel Johnson, and that in his bedroom was 'Dr. Johnson's own bookcase and secretaire; with looking glass in the panels which often reflected his uncouth shape. His own bed is also in the house; but I do not sleep in it.' [I, 508]

On subsequent stays FitzGerald began to find Goldington cold and uncomfortable, as Bedford had never seemed before Browne was married. His letters had to be 'short and meagre', since he had to 'write in a cold room, *wishing* for a fire, but of course not able to command, or hint, one in a friend's house'. [I, 545] His comfort had not been so neglected, he thought, in the old days. Soon he stayed as often with the elder Brownes in Bedford as in Goldington.

It was hardly to be expected that FitzGerald would ever become enthusiastic about Mrs Browne, and we know that he always felt that she was rather ungenerous about money, but the complete frankness with which, after Browne's death, he wrote to the widow about his love of her husband indicates – among other things – how little he had come to resent her. What Mrs Browne thought of him in return is another matter; if she left any written opinion, it is not available. She was a conventional woman, and it is clear that she wanted to forget Browne's family background in trade and the mortgage he had given FitzGerald, which she was greatly concerned that their neighbours might find out about. According to family friends, she felt that FitzGerald was too closely connected with both those matters. Her reserve with FitzGerald may have had a tinge of concern over the nature of her husband's friendship with him, and that in turn perhaps accounted for the disappearance from view after Browne's death of the correspondence between the two men. All the same, she must have been moderately hospitable and friendly, since FitzGerald continued to write to her long after her husband had died.

CHAPTER VI

Cowell and Barton

Browne apparently announced his impending marriage on Good Friday, 1844. The next day FitzGerald rushed off to 'beastly London', which stank 'all through of churchyards and fish shops'. He never specified what had prompted such profound disgust with the smell of mortality, but its occasion suggests that it was unconsciously connected either with Browne's capitulation to marriage and 'Damned Riches' or with an unacknowledged sense of being ungenerous in his reactions to Browne's engagement. Perhaps both.

Four days later he was 'still indignant at this nasty place London' when he went to Chelsea, seeking sympathy from Carlyle, who could usually be relied upon to thunder against the city:

> I smoked a pipe with Carlyle yesterday. We ascended from his dining room carrying pipes and tobacco up through two stories of his house, and got into a little dressing room near the roof: there we sat down: the window was open and looked out on nursery gardens, their almond trees in blossom, and beyond, bare walls of houses, and over these, roofs and chimneys, and roofs and chimneys, and here and there a steeple, and whole London crowned with darkness gathering behind like the illimitable resources of a dream. I tried to persuade him to leave the accursed den, and he wished – but – but – perhaps he *didn't* wish on the whole.

But beyond the stink of London hovered a reminder of another and unsullied world when 'a cloud comes over Charlotte Street and seems as if it were sailing softly on the April wind to fall in a blessed shower upon the lilac buds and thirsty anemones somewhere in

131

Essex; or, who knows?, perhaps at Boulge. Out will run Mrs. Faiers, and with red arms and face of woe haul in the struggling windows of the cottage, and make all tight.' [I, 431–2]

'My heart sucks at the fresh air from afar,' he sighed in London [I, 436], writing as if dispossessed of Eden. 'I long to spread wing and fly into the kind clean air of the country. I see nobody in the streets half so handsome as Mr. Reynolds of our parish: all clever, composed, satirical, selfish, well-dressed.... I get radishes to eat for breakfast of a morning: with them comes a savour of earth that brings all the delicious gardens of the world back into one's soul, and almost draws tears from one's eyes.' [I, 433]

In nothing was FitzGerald more typically Victorian than in the implicitly moral distinction he made between London's clamour and the quiet of the countryside. He always returned to the neighbourhood of Woodbridge as to a state of grace, although he could also soon become bored there. But in this spring of 1844 his letters were full of a desperate urgency to go back there and to the prelapsarian innocence that seemed part of it. It was almost as if he were trying to recover an Adamic purity of his own.

He has always been celebrated for his word sketches of East Anglia, but often his real subject seems to be not that flat, sea-bordered landscape but an interior paysage, the reflection of his own mind, for he was no more writing specifically of Suffolk than he was attempting to recreate a factual Persia in the imagery of his version of the *Rubáiyát*. Like so many contemporary writers, he tells us as much of his emotions as of the world around him that he is ostensibly describing.

'London melts away all individuality into a common lump of cleverness,' he wrote to Frederick Tennyson from Boulge. 'I can still find the heart of England beating healthily down here.... I read of mornings – the same old books over and over again, having no command of new ones: walk with my great black dog of an afternoon, and at evening sit with open windows, up to which China roses climb, with my pipe, while the blackbirds and thrushes begin to rustle bedwards in the garden, and the nightingale to have the neighbourhood to herself.... How old to tell of, how new to see!' [I, 441–2]

In such a mood little else in all Europe was comparable to East Anglia. When Tennyson wrote that he had been disappointed in

Switzerland, FitzGerald asked, 'How could such herds of gaping idiots come back enchanted if there were much worth going to see? I think that tours in Switzerland and Italy are less often published now than formerly: but there is all Turkey, Greece, and the East to be prostituted also; and I fear we shan't hear the end of it in our lifetimes. Suffolk turnips seem to me so classical compared to all that sort of thing.' [I, 550]

It must have seemed to his friends that FitzGerald was comfortably insulated from reality by his private income when he took offence at the worship of money he associated with London and thought he had glimpsed in Browne. But within his own family he found enough reason to flinch from that aspect of contemporary life. His father's attempt to increase the already enormous family holdings proved what Mammonism could lead to. Since 1836 Mr FitzGerald had increasingly neglected the upkeep of the other family properties in favour of Pendleton, near Castle Irwell, into which he poured money for coal mining, with little return. In 1843 there was a disastrous flood that seemed to be the last straw, as FitzGerald told Carlyle:

> My Father, after spending £100,000 on a colliery, besides losses by everlasting rogues, runaway agents, etc., has just been drowned out of it by an influx of water. So end the hopes of eighteen years; and he is near seventy, left without his only hobby! He may perhaps be able to let it to a Company at a low rent, that they may pump out the water. But he is come to the end of his purse. [I, 398]

Even this huge loss was far from exhausting the family fortunes, and Fitz knew that his own future was ensured by the money belonging to his mother that her trustees had never confided to her husband. But there were others who had been persuaded by Mr FitzGerald to invest in the mining company, and their terror was frighteningly like that of the Tennysons when Dr Allen's company was ruined. Actual bankruptcy for the company and Mr Fitz-Gerald still lay in the future, but the present disaster was real enough.

Chief among the victims, from FitzGerald's point of view, was his sister Eleanor Kerrich at Geldestone, whose husband had been one of the heaviest investors in the Pendleton Colliery Company.

'Over that house hangs a black cloud; and I see no symptom of its clearing away,' FitzGerald told W. B. Donne. 'Kerrich has got into the same state of mind that made his Father and Grandfather put the pistol to their heads. Perhaps to do this would be best; he is miserable himself. His wife and children are very unhappy; he is not at all fit to manage them, or his affairs: and yet not ill enough to have that charge taken from him.' [I, 572] Kerrich had to be taken to London to recuperate, and his wife, reduced to comparative poverty, assumed the management of the estate, 'a thing not agreeable to the good feminine nature'. To her FitzGerald gave all the money and advice of which he was capable.

At the very time that FitzGerald became so newly intent upon regaining the innocence of the country, he had a brief spurt of religious enthusiasm, and significantly both these impulses manifested themselves at Bedford on the Good Friday when Browne announced his engagement. Two years before that, Fitz-Gerald had first attended the Evangelical chapel built for the Revd Timothy Matthews in Bedford, and had been so impressed by his eloquence even then that he said he was '*entêté*', and had followed Matthews into the open street to hear him preach.

'Oh this wonderful wonderful world,' he wrote in 1844, 'and we who stand in the middle of it are all in a maze, except poor Matthews of Bedford, who fixes his eyes upon a wooden Cross and has no misgiving whatsoever.' On Good Friday Matthews pleaded with his congregation to acknowledge Christ's redemption, 'and first one got up and in sobs declared she believed it: and then another, and then another – I was quite overset: – all poor people: how much richer than all who fill the London Churches.' In his sudden wave of emotion FitzGerald confessed himself 'almost as much taken aback' by Matthews's oratory 'as the poor folks all about me who sobbed'. [I, 432, 430]

It was the kind of overt emotionalism that FitzGerald normally hated, and its attraction indicates how 'overset' he was at the time. Probably he never realized that his brief spell of religious fervour and his urgent need of the healing qualities of a rural life had anything to do with his hurt over Browne's marriage, but their concurrence is obvious enough to us now.

Once the worst of his disappointment over Browne had worn off, his short burst of piety disappeared, and he returned to the formal, largely social duty of attending Sunday service in Boulge Church with 'hat, gloves, and prayer-book. I always put on my thickest great-coat to go to our Church in: as fungi grow in great numbers about the communion table.' [I, 408] He was consistently respectful about religious services, but his strongest statements on the matter concerned his feelings of irritation with the 'Puseyite Parsons' with their 'new chancels built with altars, and painted windows that officiously [display] the Virgin Mary, etc.' [I, 574]

Since the old creed had been effective for two centuries, it was probably best for the present: 'I think we may be well content to let it work still among the ploughmen and weavers of to-day; and even to suffer some absurdities in the Form, if the Spirit does well upon the whole.' [I, 580] He had scant faith in immortality, saying that he would be content to settle instead for rest.

The speed of his recovery from religious enthusiasm was doubtlessly increased by the knowledge that his own brother, John FitzGerald, a lay preacher with distinctly odd beliefs and habits, was Matthews's chief deputy. Edward FitzGerald loved his elder brother and regarded his eccentricities with amused tolerance, but he found it almost impossible to be around him for long. John was a strange mixture of great generosity and the curious kind of abrasiveness that is often reserved for the philanthropic. He was much concerned at Pendleton with the education of the children of the miners in the colliery, but he seemed to be so almost as a way of dissociating himself from his father's business venture. When in 1843 Mr FitzGerald's mine was ruined by flooding, Edward wrote that 'to make amends for this, my brother has just had nineteen people baptized in the Naseby Reservoir – 1500 looking on.' [I, 398] He used to take Matthews with him to Naseby, and the two men, wearing plain black gowns to show the complexion of their churchmanship, held open-air temperance services in the area lying between the churchyard and the public house, the FitzGerald Arms. John gave away thousands of pounds in charity to the lower classes, but he was 'high' to those nearer his own rank who had not gone to a university, refusing to have them at table with him and giving no more than two fingers when saying goodbye to them.

As an undergraduate at Cambridge John had been excessively religious, but an attack of fever weakened his eyes and kept him from going into the Church, as he had planned on doing. Not that his

135

destiny as a preacher was apparent to others, for he had a bad 'sissing' or whistling in his speech that alternated with a clicking of his teeth; the congregation at a lunatic asylum near Boulge to whom he ministered used to imitate him audibly when he was in the pulpit. While lecturing or preaching he would abstractedly take out the contents of his pockets and place them neatly on the lectern, then slowly remove his boots and stockings, which he would carefully examine without interrupting his discourse. Once, while walking, his brother Edward and a friend came across a deserted encampment in which there was a trail of discarded boots and waistcoats. 'It looks as though gipsies have been about,' said the friend, to which FitzGerald replied, 'Yes, or more likely still, my brother has been preaching here.'[1] He was a huge man weighing eighteen stone, and the vehemence of his sermons could seem threatening when he gesticulated; to make a point he would wave the lighted candles from the pulpit, spattering hot wax all over the front pews. He became so absorbed in his lectures that he would go on for hours, and his introductions of other speakers were dreaded, since his preliminary remarks took up the whole evening. In spite of his patent disqualifications, John attracted surprisingly large congregations and audiences, who were drawn both by amusement at the 'crazy preaching squire' and by genuine emotion at his only too sincere inveighing against drink, slavery, and anything that smacked of Rome. In the spring of 1844 he came to stay at Boulge and lectured twice a week in Woodbridge on 'the Prophecies' to audiences that overflowed the little theatre.

'John means well, but he adopts extraordinary methods to attain his ends,'[2] said his brother, who dreaded the time when John would inherit Boulge and live there permanently; it would be almost impossible to stay in the cottage at the gates of the park, since John had not the slightest notion that there was an hour of day or night when Edward would not welcome his company. 'My brother John, after being expected every day this week,' Fitz said in amused exasperation at one of his visits to Boulge, 'wrote positively to say he could not come to-day: and accordingly was seen to drive up to the Hall two hours ago.' [I, 426] Edward, who was nearly made mad by his uninterrupted conversation, used to say plaintively, 'I wish my brother wouldn't always be talking about religion', but John never tried seriously to convert him.

'The difference between John and me, is this,' FitzGerald once said: 'John goes and does things that he knows nothing about – the most unheard-of things – and thinks he's perfectly right; while if I want to do anything, I go to some one who understands and get advice, which, as a rule, to my misfortune, I don't follow.'[3] Although the two brothers constantly criticized each other, they did not want anyone else to do so. In Woodbridge FitzGerald once heard a woman speaking of John's eccentricities; turning around, he said quietly but sternly, 'He is my brother, madam.' He was incapable of harbouring resentment against John, and the worst he could say was that they were 'very good friends, of very different ways of thinking'. [IV, 211]

In 1844 FitzGerald became thirty-five: young enough by most standards, but his letters show he felt he had turned a corner into middle age, with little to look forward to. Reluctantly he tried to settle down in Boulge, for Browne's marriage had robbed him of his usual travelling companion. 'I meditate a little trip somewhere, and now my old summer swallow is going to pair off, I must look for fresh quarters. Such is the state of a bachelor whom his partners desert one by one.' [I, 447] As he reviewed what the past year had brought him, he considered, not more than half-jokingly, the most desperate of solutions to his loneliness: 'If I were conscious of being stedfast and good humoured enough, I would marry tomorrow. But a humourist is best by himself.' [I, 468]

Perhaps the most striking feature of the chronology of his life is the way that one close friend succeeded another as the focus for his affections, so that they seldom overlapped for long. It is improbable that he planned or even recognized the pattern, but his need of concentrating his emotions on one other person was so great that he almost immediately replaced anyone who had dropped out of that special relationship. At least twice he attempted disastrously to cure his loneliness with the wrong person: in the case of his wife it was probably with the wrong sex as well.

Without much enthusiasm he planned on spending Christmas of 1844 with his mother in Brighton, leavening the tedium with a subsequent month in London. Before leaving Boulge he attended a gathering of some of the local literary circle at the home in nearby Playford of Mrs Biddell, whose husband was a cultivated gentleman farmer and friend of FitzGerald. Among the other guests were three who were to have important roles in his life. Two were family friends whom he was accustomed to seeing: Bernard Barton's daughter Lucy, and Elizabeth Charlesworth, with whom he had enjoyed imagining himself in love a decade before. A fairly accurate measure of his feeling for her can be taken from the fact that they had often met in the intervening years, either when she was visiting his sisters or when he called on her parents, and that there had been no recurrence of his feelings. A few years before, FitzGerald had called on her to help in sending information about Naseby to Carlyle, to whom he ungallantly but accurately described her as a 'very famous girl (now 30) with whom I used to be slightly in love as I supposed'. [I, 429] The passing years had not raised his temperature over Miss Charlesworth.

Both Lucy Barton and Elizabeth Charlesworth wrote pastel verses that were perfectly adequate for reading at an evening party in the country, as they often did. What FitzGerald found far more interesting was the conversation of a young man from Ipswich, only eighteen years old, whom he was meeting for the first time. Edward Cowell's family had been moderately prosperous until the death of his father two years earlier, and Edward had been a brilliant pupil in Ipswich Grammar School. At his father's death he had to leave school and take a place in the family counting-house, but business claimed only part of his mind, for his real love was languages. At fourteen he had become so interested in Persian poetry that he taught himself the language, and by the time he was sixteen he had published translations from Persian in the *Monthly Register* and the *Asiatic Journal*. At eighteen he also knew Greek, Latin, Italian, French, German, Old Norse, and was making progress with Sanskrit, which he had begun learning at fifteen from a grammar he found in a book shop. What FitzGerald found so appealing in Cowell was that his interests were not solely philological, for he learned languages as a way to unlock literature rather than as an end in themselves. The year that had seemed to FitzGerald to begin with renunciation closed on a new friendship that deeply affected both his personal life and the course of literary history.

Cowell never occupied the place in FitzGerald's life that Browne had filled until his marriage. He was good-looking, but Fitz-Gerald's letters indicate that he felt few of the same disturbing emotions for him that he had for Browne. What they had in common was a far rarer thing: a deep mutual intellectual admiration. A quarter of a century later FitzGerald said, 'I have met and known many learned and clever men but Edward Cowell is the *greatest Scholar*.'[4]

In the company of his elders Cowell had a surprising ease, and though he was only half FitzGerald's age, he treated him simply with the modesty and politeness due to an equal. His maturity in judging others was as unusual as his precocity at languages, and he instantly recognized the depth of mind behind the slightly farcical exterior FitzGerald presented to the world. 'I should like you so to know him,' Cowell told his mother, 'he is a man of *real* power, one such as we seldom meet with in the world. There is something so very *solid* and *stately* about him, a kind of slumbering giant, or silent Vesuvius. It is only at times that the eruption comes, but when it *does* come, it overwhelms you!'[5]

Within a month of their meeting Cowell had written to Fitz-Gerald, unselfconsciously lapsing into French and Greek in the letter. Fitz took it as a compliment, although he admitted that his own 'kind of Scholarship lies much on the surface – soon come soon gone', and it took him a good bit of swotting to unravel all Cowell's asides about Homer, Plato, Tacitus, Virgil, Sallust (of whom he was hearing for the first time), and Rabelais. FitzGerald's reply was the first of more than three hundred letters he was to write to Cowell. The slightly schoolmasterish tone of his letter suggests that it took him longer to forget the difference in their ages than it did Cowell, but soon their intellectual positions were reversed and FitzGerald had become pupil to the younger man. He hardly recognized it at the time, but at thirty-five he was finding his real artistic bent at last.

Five months later Cowell came to Boulge for his first stay, after being asked several times by FitzGerald. The happiness of the invitations indicates Fitz's delight at having him as a guest and the charming anxiety with which he tried to put Cowell at ease over any social awkwardness: 'Wednesday, and any hour of Wednesday, will suit me perfectly. As to dinner, I dine at all hours; and sometimes at none; but you shall dine at any hour you please.' The cottage ought to be comfortable, for summer had made it 'very dry now; my garden beginning to show roses; and I will cause a piece of lamb to be roasted which, with the help of salad, shall serve us for dinner. Will that do for you?' Mrs Faiers would probably not 'succeed in the pastry or confectionary [sic] line; she has no head for "subtilties".... I hope you will stay over Thursday at all events. Your one clean shirt will be quite clean enough for that. Here is no one to note dress.' He asked Cowell to bring his own share of the entertainment 'in the better shape of quotations from old books which I shall never read; your Greek cup of tears and laughter is very delightful, and will grace any table.' [I, 496,498]

The breadth of Cowell's reading was a constant stimulus, and their letters bristle with references to Homer, Pliny, Tacitus ('Do *you* think Tacitus *affected* in style, as people now say he is?'), to Dante and Milton, showing how much FitzGerald's interests were growing under Cowell's influence. 'Sophocles is a pure Greek temple; but Aeschylus is a rugged mountain, lashed by seas, and riven by thunderbolts – and which is the most wonderful, and appalling?' [I, 613–14] Nor were their speculations confined to literature alone. 'I often think,' wrote FitzGerald, 'it is not the poetical imagination, but bare Science that every day more and more unrolls a greater Epic than the Iliad – the history of the World, the infinitudes of Space and Time!' [I, 566]

Once FitzGerald had started brushing up his languages, Cowell began what was to prove his most important influence on the older man. In 1848, at his request, FitzGerald sent two translations he had made of sections of Livy and Lucretius, saying of the latter, 'I suppose I could translate a good part of it very fairly: but the *great bits*, which alone keep alive Lucretius to most men would require a great poet to render.' [I, 601–3, 607] He was right in being modest about his efforts, but the translations show an assurance in verse that is completely lacking in his earlier poetry. Also at Cowell's suggestion, he began the study of Spanish, so that he could read Calderón.

Although Cowell seemed the precise opposite of Browne in nearly every other way, in FitzGerald's eyes they had in common at least one important trait: neither of them had been spoiled by a conventional university education. With Cowell he discovered the pleasures of shared intellectual experience of a sort he could never have known with Browne, but it was largely a self-taught intelligence that Cowell brought to them. However, given the chance,

140

FitzGerald was a remarkably constant friend, and he never failed in his deep affection for Browne, even if it could not be restored to its original somewhat fervid state; it says a good deal about his temperament that he came through his disappointment without bitterness. Perhaps because they were associated with Browne, the virtues of a healthy, sporting life in the open air always remained at least as admirable to him as those of the study. Their rival claims, exemplified in Browne and Cowell, greatly occupied him during the late 1840s, and he began writing a discussion of the matter, obviously modelled on the Platonic dialogues he had been reading. *Euphranor* was not published until 1851, but for several years Fitz-Gerald talked of its problems with friends, particularly Cowell; 'such trials of one's own show one the art of such dialogues as Plato's, where the process is so logical and conversational at once: and the result so plain, and seemingly so easy. They remain the miracles of that Art to this day.' [I, 552]

Learning to accept without flinching the loss of Browne's intimacy stood FitzGerald in good stead the year after he met Cowell. In October 1845 Cowell announced that he had proposed to a woman he had known for about two years, and that he had been accepted. Even more startling than the news of the engagement of the nineteen-year-old was the name of his fiancée, for it was Elizabeth Charlesworth, daughter of the rector of Flowton, near Ipswich, the woman with whom FitzGerald had once thought he was in love. He is said to have exclaimed in surprise, when told that Cowell was engaged, 'The deuce you are! Why! you have taken my Lady!' Rather more generously, he wrote later, 'You are a happy man and I envy you.'[6]

By now Miss Charlesworth was over thirty and not less plain than FitzGerald had said in 1835. It is unlikely that he was deeply wounded at losing her, although his feelings about the possibility of losing Cowell's friendship are another matter, since he had already seen with Browne the demonstration of the old truth that marriage cancels all previous friendships, at least until they are re-established. Since his intimacy with Cowell had been founded upon common intellectual and artistic interests, a firmer basis than that on which his friendship with Browne rested, they remained good friends for years, and their correspondence continued until FitzGerald's death.

The Cowell marriage in 1847 put FitzGerald into a peculiar tri-angular relationship with them. Ostensibly he was equally friendly with both, but the frequency of his protestations of disappoint-ment at losing his old 'flame' suggests that he was trying too hard. He liked, too, to remember such sentimental details of their old friendship as the colour of the ribbons she had worn, and there were occasional gusty, not very convincing hints in his letters that he still felt his old attachment to her, but it is improbable that either she or Cowell was taken in by them, even if Fitz himself was. On the whole, however, he followed the sensible course of slipping into companionship with both, suggesting himself as guest if they neglected to do so, and feeling that he had lost little by their marriage except his primacy in Cowell's considerations. There was not much he could have done about it, and there was no point in experiencing again the pain he had felt at Browne's marriage. As part of his effort to keep the friendship on an even course, he often acted as reader of Mrs Cowell's poetry, tactfully revising it for her, seldom revealing how little he really admired it, so that she could feel as much his intellectual companion as her husband was.

Mrs Cowell was too shrewd ever to indicate that she so much as remembered FitzGerald's feelings about her in 1835, and she calmly accepted his frequent visits to their house at Bramford, near Ipswich, and his reiterated inclusion of himself with the Cowells as 'we three'. Only when he tried to steer her husband's professional life did she let a trace of resentment show. Since Cowell was so much the junior of the others, each of them felt certain of being his proper mentor, and there was a little jostling of each other with the faintest overtone of jealousy.

For all that one can tell from his letters, Cowell never recognized any difficulty in his wife's relations with FitzGerald, but he must have seen it and resolved to ignore it as having no final importance.

Her remaining correspondence indicates that one of Mrs Cowell's closest confidantes was Lucy Barton, and we know that FitzGerald figured in their exchanges. Since she was so close, Miss Barton was invited to Brampton in company with FitzGerald, as the two most intimate family friends. There is no reason to suspect Lucy Barton of scheming, but it was natural for her to notice that Elizabeth Charlesworth, who had been a spinster nearly as old as she, had unexpectedly married, and that such a thing was not impossible for herself. When her father died, she would be almost destitute otherwise, since both his income and his pension would cease. She could hardly help noticing that FitzGerald, who so often summoned up memories of the days when he had thought himself in love with Mrs Cowell, seemed an impressionable man with a strong sentimental bent. Nor can we blame Mrs Cowell if she thought the best thing for her own marriage, as well as for Lucy and FitzGerald, would be for him to find a wife of his own.

The more FitzGerald and Lucy Barton's father saw of each other, the better they liked and understood one another. Bernard Barton wrote of the younger man with amused understanding of his eccentricities, as on the occasion when Fitz had told him of wanting to write, and Barton described his departure for Geldestone with an 'incessant dream of getting out a Book' and then, instead, 'roaming about in copses, listening to the coo-ing of wood-pigeons & the croaking of frogs' until he forgot all about authorship. Another time he said of FitzGerald that ''Tis an odd quaint medly of humanity, but there is a good deal of humanity in him, I've a notion, when you get at it through that rugged ungainly husk. Besides he is a Specimen of a Class nearly extinct, which when wholly so will be miss'd & even mourn'd – for they have bottom in 'em – they are not of the Sham Genus!'[7]

There was an easy camaraderie between Barton and FitzGerald that allowed them to tease each other affectionately without being offensive. 'I am going to be a great Man!' Barton wrote jokingly in 1840, when he heard that four of his neighbours were naming a ship *The Bernard Barton of Woodbridge*. 'If I fail of being chronicled among the Poets of Great Britain by some future Cibber, I shall at any rate be registered at Lloyds.' To Donne he said that he had given the news 'too abruptly' to FitzGerald, 'just as he was going to sit down to dinner with me, and he jumped up, chair and all, taking that and himself into the far corner of the room, professing he could not presume to sit at the same table with one about to have a ship named after him.' It was no wonder that he said FitzGerald's 'droppings-in of an evening were like green spots in the desert'.[8]

Barton could not afford to keep a horse, and he was so lethargic that his hatred of walking became a joke between him and FitzGerald, who walked to Woodbridge to see him, rather than go without his company. More and more FitzGerald stayed overnight with Barton in Cumberland Street, either to be there for an early departure of the London coach or simply because he felt at home. And when he stayed, Lucy Barton was always there, efficiently running the household on very little money, managing the two women who worked there, often feeding Barton's guests on toasted cheese, which they charitably pretended was their favourite fare.

Barton's letters poked affectionate fun at FitzGerald's penchant for purely masculine company, humorously describing him as a desperate womaniser quite unable to live in 'womanless solitude' and an omnipresent danger to the opposite sex, even though Barton really believed he would be the last person in the world to marry. When FitzGerald wrote from Ireland of meeting Maria Edgeworth, who was more than forty years his senior, Barton insisted that he had been 'paying his addresses to Maria – of whom he wrote – almost like a Lover; I shall take it very ill of him if he has married her, and sent me no Cake.' More seriously he often noticed with real sympathy how bound Fitz was to his 'Mammie'. Fitz-Gerald wrote more frankly to Barton than to his other friends about his deep affection for Browne and his disappointment at his marriage. In 1847 Barton described FitzGerald's loneliness in his abortive attempts to escape Boulge for trips alone, and how, since he had 'no companion, and I verily believe is as comfortable at the Cottage as anywhere – I think his absence will not be a desperate long one – '.[9] Reading Barton's unpublished letters reinforces the feeling that he often understood parts of his friend's personality better than FitzGerald understood himself. It is presumably for that reason that he paid so little attention to his daughter's growing interest in FitzGerald. It would have been awkward, at best, for him to suggest that she was not likely to attract equal interest in return. Barton's understanding of FitzGerald is important because it shows how improbable it was that he tried to arrange a marriage between Lucy and Fitz on his own deathbed, as has been suggested.

Since Barton and his daughter were so close, FitzGerald naturally sent her his regards when he wrote to her father, marked passages in books that he thought she would like, and helped her in the preparation of a volume of Bible stories that she had written. In return she gave him such innocent presents as a kitten and urged her father to take more notice of his kindness. In 1847 she knitted a silk purse for his birthday, somewhat to the surprise of Barton, who gracefully pretended that it was his own gift and sent it to FitzGerald with accompanying verses:

> Poets seldom make presents, because they've no Money!
>   Could I give thee a reason more trite or more terse?
> So, in true Irish fashion, 'I send ye, my Honey!'
>   Fitting gift for a Poet, a poor empty Purse! [I, 557]

It is touching to see on how many counts she had misjudged her man. FitzGerald hated his birthdays and liked them to be passed over in decent silence, and a silk purse was exactly the kind of ostentation he had been avoiding for years. She, however, felt that FitzGerald ought to dress and behave more like a gentleman than a down-at-heel countryman, and the purse was perhaps her idea of a gentle hint. Even had these things not been true, he would still have been embarrassed at such a personal gift from an unmarried woman of his own age. For all her affection and generosity, Lucy Barton was regrettably lacking in tact, and the episode of the purse was like a preview of the misunderstandings that made their brief marriage impossible.

Barton was sixty-three, and since it would not do for 'grand-climacterical people to procrastinate' [I, 562] in such matters, Lucy wanted to have his likeness taken. Her father pretended to dread the sittings, which FitzGerald declared was 'my eye', and he suggested as artist his friend Samuel Laurence, for whom he was always trying to find commissions. He undertook all the arrangements, put Laurence up while he was in Woodbridge, and sat with Lucy for three days reading *Pickwick Papers* aloud to Laurence and the Bartons as the portrait progressed. By pretending that he had made a mistake in quoting Laurence's fee, he tactfully managed to pay a large part of it himself. It is not surprising if Lucy Barton thought him anxious to indulge her whims out of an inexhaustible income.

Although he had amassed some capital, FitzGerald was still dependent upon money from his mother, and he had constantly to be on call when she wanted him to accompany her to the opera or, less appealingly, to act as host at the dinners she was still giving at Portland Place, occasions so spectacular that even Fitz was impressed. Years later Fanny Kemble recalled that the gold dessert service in Portland Place was replaced, 'upon Mrs. FitzGerald's wearying of them, by a set of ground glass and dead and burnished silver, so exquisite that the splendid gold service was pronounced infinitely less tasteful and beautiful'. [IV, 105, n. 1] Her husband's financial troubles were no curb to Mrs FitzGerald's entertainments, since a great deal of her fortune had been legally kept separate from his; the more desperate his position, the more glittering her dinners. The 'large, hot, noisy' evenings made Fitz drink too much port or smoke a 'great black cigar', so that his London mornings were accompanied by hangovers. His mother seldom gave him advance warning about needing him, and for part of each year he had constantly to be ready for her summons to London, Brighton, or Leamington. Many of his unexpected departures from Boulge were at her request, and his position as extra man 'on duty' was too demeaning for him to admit to his friends the real reason for the trips. But, as Barton noticed, the old unhealthy ties to his mother were as strong as ever; he hated nearly everything she stood for, but he could not tear himself away, either financially or emotionally.

His observation of his mother made him unnaturally sensitive to anything resembling social snobbery in others, and for a long period in the 1840s he was shy of intimacy with Thackeray, who seemed to him to have absorbed many of the very views that his novels satirized. In the spring of 1843 he stayed for about three months with Thackeray at his London house in Great Coram Street, trying to keep up Thackeray's spirits after his wife's mental breakdown. 'It's a great comfort to have Fitz,' Thackeray told his mother, 'and we don't see too much of each other only at breakfast of mornings or for ½ an hour in the day to laugh and smoke a cigar. We only talk nonsense: but that is the best of talk and a good laugh the jolliest of luncheons.' But the next year when Fitz wanted to stay again with Thackeray, his old friend said that he could not 'live with him, he makes me too idle'.[10]

As usual, FitzGerald found it difficult to accept that someone he loved might be so busy that it was difficult to see him. Among Thackeray's engagements were occasional dinners with Mrs Fitz-Gerald, whom he apparently never saw with her son. From Brighton Thackeray wrote to his mother in 1845 of seeing 'Mrs. FitzGerald arrive in great state – four in hand an army of flunkies and ladies' maids – and piles of mysterious imperials – There's a prospect of good dinners! The old woman's compliments are however overpowering to me; and to hear how the toadies who surround her compliment *her* is a good moral lesson.' At nearly seventy Mrs FitzGerald was becoming something of a figure of fun for her make-up and the girlish white satin of which her magnificent gowns were frequently made. Thackeray sometimes glimpsed her driving alone in the park 'and looking very melancholy' or at an evening party 'covered all over with diamonds & rouge' listening to the famous contralto Alboni, quite unconscious that 'poor old Mr. FitzGerald' had fainted on the stairs of the same house 'from heat and age and exhaustion' and had been taken home in his own carriage.[11]

It wounded FitzGerald that Thackeray seemed to have gone over to the social camp that included his own mother, and that he sought solace from his troubles in the grand houses of London. 'Thackeray is progressing greatly in his line,' he wrote to Frederick Tennyson in 1848, 'he publishes a Novel in numbers – Vanity Fair – which began dull, I thought; but gets better every number, and has some very fine things indeed in it. He is become a great man I am told: goes to Holland House, and Devonshire House: and for some reason or other, will not write a word to me.' [I, 604] Fitz-Gerald's informant was Carlyle, who had a keen eye at spotting pretension that never existed. Some of the bitterness in Fitz-Gerald's remark is undoubtedly explained by the fact that when he had talked to Carlyle he was in London on business connected with his father's impending bankruptcy and hence was unusually critical of anything that might look like toadying to wealth. When he taxed Thackeray with becoming too grand, 'Old Thack' replied that what 'Gurlyle' had told him about his 'having become a tremenjuous lion &c' was nonsense. A few months later Thackeray looked up FitzGerald: 'I have cared for him tenderly and with a noble affection for twenty years.'[12] The old amiable personal relations were re-established, but FitzGerald's lingering suspicion is indicated by his carping at Thackeray's subsequent novels. *Pendennis*, for example, he found 'very clever, of course, but rather dull'. Not the most graceful of transferrals of resentment, but it acted as a safety valve, so that there was never any open conflict between them.

Perhaps FitzGerald really believed that literary men did not mind criticism of their works, in spite of the aphorism that most of them would prefer aspersions on their morals. He was so whole-hearted in his affections that he expected all-around perfection in his friends, and when he discovered their human weaknesses, he typically ascribed faults to their novels or poems rather than to their personalities. As he had done with Thackeray, so with Tennyson.

Although he never shared with FitzGerald the easy and spontaneous friendship that Thackeray did, in the 1840s Tennyson was very close to him. He was miserable from financial vicissitudes, harried by fear of his own mental state, and apprehensive about the future. FitzGerald despaired of his ever regaining his health, since he persisted in drinking a daily bottle of second-rate port and smoking filthy-smelling shag nearly continuously. Once Fitz had been in awe of him, but now he had more compassion than reverence, concluding that 'poets are an ill-starred race.' When Tennyson had fallen from the pedestal that FitzGerald had erected at Mirehouse, his poetry seemed no more miraculous than the man. At the news that he was writing a long poem in memory of Arthur Hallam, FitzGerald was sceptical: 'Don't you think the world wants other notes than elegiac now?' [I, 478]

In the period between 1845, when Fitz first heard of *In Memoriam*, and 1850, when it was finally published after seventeen years of composition, Tennyson was also working at *The Princess*, a poem that FitzGerald instinctively disliked. In 1847 Tennyson read three books of it to FitzGerald in his lodgings in Charlotte Street; Fitz was 'tired with hacking about London, and slept as he read'. [I, 559] With some reason Tennyson was offended, and he neglected to give FitzGerald a copy when *The Princess* was published at the end of the year. By the time he got around to reading it, Fitz found it mere 'elaborate trifling' and regretted that Tennyson's 'idle, selfish, and unheroic way of life has wasted away the heroic poetical faculty'; he expected never again to read a great work from him, since he had been spoiled 'by so many years of self-indulgence and laziness'. It was a judgement that some observers would have made of FitzGerald himself. [I, 589, 592]

The speed with which *In Memoriam* became widely popular

served only to confirm FitzGerald's prejudices against it, and he said on reading it that it was too repetitive, lacking the 'old champagne flavour' that he had also thought was missing from *The Princess*. Once more Tennyson neglected to send a copy of his work to the friend who had supported him a few years before, and FitzGerald had to ask at least twice before receiving one. Although it was 'full of finest things', he found the poem monotonous, with an 'air of being evolved by a Poetical Machine of the highest order'. [I, 696]

Thereafter Tennyson cared less and less what FitzGerald thought of his poetry, as Fitz became increasingly critical of it. What lay unspoken at the heart of the cooling of their intimacy, which was always stated in terms of poetical criticism not emotions, was FitzGerald's reasonable feeling that Tennyson was insufficiently grateful for the help he had received, and Tennyson's equally understandable sense that monetary dealings between friends in no way guaranteed gratitude. It was a pattern of mutual, largely unstated, recriminatory feelings that FitzGerald was to repeat with Posh Fletcher in later years, and perhaps with Browne as well.

FitzGerald was almost pathological in his hatred of the worship of money, but, like many men who had never been without it, he still regarded it as somehow personal, almost an extension of himself, and he believed that his generosity with it was as intimate as his prodigality of affection. To his poorer friends it seemed a mere accidental possession, part of what he had to bring to friendship, as they brought poetic genius, physical attraction, intelligence, or charm, and not to be openly acknowledged more than any of those even rarer contributions. Nearly every friendship into which finances entered caused trouble for FitzGerald.

CHAPTER VII

Euphranor

By May 1848 Mr FitzGerald was in such financial distress that his creditors wanted to force him into bankruptcy. Edward hoped they would not, less from worry about his father than because the creditors would ultimately be better off if Mr FitzGerald were able to continue running the mine. 'I even now doubt if I must not give up my daily two-pennyworth of cream and take to milk,' Edward wrote, although he knew he would have enough to live on unless the entire kingdom collapsed, 'and, luckily, every year I want less.' [I, 603–4]

On 5 September 1848, under the headline 'A Wealthy Petitioner', *The Times* reported that 'Mr. J. Fitzgerald, of Portland-place, Regent's Park, the Oak Lodge, Leamington, Brighton, and other places' had filed a petition to obtain the protection of the Court of Bankruptcy. 'The debts of the petitioner exceed the enormous sum of 133,000 *l*. . . . His proposition to creditors, in liquidation of his debts, is to pay 6,000 *l*. per year, secured upon the assignment of the Pendleton mines, the machinery, working utensils, &c., until the whole of his debts are satisfied, and in the case of his death then his widow, Mrs. Mary Frances Fitzgerald, is to continue an annual payment of 4,000 *l*.' Some of the individual debts were in excess of £10,000, but a sufficient majority of the creditors acceded to the proposition, so that the Commissioner 'awarded Mr. Fitzgerald protection from arrest'. His son-in-law, John Kerrich, was in debt for more than £16,000 over the Pendleton mine.

All through the autumn of 1848 and the following year the newspapers kept the world informed of the progress of the bankruptcy. In time it was established that Mr FitzGerald's debts

150

actually totalled about £198,000, but the situation was slightly less critical than the figure suggests because out of the total he owed £10,000 to his wife and to each of his seven children, and in addition Mrs FitzGerald's trustees held a £61,000 mortgage on the Pendleton works, so that the amount owed outside the family was probably about £60,000. And, as *The Times* pointed out repetitively, 'the assets are considerable.'

On 17 January 1849 'A claim for 10,000 *l.* was urged on behalf of Mr. Edward Fitzgerald, son of the bankrupt', who held a bond from his father. According to *The Times*, 'Mr. E. Fitzgerald was examined, and it appeared from his statement that the consideration for which the bond was given was cash which was obtained out of a reversionary interest to which witness was entitled.' By the end of May Mr FitzGerald had already paid over £15,000 to his children in interest on his debts to them. The interest on his own capital was an important part of what Edward had been living on, and its diminution was a severe inconvenience. Ultimately he would have more than ample income from his mother's estate; 'in the meanwhile I keep on the windy side of care, and don't care half so much for all these matters as I should for my finger aching.' [I, 609] Perhaps he was whistling to keep up his courage, but he was straightforward in saying that lack of money worried him but little.

There was a veiled suggestion that something more than simple debt was involved in Mr FitzGerald's bankruptcy, but what it was is no longer apparent. The only hint concerns a 'ludicrous incident' that occurred at the meeting on 21 June 1849. 'An attempt was made to prove a claim upon an alleged annuity. In support of the claim a letter was produced, on the back of which was written that the consideration for the annuity was that the annuitant should "hold his tongue." The claim was not established.'[1]

The warmth of their response to his trouble shows how much FitzGerald's friends loved him and admired his refusal to be downcast. Both James Spedding and Frederick Tennyson offered him as much money as he might need until his father's affairs were settled. Bernard Barton, who hated to speak of the bankruptcy to Fitz because his own bank was one of the creditors, hoped that at least 'the *Interest* on this *Bond* will continue to be paid – and what is yet to come to him on the death of his Mother, as well as to his

Brothers & Sisters, will still be something handsome. . . . I only grieve that with his liberality & generosity, & constant readiness to do good, his means should be circumscribed. . . . The matter has vexed him much more for others than himself, indeed I hardly know any so utterly regardless of Self. . . . through the whole affair I have never seen him, for himself, in the least cowed, or even deprest in spirit. I always thought highly both of his heart & head, and I now rate them more highly than ever.'[2]

With his usual generosity FitzGerald sold his father's bond to pay off three of the creditors who seemed most in need, and equally typically he refused to give anything to those who had pressed too hard for bankruptcy proceedings. The furnishings of Boulge Hall were sold to raise money, but the house was retained, since it belonged to his mother's trust. Some of the furnishings of Boulge Cottage went under the hammer, too, but he bought in 'eight chairs, one bed, one table, and twelve towels', as well as several paintings from the main house. His own possessions in the cottage were, of course, not sold. For a time he expected to leave Boulge; the 'diminution of wealth and reputation' was of no consequence to him, but he knew that if he stayed he would be surrounded by creditors looking for help, which he was determined not to give. Even worse would be the old friends trying not to show reproach in their faces: Squire Jenney, for example, had lost £50,000 in Mr FitzGerald's crash. In the meantime FitzGerald sought to raise money on his expectations, to pay for his current expenses. Knowing that the family would ultimately have plenty, 'we should be base to fret ourselves now.' [I, 616]

Far worse for FitzGerald than the loss of money was the notoriety surrounding his father's ruin, for a bankruptcy involving sensationally large amounts was naturally reported in gloating detail in the newspapers. To a man with such a strong feeling of privacy the publicity must have been painful indeed, but he behaved very well, as Barton indicated. The knowledge, however, that his father was ultimately responsible for the whole affair further weakened his ties with him.

There is little evidence of what Mrs FitzGerald thought of her husband's bankruptcy, but she must have been expecting it for years. Mr FitzGerald was reported to have kept a mistress in London, as her father had done, and if so, that fact would undoubtedly have coloured her feelings about his troubles. She increased her allowance to at least one of her daughters but apparently not to the other children, although her own fortune was still so large that at her death a few years later, she was reputed to have left about £1,000,000. In April 1849, in the midst of the proceedings against her husband, she was formally separated from him. She allowed him to stay on at Boulge, which was still her property, and for her own country seat she began restoring the castle on Little Island. As her London residence she took a large house in Ham, near Richmond, in which she lived the last few years of her life when she was not in Brighton or Ireland. Mr FitzGerald stayed in Portland Place for a time, then removed to Regent's Park Terrace in Camden Town.

Barton's remarks about FitzGerald's courage in the face of disaster indicate the affection they had come to feel for each other. On an infinitely smaller scale, but perhaps even more important for him, Barton knew what the loss of money meant. Only a few days before Mr FitzGerald filed his petition of bankruptcy, Barton had discovered that almost all of his own savings, 'a little nest-egg of about a thousand pounds', which he had entrusted to a relative for investment, had been lost, and that the interest of £50 it brought in was 'clean spunged out'. In telling Donne of the catastrophe, Barton was full of praise for the way in which Lucy had taken the news, 'bravely & beautifully – and says we can fadge without it – so we shall cut & pare down ... giving up our Garden, & keeping one girl in the place of two – all which may be done with no great hardship – or attracting much if any notice on the part of our Neighbours.'[3] Barton was in poor health and knew that at his death his salary, his pension, and now his savings would all be gone, leaving Lucy penniless.

Instead of going to London or Brighton in 1848 to have Christmas with his mother, FitzGerald spent the holiday with the Bartons. 'I know not where he could go to be more appreciated, or more highly loved & esteemed, and I believe he has a lurking love of old familiar haunts,' Barton wrote in anticipation of his coming. By now FitzGerald was like a son to him, surely included in the 'one or two special friends' to whom Barton had confided the story of his own loss of money. At Christmas FitzGerald found that Barton had declined noticeably: 'less spirits, less strength: but quite amiable still'. He was short of breath, and his doctors suspected trouble with his heart. Two months later he died, looking 'very demurely to the necessary end of all life' but maintaining his sense of humour to the last.

FitzGerald went to his funeral, wrote Barton's obituary for the *Ipswich Journal*, and helped Lucy sort out her father's effects in preparation for a sale of his books and pictures. Barton, he wrote to Donne, left 'very little worldly goods behind him; and we do not yet know what Miss B. will have or what else she is to do with herself'. [I, 632] 'We' probably included Richard Jones, the local surgeon, and his wife, close friends of Lucy, but it also shows how much FitzGerald was involved in helping her. Not only was Lucy left penniless, but she had also inherited debts from her father and had no way to pay them. It was FitzGerald's suggestion that she assemble a volume of selections from her father's poems and letters in order to earn money to pay the debts, and when she protested that she was unable to do so, he undertook most of the work himself, although he left Lucy's name alone on the title page. To preface the volume he contributed a brief and elegant memoir of Barton, a model of what such writing should be, and he sorted out nine volumes of Barton's verse, to leave only the best. Even those badly needed editing, so he cut most of the ones that remained, trying 'with a change of a word, or even of a line here and there, to give them logic and fluency'. To his surprise he thoroughly enjoyed the task: 'It is wonderful when you come to look close into most of these poems to see the elements of repetition, indistinctness, etc. which make them diffuse and weary. I am sure I have distilled many pretty little poems out of long dull ones which the world has discarded.' Regretfully he admitted that he was not a real poet and could not make a single whole poem as good as Barton's best, 'but I have faculty enough to mend some of B.B.'s dropped stitches'. Artistically he knew he was correct, but 'whether I am right in *morals* to use a dead man so I am not so certain.' [I, 633]

FitzGerald's editing of the poems was so rigorous that it might better be called rewriting. It was the first public appearance of his remarkable ability at reshaping other men's work, seeming in retrospect to have been a preparation for his later translations. As he told Frederick Tennyson, he was aware he lacked originality, but he considered that he had 'the old woman's faculty of judging of them: yes, much better than much cleverer and wiser men; I pretend to no Genius, but to Taste: which, according to my aphorism, is the feminine of Genius.' [I, 664]

Nearly every letter he wrote in the summer of 1849 referred to his admiration of Lucy Barton's bravery, repetitively calling her 'poor' Miss Barton or 'noble' Miss Barton, but nowhere did he hint at tender emotions for her or any close connection between them. He spent most of the spring and summer in Boulge, helping correct proofs of the Barton book. 'Miss B. is so bothered and bewildered she has scarce time or thought to bestow on it. She has been selling all her furniture by auction, poor thing: and is going to take a situation as Governess – at Mrs. Hudson Gurney's, I believe. Is it not noble of her to insist on paying all her Father's debts?' [I, 648] After the sale she went off to Keswick Hall, near Norwich, where she occupied an anomalous position somewhere between family friend and chaperone to the Gurney nieces. There she stayed for seven years.

Lucy had taken some time to make up her mind about accepting the position with the Gurneys, hinting that she had turned down at least one other offer and that the future held still more: 'It seemed to me that the *Gurney home* offered enough of *occupation*, and promised also the *repose* which I really need. At any rate, if my engagement with them does not seem a permanent one, I shall not be *less* fit for any thing else when I give this up, but I must remain there longer than I think for: I have tried to decide for the best, and must now leave it.'[4]

By the spring of 1850 FitzGerald's attitude to Lucy had undergone a radical change, perhaps connected with her unspecified alternatives to staying with the Gurneys. When Frederick Tennyson rallied him about Elizabeth Cowell and his continuing protestations of sorrow at her loss, FitzGerald had to admit that in spite of his avowals, he was in no danger of drowning himself because she had married Cowell. 'The fact is it is not the loss of her alone that makes me hate myself for a fool, but other contingencies which may flourish into worse, and might make me prefer the pond.' [I. 667] What had happened was that in the meantime he had promised to marry Lucy Barton, and that he felt frightened, trapped, and resentful.

There are at least two 'authoritative' accounts of how he got into

155

IX Lucy Barton.

such a scrape, but they are entirely different from each other, and the whole truth is probably beyond recovery now. FitzGerald's grandniece recorded the family tradition that 'in his agony, as he was passing, Bernard Barton joined his daughter's and Fitz-Gerald's hands and gave the momentarily associated pair his blessing',[5] presumably to ensure that Lucy would be taken care of, and that FitzGerald felt thereby morally committed to marry her. The edifying tableau is not impossible, but its sentimentality sounds a long way from Barton's usual amusement at hackneyed situations. Besides, he was keenly aware, as his letters show, of the nature of FitzGerald's emotions and his complete disinclination to marry. What clinches its improbability is that for more than a year after Barton's death Fitz gave no indication of any close relationship with Lucy or even that her departure for Norfolk had any personal significance for him.

The account of the Barton family seems slightly more plausible, even if it is told in a style as melodramatic as Miss Kerrich's. F. R. Barton wrote that FitzGerald had promised her father to take care of Lucy, but when he offered money to her, 'her sense of propriety forbade her to accept.... He accused himself of having committed an indelicacy – a breach of good taste.... He must make amends at any cost. And so, heedless of the consequences, he proposed and she – blind to the distraction of mind that had impelled him – accepted his offer.'[6] But this is to assume that somewhere in the tangle FitzGerald made a deliberate proposal, which is highly improbable in view of his hatred of matrimony. He loved to give the impression that he was susceptible to marriage, but only when there was no danger of its taking place.

What actually happened can only be guessed at, but it seems, in light of both their personalities, that it was a tragicomic misunderstanding between a woman who had had no romantic experience of men, and a man who knew next to nothing about women. Probably Lucy Barton assumed that FitzGerald's constant help to her was his own shy way of indicating affection, and that his offer of financial help was a gauche proposal, one that confirmed all the special feelings about him she had been nursing for several years, a proposal she accepted without his having made it. We know from FitzGerald's talk of Elizabeth Charlesworth, a decade before, that he liked to fancy himself in love, without much sense of the expectations he might be raising in the woman involved; it is most unlikely that he intended his kindness to Lucy Barton to make her fall in love with him, and when she accepted the proposal that had never been offered, he was so inexperienced that he probably saw no way of disentangling himself. What is certain is that as time passed, he became increasingly resentful of having been ensnared, as he saw it, while she looked forward happily to her eventual marriage with a man who she believed had finally overcome a crippling bashfulness with woman.

They must both have realized that it would be a long time before they would be married, for in 1849 his father's bankruptcy was a legitimate excuse for him to drag his feet. There is little evidence of what understanding existed between them during her seven years at Keswick, although it is certain that she wrote to him at least occasionally. In 1868, looking back at his engagement and marriage, FitzGerald told a friend that when he realized how unsuited they were for each other, 'and *love* between two of their age and feelings being out of the question, he *suggested* through a letter to Mrs. Jones a breaking off of the engagement – but Miss B. on receiving this letter from Mrs. J. returned it to him saying *she* had no fears for the future, but that he was always looking on the worst side etc. Then she holding in that mind and he on his Mother's death coming in for a fortune, what could he do?'[7]

The circumstantial quality of FitzGerald's account makes it sound more believable than the statement of his niece that Lucy Barton had offered to release him before their marriage, and that he refused the offer.[8] After 1850 her name virtually disappears from his correspondence, as he returned to his bachelor life, as if hoping that if he ignored it, the spectre of marriage would go away. Both of them were honourable, decent-hearted persons, but it would be difficult to find a better example of how easily artlessness and naïveté may be as destructive as malice.

Had FitzGerald not already been sore from feeling manoeuvred into an engagement with Elizabeth Cowell's best friend, he might have behaved somewhat differently in 1850 and 1851. Like Lucy, Mrs Cowell was a devout Evangelical, and she had always wanted to be a clergyman's wife, like her mother before her. Although her husband was also religious, he had become so involved in the study of Oriental languages that it was improbable that he could be persuaded to study for Holy Orders; the next best thing was for him to take a degree at Oxford or Cambridge, which she proposed to him when his brother was old enough to take his place in the family counting-house. She shared her young husband's interest in language, she read Latin and Greek already, and the major part of her honeymoon at Dover had been taken up with their joint study of Sanskrit.

Not surprisingly, Cowell was unenthusiastic at first about going to Oxford; by the time he could take up residence, he would be a twenty-five-year-old among teenagers, and his wife would be nearly forty. None of that altered her determination in the least. In the summer of 1850 they went to Oxford for a week to attend the degree ceremony with Cowell's school friend, George Kitchin, who had taken a double first. 'It does promise to have the most *important* influences upon our future life,' wrote Mrs Cowell, for her husband's mind was 'more and more settling into the wish to go to college'. By the end of the summer Cowell had agreed to matriculate in November and go into residence early in 1851.

FitzGerald gave the Cowells letters of introduction in Oxford, and since he still thought he might move from Boulge to be away from his father's creditors, he for a time considered renting the Cowells' house during their stay in Oxford. Mrs Cowell may have thought that Oxford would provide a welcome break in their close association with FitzGerald, but in the early autumn all was still peaceable; according to her, Cowell 'was having the hottest correspondence just now in Latin with E.F.G.', and FitzGerald still referred to her as 'the Lady of my old Love'. At the end of October he went to stay with them at Bramford; he read Euripides with Cowell and tactfully went for walks when his host was working at mathematics. A week later, however, Mrs Cowell reported indignantly that 'some evil influences are persuading Edward to give up college altogether and trust to Oriental studies alone for a career.'

The malign powers were FitzGerald and W. B. Donne. Worst of all, as Mrs Cowell saw it, it had all come about through her 'own wretched fault!'. Cowell had insisted that she say nothing of his Oxford plans to others, but she was so proud of having persuaded him to go that at last she had been given permission to 'send word by E.F.G. to Mr. Donne, who, being a great scholar, I thought would rejoice in it'. '*Par malheur*' Donne suggested that Cowell was already well embarked on Oriental studies, and that he would have to abandon them temporarily in Oxford to concentrate on Latin and Greek. Because he had no influential connections there, finding a chair in Oriental languages would be difficult, since 'such Professorships ... are given, *not to merit*, but by interest and party prejudice.' Far better, he thought, for Cowell to concentrate on Sanskrit, then try for a chair at one of the London colleges, where they were awarded by merit, 'and an University degree is not insisted on'.

Perhaps Mrs Cowell thought that Donne and FitzGerald were insinuating that her own rather unusual marriage would be a social hindrance to Cowell in Oxford, for she was indignant at the suggestion that her husband 'try for something (of all *nonsense* to

159

talk!) in the wretched Scotch or London Universities ... the mischief of it is that to prove their point they so *distort* College life, in the dreadfully long letters E.F.G. is rousing up his languid energies to send us, that Edward, who was just beginning, to my heartfelt thankfulness, to *rise* to the occasion, and really feel the fitness of his tastes and energies for the career before him, is now almost wholly turned back again.... I wrote to try and stop [Fitz-Gerald's] writing, or using such influence, but *quite* in vain; it only brought on fresh arguments.'

Angrily Mrs Cowell wrote a few days later that Donne and Fitz-Gerald had been pressing her husband to go to Donne's house at Bury 'to *argue* the point with them, and I have been *just* able, day by day (*Sanscrit* and *I* have, as he is intensely hard at work) to persuade him *not* to go or write'. She admitted that both Donne and FitzGerald meant well 'and are both really men of the highest principle, as far as a *man* can be, who doubts if Scripture be altogether the highest guide ... but they are men *totally* incapable of appreciating Edward's higher qualities'.[9]

FitzGerald certainly had Cowell's best interests at heart, but he was not uninfluenced in determining them by his own reluctance to lose the companionship of the one man who had meant most to him since Browne's marriage. 'With whom shall I change a word on Aeschylus now – from whom shall I learn anything about Persian Spoons? But every day I get more dogged in expecting less and less of Life.' He made one last attempt to keep him in the vicinity by suggesting that Cowell apply for the headmastership of the Bury St Edmunds Grammar School. After a considerable silence Cowell wrote to say that in spite of the advice he had received, he was going to Oxford the following year. With only a nearly imperceptible flick at Mrs Cowell, FitzGerald replied good-naturedly: 'I had begun to suppose your Wife had forbid you to write to me, for fear of my bad communications corrupting your good designs. You both so far misunderstood me that I had no desire to *stop* your Oxford plans for good and all, but only to advise you to consult so capable a man as Donne before you decided ... you may have heard as good advice to a contrary effect from others which quite justifies your decision.' He signed the letter, 'Yours, and the indignant Wife's, ever E.FG.' [I, 688–9]

Cowell, FitzGerald told Frederick Tennyson, would be the 'best

Scholar in England. Not that I think Oxford will be so helpful to his studies as his counting house at Ipswich was. However, being married he cannot at all events become Fellow, and, as so many do, dissolve all the promise of Scholarship in Sloth, Gluttony, and sham Dignity. I shall miss them both more than I can say.' [I, 695] By now he had learned painfully how rare close friendships are, and he was not going to endanger that with Cowell by further antagonizing his wife, even though she had seemed as rough-shod in getting her own way as Lucy Barton was. Once she had won the battle, Mrs Cowell could afford to be generous. After this Fitz-Gerald was as thick as ever with Cowell over literary matters, and he stayed with them at Oxford and elsewhere, but the first flush of intimacy was over. Mrs Cowell apparently kept Lucy Barton informed of his doings for the next six years, and it was probably she who kept him up to the mark until he finally married Lucy. (One can only wonder whether she did so out of loyalty to Lucy or as revenge on FitzGerald.)

Three years in Oxford, with a wife to support, must have put a severe strain on Cowell's finances when he gave up the income from the counting-house, since there is no evidence that he had money of his own, and his wife certainly had none. After Cowell left Oxford, FitzGerald thought he might need support and offered money to him so spontaneously as to suggest that he had done so before. In 1851, when Cowell became an undergraduate, Fitz could count on a fixed income, as his father's bankruptcy was at last on the verge of settlement, and it is possible that he contributed to the Cowells' support in Oxford. If so, his action would have been of a piece with his embarrassed generosity to other friends such as Thackeray, Tennyson, and Browne. Even in the depth of his own financial worries, he insisted on continuing small payments to several indigent old people in the neighbourhood of Boulge, referring to them as his pensioners. No one could have been more genuinely charitable, but he always had trouble understanding that close friends whom he helped might not take as much pleasure in his generous transactions as he did.

Some of the documents concerning Mr FitzGerald's financial troubles are inaccessible, so that it is difficult to be certain of details, but he seems to have been discharged as a bankrupt by the end of 1851, after three years of negotiations that left Fitz with a permanent dislike of the law. One creditors' meeting was 'filled with miserable, avaricious, hungry, angry, degraded, cunning faces', sharp voices 'grinding disreputable reports and surmises – a drunken greengrocer clamouring for two years' pay, etc.'. [I, 614] A full year of dealing with another lawyer to set up an annuity on his reversionary interest 'ended only in his bringing me in a long bill for doing nothing'. [I, 658–9] When his father's affairs were settled, FitzGerald confided all his own finances to the care of Spedding, with a sigh of relief at having his estate at last 'in the hands of a *Gentleman*'. [II, 40] He told Frederick Tennyson that he was no worse off than he had been for the past three years, and by April 1852 he made a will in which he left Thackeray's daughters £1,000, apologizing that it was such a small sum, since most of his money would be needed elsewhere, which suggests that the whole affair had still left him in fair shape financially.

The only peripheral advantage to all the meetings that he had to attend was that they gave him occasion to be in London, seeing Thackeray, Tennyson, Carlyle, and Spedding, whose calm and judicious nature he came to love more and more, even though he still liked to tease him about his passion for Jenny Lind and to poke fun at Spedding's high, bald forehead that he claimed would keep him from ever being scalped, since Red Indians would have nothing to hold on to. Tennyson was married in 1850, the year he became Poet Laureate, and though FitzGerald frequently went to Twickenham to see the poet and his new wife, he never took greatly to Mrs Tennyson and felt that she had unduly tamed the rough Lincolnshire manners of his old friend, thus speeding the decay of his poetic powers. FitzGerald's manner must have been transparent when he was not fond of someone, and Mrs Tennyson's remarks about him after his death indicate that she had never had any more liking for him than he had for her. By the end of 1851 he wrote of making a 'call on Alfred the Poet with Spedding. Somehow I have no curiosity to see him any more.' [II, 43]

Like most persons who knew Carlyle, FitzGerald veered wildly in his regard for that wayward genius. On good evenings they would lie calmly on the carpet on either side of Carlyle's fireplace, pulling on their pipes and talking, but too often Carlyle would only grunt in reply to FitzGerald's remarks and send out a great puff of smoke. 'He smokes indignantly,' FitzGerald complained. [I, 504] Even worse were the times when Carlyle set off on hour-long diatribes of increasing violence that made Fitz think he was 'more wild, savage, and unreasonable every day; and, I do believe, will turn mad'. [I, 534] On such occasions there was little FitzGerald could do but release his frustrations by actions equally eccentric. One evening he was so put out by Carlyle that he was delighted to say good night: 'An organ was playing a polka even so late in the street and Carlyle was rather amazed to see me polka down the pavement. He shut his street door – to which he always accompanies you – with a kind of groan.' [I, 472] In 1848 Fitz said he had seen Carlyle but once; 'he was very grim, very eloquent; and altogether I have not been tempted there again.' [I, 623]

But, like Carlyle's other friends, FitzGerald found him so interesting that he always returned, even when he knew that he was being used, as he had been over the matter of Naseby Field. During one year Carlyle's letters were full of a six-year-old black gelding that FitzGerald had arranged for him to buy for £35 from William Browne. Carlyle rode him two hours daily, to 'see the green fields by means of him: but at bottom he is still rather a dangerous piece of goods for me! He improves in strength; has excellent paces (when he likes to put them forth), hoofs of brass; is fleet as a roe; – neither do I think the creature has any radical vice or ill-nature in him: but he is in fact *unbroken*.' Bobus, as Carlyle named him, had 'to be forcibly flogged and kicked along or he will not go at all', and then he would streak away 'like a Cat travelling on hot iron!' After Carlyle had complained long enough, Browne (the 'most courteous and obliging of men') took him away to perfect him 'in all manner of equine behaviour' before bringing him back 'thin and rough, but airy as a Kangaroo'. Carlyle seldom lost a struggle through lack of perseverance, but Bobus proved too much for him and had to be sold to a 'much admiring neighbour of my Brother's' in Annandale for the exact price he had originally cost.[10] Letters like Carlyle's, however, nearly made up to FitzGerald and Browne for the trouble he had caused them.

With good reason FitzGerald had been pleased with his memoir of Barton, and it turned his thoughts to further writing. 'I have been obliged to turn Author on the very smallest scale,' he told Frederick Tennyson [I, 657] with evident pleasure. But he recognized his limitations in prose: 'I have what Goethe calls the "Barber's talent" of easy narrative of easy things – can tell of Barton, and Chesterton Inn, but not of Atreus, and the Alps. Nor do I pretend to do so.' [II, 3] He also took a cold look at his own poetry that must have cost him a twinge or two: 'I do not care about my own verses.... They are not *original* – which is saying, they are not worth anything. They may possess sense, fancy etc. – but they always recall other and better poems. You see all *moulded* rather by Tennyson etc. than *growing* spontaneously from my own mind. No doubt there is original feeling, too; but it is not strong enough to grow up alone and whole of itself.' [II, 14] He still seemed to himself a long way from being a true writer.

In 1846, under Cowell's influence, he had begun writing a modern 'Platonic' dialogue on the subject of contemporary education and how it had warped young men's minds by teaching them only bookish subjects. After a few weeks of desultory work, the 'spirit of light dialogue evaporated' during an attack of influenza, and the manuscript was shoved to the back of the drawer.

The whole subject was revived in his imagination during the acrimonious correspondence as to whether Cowell would benefit from going to Oxford. As FitzGerald waited for an answer to his letters, he took a short trip to Cambridge, already established as the setting of the dialogue, which was so far called *Phidippus*, for the character based on William Browne. 'I came back last Saturday,' he told Cowell, 'and, happing on that famous scribble of "Phidippus" in my desk, I seized it, and during the week past have licked [it] into a sort of shape – so as I would like to show it you: though there is much in it you would disapprove.' [I, 689] A few days later he reported that he had bundled it off to the printer, although he knew it needed more work. 'I should be well content if it paid its expenses, at the same time doing no harm.... Your wife would hate it.' [I, 690]

At the last moment he changed its name to *Euphranor*, after the character who had usurped the larger part of the interest of the book. As might be expected from the circumstances of its composition, it is a highly personal document, and though none of the characters is a direct portrait, at least two are recognizable as very near relatives of Browne and Cowell. 'Lexilogus' thin, pale, and spectacled face', although it does not resemble Cowell physically, is obviously a version of him, at least as he might become at the university, and his fire screens with representations of 'the old Church – the Yew tree – the Parsonage' glance at the Cowells' house in Bramford. There is no way of knowing how much the character was changed at the last moment, but it is easy to see why Fitz-Gerald did not expect Mrs Cowell to appreciate it. Phidippus, modelled on Browne, who from the first had been intended as the central figure, has diminished to a purely visual part of the narrative, making his entrance late in the book on a splendid black Yorkshire mare, 'plunging, and blowing out a peony nostril after her flying fellows', as if leaping from a Stubbs painting or one of Carlyle's letters. Once the mare is stabled, Phidippus has little to do but show Lexilogus how to master the 'side-roll' at bowls, at which William Browne had been expert.

FitzGerald seems to have recognized that Phidippus shared with his original the awkwardness of not being very interesting to anyone but his creator. The burden of the argument is sensibly shifted to the shoulders of the newly eponymous character, Euphranor, who debates with the narrator about the function of education (to tell truth, there is remarkably little difference between them). What lies at the heart of the dialogue is the early Victorian interest in the rebirth of chivalry in modern guise, the nineteenth-century attempt to graft medieval virtues on to contemporary values. Among the other writers invoked are Carlyle, Tennyson, above all Kenelm Digby, in their various recreations of modern chivalry. In 1838 FitzGerald had given Browne a copy of Digby's *Godefridus*, the first part of *The Broad Stone of Honour*, his treatise on the recreation of noble medieval values in England, and the book is used as the cornerstone of FitzGerald's dialogue. 'Chivalry', Euphranor reads aloud from it, 'is only a name for that general Spirit or state of mind, which disposes men to Heroic and Generous actions; and keeps them conversant with all that is Beautiful and Sublime in the Intellectual and Moral world.'

FitzGerald's first subtitle for *Euphranor* was *A Dialogue on Youth*, which accurately indicates its focus on the grace, gallantry, and beauty of young men whose bodies are not warped to feed their minds. The reader feels uncomfortably that FitzGerald is endowing them with everything that he would like to have been himself. The dialogue does not wholly neglect learning, and the text itself reflects FitzGerald's own broad reading, but learning comes off a very poor second to rowing, riding, or boating. The ideal emerging from the dialogue is a re-establishment in the public schools and universities of the spirit of the Greek gymnasium beside training in military arts and even a 'piece of Arable to *work in*'. The result sought was a 'sense of Order, Self-restraint, and Mutual Dependence'.

The tenor of the argument is familiar from a dozen other sources in Romantic attempts to bring to rebirth the spirit of chivalry in a mercantile world, but it is urged with wit, charm, and a shrewd use of lush language that stills one's objections to some of FitzGerald's tenets. The point is demonstrated at the end of the dialogue, a passage that Tennyson enormously admired. The narrator leads his friends through the water meadows back to Cambridge, and by the deliberate diminution of sound and the slowing of rhythm to a stylistic resolution FitzGerald keeps one from reflecting on whether the best part of a university is after all a boat race on the Cam:

> Then, waiting a little while to hear how the winner had won, and the loser lost, and watching Phidippus engaged in eager conversation with his defeated brethren, I took Euphranor and Lexilogus under either arm, (Lycion having got into better company elsewhere,) and walk'd home with them across the meadow leading to the town, whither the dusky troops of Gownsmen with all their confused voices seem'd as it were evaporating in the twilight, while a Nightingale began to be heard among the flowering Chestnuts of Jesus.

As pure argument it may cheat, but it is an effective close to the work.

The little book was printed at FitzGerald's expense and published by William Pickering, appearing anonymously in January 1851. It sold well enough for there to be a need in 1855 for a 'new Version (rather than new Edition)'. [II, 175] For such a modestly produced book, it was a surprising success with the reviewers, including Cowell and Spedding, as well as a number of others who surely did not recognize his references to Browne and Cowell, his sly insertion of private conversations he had had with

Tennyson, Carlyle, and Charles Merivale, or his covert apology for
having misjudged 'Daddy' Wordsworth at Mirehouse. The *Gentleman's Magazine* said it would be read with pleasure 'by all who
desire to see around us not a race of mock heroes studying and
striving to revive the thoughts and imitate the customs of the
worthies of the Middle Ages, but men suited to enjoy and defend
the many blessings which increased light and liberty have given us
over our forefathers.' To FitzGerald's shyly expressed pleasure, the
Spectator 'praised moderately – the poor old Literary Gazette
more warmly'. [II, 10]

Having once made the plunge, FitzGerald found that writing
and publishing were completely to his taste, since he was now convinced that he had as much talent as several of his friends who were
already established as novelists, poets, or essayists. Only a year
after *Euphranor* appeared, he had 250 copies of another volume
printed at his own expense and once more published by Pickering:
Polonius: A Collection of Wise Saws and Modern Instances.

FitzGerald had always been an inveterate keeper of common-
place books, note books, and scrap books, many of which may be
seen today in the Christchurch Museum in Ipswich. *Polonius* was
derived from remarks by friends, the commonplace books he had
kept on his reading, and aphorisms that had occurred to himself: it
represented the loose change of his thought. Despite the self-
defensive title, he aimed above all at variety and said that he 'meant
it to be the best little Book of its kind extant. I am not *sure* it be not
– but it is not so good as I intended.' [II, 48]

The quotations in the book are arranged under 139 loose
headings that are intended more for punctuation than exact defin-
ition of ideas. The range of FitzGerald's reading is impressive, the
more so because it is so unostentatious. More than a hundred
authors are quoted, in five languages, of which only the plentiful
Greek selections are usually translated. Some are identified, many
are not. Bacon and Newman appear frequently; more unusually,
Selden is well represented; perhaps the largest number of quotations are from Carlyle (and probably from FitzGerald himself,
although their lack of identification makes attribution uncertain).
They vary considerably in length, but FitzGerald gave his real
love to apophthegms, the pithier the better. 'The quick decision of
one who sees half the truth' bears no identification, but FitzGerald

elsewhere wrote that it was a casual remark made by Tennyson. 'He was scant o' news wha tauld his father was hanged' is exactly the kind of remark FitzGerald liked to repeat in conversation.

Polonius contains what is apparently the first record of Fitz-Gerald's favourite anecdote, one told by John Wesley, which FitzGerald repeated on numerous occasions in letters and conversation when he was annoyed by pretension: 'A gentleman of large fortune, while we were seriously conversing, ordered a servant to throw some coals on the fire. A puff of smoke came out. He threw himself back in his chair, and cried out, "O Mr. Wesley, these are the crosses I meet with every day." Surely these crosses would not have fretted him so much if he had had only fifty pounds a year instead of five thousand.'

FitzGerald sensibly recognized that wit and humour are often difficult to distinguish from either reasoned morality or a bottom of exact good sense. We understand the 'grand Truisms of life' only 'as years turn up occasions for practising or experiencing them', he wrote in the Preface. 'For in proportion as any writer tells the truth, and tells it figuratively or poetically, and yet so as to lie in a nutshell, he cuts up sooner or later into proverbs ... and gradually gets down into general circulation.' Not surprisingly Carlyle turns up on page after page, in such examples as 'What is to be undergone only once we may undergo: what must be comes almost of its own accord. The courage we desire and prize is, not the courage to die decently, but to live manfully.'

For anyone who knows FitzGerald's other writings, it is great fun attempting to spot the quotations in *Polonius* that are his own. 'Taste is the feminine of genius' is easily recognizable and comes directly from a letter to Frederick Tennyson (see p. 155). And nothing could be more typical of his attitudes than 'One may conceive that Handel is wholesomer for a people than Bellini.' Some are questionable, although they have the ring of his habit of making maxims of what he thought were his own failings, such as 'The beginning of self-deception is when we begin to find *reasons* for our *propensities*.' The most revealing but teasing quotation in the book is the only one that is repeated; once it occurs under the heading of 'Solitude', once under 'Melancholy and Madness', both of which haunted him and presented more temptations than most other failings: 'Be not solitary, be not idle.' It probably owes its origin to a letter from Johnson to Boswell, but it had rattled around his head so long that it had taken on a new and more admonitory form. It is improbable that he remembered its source or even realized that he had repeated it in *Polonius*.

'I doubt it will be but a losing affair,' he wrote in self-deprecation, 'but I had long had a desire to put out such a thing: life flies: the venture is not very much: and so an end.' [II, 50] Nor was he wrong. Apparently it was never reviewed, and it was soon forgotten except by friends and by himself. It remains, however, a delightful book, to be taken in small doses like most such collections, and telling us in other men's words as much about FitzGerald as if he had been a confessional writer.

CHAPTER VIII

Death of FitzGerald's Parents

Ever since 1848, the beginning of his bankruptcy proceedings, old Mr FitzGerald's health had been failing, and he suffered from recurrent bladder trouble. In the spring of 1852 he was ill for three weeks and in March, only a few months after his affairs had at last been set in order, he died at the age of 76, probably of a heart attack. Edward's few references to his death indicate that he felt more pity than sorrow. 'I do not think I told you my Father was dead,' he wrote to Frederick Tennyson some three months after the event, 'like poor old Sedley in Thackeray's Vanity Fair, all his Coal schemes at an end.' Since Thackeray was already writing the novel at the time Mr Fitzgerald first faced bankruptcy, perhaps some aspects of his personality and situation had crept into the fictional character, but it is more probable that Edward FitzGerald saw in the pathos of his tired old father a reflection of the defeated Sedley, reduced at the end of his life to acting as a coal agent. 'As he lay in the stupor of Death,' Mr FitzGerald was haunted by memories of his colliery and murmured, 'That engine works well' with his last breath. [II, 57]

If one obituary of Edward FitzGerald is to be believed, he received £30,000 at his father's death.[1] What makes it seem improbable is that his poverty had been the ostensible reason he could not marry Lucy Barton, and since such a large sum could hardly have been kept secret, he would surely have felt obliged to fulfil his engagement to her if he had inherited it, as he ultimately was after his mother's death.

Because Mrs FitzGerald had already set up her own residence elsewhere and was anyway too old to come back to Boulge, in 1853 she turned the estate over to Edward's brother John, chief of his parents' heirs. It was what FitzGerald had feared ever since moving into the cottage; almost immediately its rural calm was shattered. John began organizing his own charities near Boulge. Since the family did not own the presentation of the parish living, he could do little to influence the rector, who was as High Church as John was Evangelical, so one of the outbuildings of Boulge Hall was converted into a chapel that was ostensibly intended for the private use of the family but actually became the centre of anti-Puseyite churchmanship in the neighbourhood of Woodbridge. The contentiousness that Edward hated in organized religion was beginning to engulf the parish.

'Did I tell you I really was about to leave this Cottage?' he asked Stephen Spring Rice in May 1853, 'before the Winter if I can exert myself. But I have not yet fixt on a new abode.' [II, 89] As usual, he had difficulty in making up his mind over such practical matters, and now the decision was complicated by the possibility of marriage, which he had been trying to forget. It would be unwise to buy another cottage suitable only for a bachelor, and equally undesirable to take a house large enough for a wife, which would only be inviting matrimony. In the meantime he began selling pictures and books, and 'in general lightening my wings for a flight when I have decided *whither*'. [II, 102]

The previous tenant of the home farm at Boulge was Job Smith, who had moved to Farlingay Hall, a large and beautiful farmhouse halfway between Boulge and Woodbridge (nowadays it is on the edge of the town itself). In desperation FitzGerald decided to take rooms temporarily with the Smiths; he stored his goods in the garrets of Farlingay, found Mrs Faiers and her husband places with John FitzGerald, and left Boulge forever. Smith 'and his Wife, a capital housewife, and his Son, who could carry me on his shoulders to Ipswich, and a Maid servant who, as she curtsies of a morning, lets fall the Teapot, etc., constitute the household'. [II, 150] It became the most permanent base he had for the next three years, since he spent long periods in London, frequently visited the Cowells in Oxford, and stayed with Crabbe at Bredfield Rectory for weeks at a time.

As early as 1849 FitzGerald had written of how his 'head sometimes runs on that grand grotesque Play' of Calderón that Cowell had translated for him, and he vowed to read it in the original one day. [I, 644] A year later he had 'begun to nibble' at old Spanish ballads and had 'bounced through a play of Calderón with the help of a friend'. Once, he believed, Calderón had been overrated, but now it was the 'fashion to underpraise him'. [II, 63] The idea of making his own translation was already forming.

He continued to consult Cowell over obscure passages, but he had no trouble in understanding 'the *whole*: plot and dialogue too'. [II, 65] By October 1852 he had resolved on half a dozen plays, and only nine months later, in July 1853, they were published as *Six Dramas of Calderon, Freely Translated by Edward FitzGerald*, which says something of both the efficiency of publishing in those days and FitzGerald's energy when his interest was stirred. It was the only one of his books that was ever published under his own name.

He was worried of course by the old problem of translation, of whether respect for the author or the reader was more important, whether to be scrupulously faithful to the text or to attempt by modernization to create in his own readers a response that would be parallel to that of the original audience, even if it was not precisely the same. In his preface to the plays he said that he did not 'believe that an exact translation of this poet can be very successful', since the seventeenth-century Spanish sounded bombastic to modern ears. He had 'tried to compensate for the fullness of sonorous Spanish, which Saxon English at least must forgo, by a compression which has its own charm to Saxon ears'. Since he had ventured to be so free with Calderón, he stressed that he had not 'meddled with any of his more famous plays', only with six out of the more than a hundred dramas that were not well-known in English and deserved to be.*

FitzGerald used to say that Tennyson owed it to the world to translate at least one of the great Greek plays, since every generation needs its own version in the poetic style that is most immediate to contemporaries, so that the classics do not become museum pieces. Most readers find no trouble in responding either to older works or to modern translations of them, but it is difficult to accept translations of an intermediate period that speak more of

---

* *The Painter of His Own Dishonour, Keep Your Own Secret, Gil Perez, the Gallician, Three Judgments at a Blow, The Mayor of Zalamea,* and *Beware of Smooth Water.*

the age of the translator than of the author and so seem outdated. A century later FitzGerald's translations of Calderón tell us as much about the influence (often a pernicious one) of Shakespeare upon the Victorians as it does about the Spanish dramas, and it is the echoes, conscious and unconscious, of Shakespeare in FitzGerald that make appreciation of his Calderón difficult today.

The problem became particularly acute for him because Shakespeare and Calderón were contemporaries, so that it was tempting to make them speak a language that was at least similar. FitzGerald did not make it easier by writing five of the six plays primarily in blank verse, which was the usual Victorian solution to poetic translation of drama. It was a hurdle that Arnold and Tennyson and dozens of lesser poets stumbled over and that Browning and Swinburne only narrowly skirted. But one suspects that FitzGerald was right to say that each generation needs its own versions, and probably poetic drama sounded best to the Victorians if it resounded with Shakespeare. Today, when we are less preoccupied with Shakespeare, the echoes in these Calderón plays tempt us into an outrageously unfair comparison between FitzGerald and Shakespeare, in which the translator is bound to be diminished. It is only some forty years ago that an expert on FitzGerald praised his Calderón translations for being 'written in a Shakespearean blank verse that is both musical and vigorous'.[2] For modern ears Fitz-Gerald did not go far enough in making Calderón sound our contemporary, so that we hear him not only through the heavy curtain of the English language but also through successively muffling overtones of Victorianism and Shakespeare, and all contribute to the lack of immediacy. The unpliable result is a language that makes it impossible to distinguish the speech of one character from that of any other.

FitzGerald himself was pleased at the likeness between Shakespeare and Calderón, as he saw it and as he increased it by the addition of songs that are intended to sound Elizabethan. In *Keep Your Own Secret* the gracioso, or comic lord of misrule, is Lazaro, who is only too obviously related to Falstaff in his lying account of the constantly increasing number of men with whom he has fought. To the text FitzGerald added a footnote: 'One cannot fail to be reminded of the multiplication of Falstaff's men in buckram, not the only odd coincidence between the two poets. Lazaro's solution of the difficulty seems to me quite worthy of Falstaff.'

However difficult appreciation of it is for us, FitzGerald's translation was effective for his contemporaries, particularly in its Elizabethan echoes. Unfortunately, his volume appeared at almost the same time as another Calderón collection of translations by D. F. McCarthy, and only three years before FitzGerald's old Cambridge acquaintance, Richard Chenevix Trench, newly Dean of Westminster, published a translation of two of Calderón's plays. Reviewers are seldom eager to get their hands on translations still smoking from the press, and FitzGerald's volume had to wait to be bracketed with McCarthy's at first and finally with Trench's as well. He was afraid that his attempts to modernize the plays would not meet with general approval, and he was right. Shortly after publication the *Athenaeum* was severe on his meddling with the originals and for that failing refused to review him at length. The *Literary Gazette* thought he translated with 'zeal and carefulness, and displays some ingenuity in the difficult task'. In spite of that tepid praise the reviewer could not 'conscientiously recommend Mr. Fitzgerald's "free translations" as giving a just estimate of the spirit and point of Calderon. The reader will, however, obtain some idea of that fertility of invention and skill of arrangement which have placed him at the head of all continental writers for the stage.'

FitzGerald was so unhappy at the early reviews, however expected, and in particular the 'determined spit' of the *Athenaeum*, that he regretted he had ever published. Some of the sting was taken out three years later by the *Saturday Review*, which compared the versions of FitzGerald, Trench, and McCarthy; of them all, 'Mr. FitzGerald's, by the freedom and raciness of the style, and by the skilful adoption of the tone and manner of our elder and best dramatic poets, will perhaps excite in readers unacquainted with the original, the highest admiration of Calderon.' It helped, even if a certain reluctance shows through the interstices of the words.

In 1857 *Fraser's* found the 'freedom, vigour, and liveliness of Mr. Fitzgerald's translation ... almost impossible to commend too highly: he possesses the true art of compensation; and his version reads like an original composition of the best days of the English language.' FitzGerald found it 'very handsome', although he realised that W. B. Donne had written the review and could be counted on to say nothing wounding. Modestly FitzGerald said, 'I find people like that Calderon book.' [II, 266]

Even *Fraser's* and the *Saturday Review* suggest that the language of the translations was that of another age, not FitzGerald's. Finding his own style was a slow process, but he was headed in the right direction, for he sensed that his particular talent lay in handling materials taken from other writers with the quirky originality of his own mind. Barton, *Polonius*, and Calderón all moved him nearer his goal.

FitzGerald spent Christmas with his mother in Brighton in 1852, then went along the coast for a short stay with Tennyson and his wife in Seaford. In reporting the visit to Cowell in the last days of the year, he said that he had been trying to convince Tennyson of the necessity of learning Persian, and he signed the letter in Persian script.*

The signature shows something of FitzGerald's celerity when he was absorbed in a subject, since he had begun studying the language less than three weeks before, during one of his periodic visits to the Cowells in Oxford. Learning Persian was a way of encouraging Cowell to keep up his Oriental studies, and it also provided 'a point in common with him, and enables us to study a little together'. [II, 117] Once he was away from Cowell's immediate proximity, he continued Persian grammar, but his enthusiasm flickered and nearly went out.

It was not until January 1854 that he could write: 'This Persian is really a great Amusement to me.' What had set the spark alight again was his appreciation of Sir William Jones's Persian and Arabic grammar, of which the 'Poetic Taste' made learning the language 'as delightful as possible'. [II, 118] From that time on, his letters to Cowell were full of questions about Persian grammar and literature. Since many of the translations he used were in German, he quietly learned that language along the way, making 'two Birds kill each other for my benefit'. [II, 137]

In the summer of 1854 he began working on *Salámán and Absál*, Jámí's fifteenth-century Persian allegorical poem, which Cowell

---

*Tennyson was interested in learning Persian, but his wife, fearful that the characters were bad for his eyes, hid his texts and persuaded him to play badminton instead.

had pointed out to him. Largely he began it out of sheer delight in being with Cowell. He put it aside, however, until January of the following year, then picked it up at the time of his mother's death, after which he worked so hard at it that he had a 'metrical abstract' of it two weeks later, and had it ready for publication in April.

Aside from the pleasure it gave him to work with Cowell, *Salámán and Absál* may seem a strange poem to engage FitzGerald so deeply, but there were other considerations that made it attractive. In the first place, he resumed work on it in part as a congratulatory present for Cowell, who had just taken the first in classics that FitzGerald had expected. Mrs Cowell was naturally jubilant, since the degree proved how right she had been in overriding FitzGerald's objections to her husband's matriculation as a mature undergraduate. In spite of the excellent degree, however, Cowell was unable to find a regular teaching position, and he had to rely on intermittent tutoring and work in the Bodleian Library. To FitzGerald it seemed that it was he not Mrs Cowell whose predictions had been fulfilled. A translation of *Salámán and Absál* was recognition of Cowell's help and erudition, and if it was properly presented, the acknowledgement to Cowell might help him in his academic career.

Probably equally important, although surely far less consciously considered, was the actual period at which he resumed work on the poem, just at the time of his mother's death. The drudgery of translation helped keep his mind off her loss, and the underlying meaning of the poem engaged his own feelings about her death.

Salámán and Absál, an Allegory Translated from the Persian of Jámí is precisely what FitzGerald's title proclaims it. The narrative is that of the Sháh of Yúnan, who is unmarried but wants life's greatest blessing, a son to succeed him. The advice of his Sage is that a wife would put him in leading-strings and cuckold him when he was old. When an alternative means of fathering a child is left to a combination of the Shah's own Will and that of Supreme Intelligence, miraculously

> from Darkness came to Light a CHILD
> Of carnal composition unattaint.

Since the baby is motherless, he is given to a wet nurse named Absál,

> So young, the opening roses of her breast
> But just had budded to an infant's lip

and she was as beautiful as 'a Moon of beauty full'. When Salámán has grown to young manhood ('of his fellows he the Fairest'), Absál, most lovely of her sex, tempts him with her beauty and they fall in love. Salámán's father orders him to give her up, but the lovers flee, first to a paradisal island, then to the Wilderness of Death. Salámán builds a funeral pyre on which he leaps with his nurse-mother-lover, but the magic flame devours her only, leaving him untouched,

> all the baser metal burn'd
> And to itself the authentic Gold return'd.

The Prince goes back to his father, learns to forget his old love and to devote himself to the 'Planetary and Celestial Venus', and, when he is so purified, 'Then was his Head worthy to wear the Crown.'

Jámí's obliging explanation of the allegory, in FitzGerald's verson, is that the Prince is the soul 'from no Womb of Matter produced', Absál the 'Sense-adoring Body', which, though a slave to the blood, teaches the soul the knowledge and delight 'of things of SENSE'. The island is the false paradise of 'Sensual passion', whose pleasures soon expire. The Prince's reconciliation with his father is the return 'Of the lost SOUL to his true Parentage', and his sucession to the throne is the soul's final reign as 'One with the LAST and FIRST INTELLIGENCE'.

> This is the meaning of this Mystery,
> Which to know wholly ponder in the Heart,
> Till all its ancient Secret be enlarged.

The allegorical content of the poem is clear enough, but what is slightly puzzling, preventing our easy acceptance, is the first level of narrative and characterization. When allegory is most satisfactory, the human, literal level of action is as coherent as the level of meaning lying behind it, so that the two merge into an extended metaphor. For Westerners what is obscure in this poem is the relationship between the lovers. It is easily believable that a young man should fall in love with a beautiful woman presumably only some twelve to fifteen years older than he, even if she has been his wet nurse, and perhaps that he should both make love to her and also accept finally that to do so is wrong. What is harder to swallow is that the poet should find the whole romantic episode so unremarkable that it is unnecessary to take any notice of its peculiarities. FitzGerald was of course not responsible for the original narrative, but what seems worth consideration in a biography is why he should have been attracted to it and whether it had any special significance for him.

In pondering or enlarging the meaning of the poem, as its conclusion exhorts us to do, a reader would probably be mistaken in tracing exact parallels between FitzGerald's own life and the narrative of the poem; certainly there is no suggestion that he ever noticed any himself. None the less, they are so striking that it seems impossible to overlook the likenesses between the necessary liberation of the son by the ritual death of the nurse-mother-lover and the dissolution of the ties between FitzGerald and his own mother. One can only wonder if the parallels are not what gave the poem particular, if unrecognized, meaning for FitzGerald and provided him with the energy to complete it in a fortnight.

His version of the poem is far more accomplished than his Calderón plays, largely because the reader does not always sense Shakespeare breathing down the translator's neck, so that the language moves with freedom, even though much of it is still in blank verse. It is perhaps a knowledge of FitzGerald himself that makes him seem more at ease in a universe removed from traditional Christian *mores*, which had been a constant impediment to his version of Calderón. 'I am more and more convinced of the Necessity of keeping as much as possible to the Oriental *Forms*, and carefully avoiding any that bring one back to Europe and the 19th Century,' he wrote. 'It is better to be orientally obscure than Europeanly clear.' [II, 164]

To Cowell, who had advised him constantly, he wrote that he had hacked mercilessly at his own verbiage, 'lightened the Stories, as you desired; cut out *all* the descriptions of Beauty etc. which are tedious and are often implied; and I think advantageously condensed and retrenched the Love-making'. [II, 192]

He took the finished manuscript to *Fraser's*, but the publisher, John Parker, thought it too long and doubted that 'it would be of a nature to suit his Magazine'. [II, 161] When it was rejected, Fitz-Gerald put the poem away for a year, although he still liked it 'as a whole, better than anything I have yet seen in Oriental Poetry'. [II, 192] At the beginning of 1856 he had it privately printed and given to Parker for distribution. FitzGerald remembered the reception of his Calderón translations by the critics as being more severe than it actually was, and he protected himself by anticipating the worst. *Salámán and Absál* was not widely noticed, but the reviews were moderately favourable, and by then FitzGerald had moved on to other projects, particularly the study of Háfiz and of a set of *rubáiyát* or quatrains by Omar Khayyám, the manuscript of which had been found for him by Cowell in the Bodleian Library.

Before sending the manuscript of *Salámán* to the printers, Fitz-Gerald added to it a graceful prefatory letter to Cowell that had not been in the version submitted to Parker. As he was writing it, he told Mrs Cowell, 'came the News – and the Certain News – that you were both going to India ... then all came into my Head and Heart to write what is written – only much more, which I chipped away to what now remains for fear of too much.' [II, 223–4] The letter is full of private references of the kind that he liked to put in published works, remembrances of evenings at Bramford, 'drawing home together for a fireside Night of it with Æschylus or Calderon in the Cottage', quotations from Mrs Cowell's poetry, and echoes of Oxford, where he and her husband had sweated over the copy of 'dear old Salámán' [II, 260] they had found there. The new volume became a farewell present for the Cowells, and on 4 April he gave them a copy with an affectionate inscription. It was published anonymously, but anyone wanting to search out his name could have found an easy track through the Cowells.

Once FitzGerald had been almost completely dependent upon his friends, but now he increasingly filled his time with writing and reading as he faced up to the realization that most of them occupied larger places in his life than he did in theirs. It was still great fun to be with his intimates, but the occasions became rarer. There were, however, a few times when he renewed acquaintances that had almost lapsed, as he did with Fanny Kemble in the autumn of 1852. He had known her since he was a child, although her brother Jack had naturally been closer to him, since they went to school together in Bury St Edmunds and were both undergraduates at Trinity.

After a brief early success on the London stage, Fanny Kemble had married an American, but their marriage was so unhappy that she left him and was divorced by him in 1849. She made a return to the stage for a short time, and then turned instead to Shakespearean readings in both England and the United States.

Fanny Kemble had less than her share of the family good looks, but she had great charm and was that rarity, a correspondent who was even more charming in letters than in person. From 1867 until FitzGerald's death they wrote regularly to each other, but in 1852 he was still usually dependent for news of her upon her cousin, W. B. Donne. There was almost no facet of her life that was not normally antipathetic to FitzGerald, but they became undemonstratively fond of one another, although they still did not use each other's Christian name after seventy years of acquaintance. The mere fact of her sex was against her, so far as FitzGerald went; she was an actress; she had been divorced; she took an active part in London society; she was totally independent in her dealings with men (and with women, for that matter). She had long ago recognized that life was simpler if governed by the most fixed of routines, so by a law that she said was an immutable as those of the Medes and the Persians she kept her correspondence in order by being absolutely just: 'I never write till I am written to, I always write when I am written to, and I make a point of always returning the same amount of paper I receive'.[3]

She wore the dresses and gowns in her wardrobe in strict rotation, regardless of the occasion, so that she might turn up at a funeral in red or at a wedding in black. She had a repertory of twenty readings for her public appearances, each of which was timed for exactly two hours, and she gave them in rotation as unchanging as the order of her dresses.

In October 1852 Mrs Kemble was reading on two evenings in Ipswich, and when FitzGerald heard of it, he asked her to come to the little Woodbridge theatre, although he expected so few in the audience that he had quietly to guarantee the fee of £20 for a performance in which she took all the parts in an abbreviated version of *Richard III*. FitzGerald was not happy with the choice of play, 'But so it falls to us in her routine; and, were it even of any use to ask her to alter it, I hardly would bother her.' [II, 67]

There were a few bad moments at the beginning of the evening.

180

It was Mrs Kemble's habit to curtsey to the audience when she reached the platform, and when she did so on this occasion, Fitz-Gerald rose politely and bowed back. At that the entire audience got to their feet and followed his example, so that it was some time before she could recover from her confusion and amusement. Fitz-Gerald was not enchanted with her acting, although he admired her vigour in the male roles: 'She called out so loud for a horse in Richard that little Mr. Maclean hasn't recovered [from] it yet. He jump'd like a pea on a trencher.' [II, 72]

After such an improbable renewal, their friendship through letters burgeoned, although they did not see each other again for another twenty-seven years. She was a great admirer of FitzGerald; she was so amused at his letters that she called them his 'Lunacies', both because of their content and because they were regularly written at full moon each month. FitzGerald was no lover of women in public life, and he was thoroughly unfair to such writers as Jane Austen, Mrs Browning, Charlotte Brontë, and George Eliot, but he never flagged in his admiration of the charm and the intellect of Fanny Kemble; 'a more honest, truthful, and generous, and loyal, and constant Woman I never knew.' [IV, 38]

FitzGerald frequently said that he was not sure of his place in Thackeray's affections, but at heart he was never really in doubt. On the very day that Mrs Kemble was reading in Woodbridge, Thackeray wrote to his old friend because he was making his legal arrangements before leaving for a six-month lecture tour in the United States: 'I mustn't go away without shaking your hand, and saying Farewell and God Bless you.... I should like my daughters to remember that you are the best and oldest friend their Father ever had, and that you would act as such: as my literary executor and so forth' in the event of his not returning. [II, 70–1] In reply FitzGerald told how deeply affected he had been by Thackeray's letter: 'I truly believe there is no Man alive loves you (in his own way of love) more than I do.' When he sat reading Thackeray's old works, 'I cry again. This really is so: and is poor work: were you back again, I should see no more of you than before. But this is not from want of love on my part: it is because we live in such different worlds: and it is almost painful to me to tease anybody with my seedy dullness, which is just bearable by myself.' [II, 75] It was a moment of rare candour on FitzGerald's part; usually it was easier

181

to pretend that he was neglected by his best friends rather than admitting that it was his own fault they had not met.

With Tennyson he usually complained that he had been deserted, although the fact is that he was even more negligent than the poet about making an effort to see his friends. In 1854, after numerous invitations, he finally went to stay with the Tennysons at Farringford on the Isle of Wight, to attend the christening of the younger son of the family. He was in good form, keeping Tennyson constantly amused, and he played Emily Tennyson's piano for hours at a time. Because she had hidden her husband's texts, he translated Persian poetry aloud to Tennyson, and he took him on walks to the sea, where he made Tennyson try his hand at his watercolours. In spite of enjoying himself enormously at the time, he never accepted one of his future invitations to Farringford, saying vaguely in excuse that the Tennysons lived too grandly for his taste.

If the world be naturally divided into those who are good hosts and those who are good guests, FitzGerald would certainly be one of the former. In 1859 he finally prevailed on Carlyle to come to stay in Farlingay, after assuring him for a year that Suffolk was considerably quieter than London. He offered a choice of Farlingay or Crabbe's vicarage at Bredfield, promising that a bed was kept ready for him at either place and that he need not even give notice of his arrival. To Chelsea he sent details of the timetables of three daily trains to Ipswich from Shoreditch that arrived in time for the coach to Woodbridge; alternatively, there was a steamer every Wednesday and Saturday, taking nine hours to Ipswich. 'The Rail to Ipswich takes three or two and a half hours.' Carlyle was to be at complete liberty; 'Pipes are the order of the house at both places', and at either he could have a 'capital sunshiny airy Bedroom'. FitzGerald suggested a stay of a week, but Carlyle was to be free to extend it or 'to go off without any sort of Ceremony'.

Carlyle had enough of half-rotten ships in Chelsea, with 'ropes breaking, sails holed, blocks giving way', so that he preferred the train, typically indicating that the waiting Woodbridge coach held few charms for him: 'If you have a gig and pony, of course it will be pleasant to see your face at the end of my shrieking, mad, (and to me quite horrible) rail operations: but if I see nothing, I will courageously go for the Coach, and shall do quite well there, if I can get on the outside especially.' He stipulated that he had to have several hours of solitude each day, 'and cannot be said ever to *weary* of being left well alone'. But he was willing to let FitzGerald drive him around the countryside: 'I calculate on getting some real benefit by this plunge into the maritime rusticities under your friendly guidance, and the quiet of it will be of all things welcome to me.' It is difficult to imagine that he had the natural disposition of a guest, although he seems not to have been a brilliant host either.

Since he was convinced that everyone else waited breathlessly for each detail of his health, Carlyle reported to his wife that the first night at Farlingay he had an excellent sleep, 'at least two sleeps added together that amounted to excellent'. The following night was less successful because of 'an adventure of cows' conspiring against the guest in the house. At 2 a.m. they 'took to lowing with an energy to have awakened the seven sleepers. No soul could guess why: but there they raged and lowed through the night watches, awoke the whole house here, and especially awoke me, and held me vigilant till six, when I arose for a walk through fields and lanes. No evil came of it, only endless sorrow of poor Fitz and the household, endless apologies, etc.' It is not hard to imagine the complaints that elicited the sorrow and apologies. The following day the inhospitable animals were removed, and Carlyle got his sleep.

FitzGerald was always good at soothing Carlyle's awkwardness, even if doing so sometimes made him impatient. He lent him a dressing gown, walked him about the neighbourhood, took him to call on the Crabbes at Bredfield, and drove him to Aldeburgh, which so enchanted Carlyle that he wrote home to recommend it to Jane for a holiday: 'Never saw a place more promising.' The sight of FitzGerald was enough to start up again all Carlyle's sleeping plans for a new marker at Naseby on the proper site of the battle, and he held tenaciously to the idea even when FitzGerald told him that his family was selling the whole estate there.

When he was safely home again, Carlyle complained that 'the stillness of Farlingay is unattainable in Chelsea for a *second* sleep', which naturally turned out to be the fault of Suffolk and 'all the kindness of my beneficent brother mortals' there, for they had 'stirred up a good deal of bile'. The vigour of his complaints probably proves how much he had enjoyed himself in Woodbridge, but he never accepted another invitation, although he told Fitz-Gerald to get a house of his own, and to reserve a room for him, '*plus* a pony that can trot, and a cow that gives good milk: with these outfits we shall make a pretty rustication now and then, not wholly *Latrappish*, but only *half*.'[4]

At the end of 1855 William Browne returned to England after service in Ireland with the Bedfordshire Militia during the Crimean War. It was the kind of life at which he excelled, and he had recently been promoted to captain. Fitz found that the boy and young man he had known had become a man with 'instantaneous Decision, [who] knows of more People and Probabilities by a Guess than I do by Years of personal Acquaintance'. On his short visits to Fitz he supplied him 'with Sense and Courage – then goes away', leaving his friend feeling, he said, as useless as a beached barge. [II, 89] '*Meeting* with old Friends is almost more sad to me than meeting with new Acquaintances,' he wrote, 'but *Parting* is so much the worse.' [II, 233]

Like anyone else who has spent long periods with the young, he felt an uncomfortable mixture of pride at the independence and maturity of Browne and a nostalgic sadness, which he knew at heart was ignoble, that his former protégé was no longer in real need of him. It was on this basis of friendship that they went in the summer of 1856 for a Continental trip of some two weeks, with George Crabbe, rector of Merton in Norfolk, and son of Fitz-Gerald's friend of the same name at Bredfield.

Except for half a dozen trips to Ireland to see relatives, Fitz-Gerald had not been out of England since his stay in Paris with Thackeray a quarter of a century before. In the interval he had not become less chauvinistic. His letters about the trip are as shot through with insularity as those of any package tourist more than a century later – or, for that matter, as his mother's impressions in 1840–1. He loved seeing the Louvre again, but Strasbourg was hardly worth the eight-hour trip; the cathedral was 'a failure: looking not nearly so high as one hears it is: and the inside quite inferior (as are all the other Cathedrals we have seen) to half a dozen of our own in Grandeur and Solemnity'. The banks of the Neckar were 'just like the Avon between Bradford and Bath'. Even the 'famous Rhine' turned out '*quite a failure*: not a bit better in its best parts than parts of the River Dart, for instance: its colour dirty; its banks inferior in *Colour*, both of Rock and Tree to much in England'; it was, in short, a 'Cockney affair'. The cathedrals of Cologne and Aix were so disappointing that he might have been better off staying at home.

FitzGerald's conclusion was that he had 'little to notch my Memory with except the pleasure of the Company I have travelled with; and the Consciousness of the Prosperity and Happiness of other Countries beside one's own'. Both Crabbe and Browne were pleasant travelling companions, but as younger men they naturally formed a pair who unconsciously reminded FitzGerald that he was nearly fifty: 'I believe I have been the only one of the Party who has made any Bother.' There was a natural sense of disappointment in his realization that his two friends, whom he had so recently introduced to each other, now had much in common from which he was excluded.

As the return trip to England grew near, FitzGerald took stock of the trip: 'Little as I really love Travel, I really look with a sort of Terror now that the Hour approaches for the Dissolution of a little Partnership which probably never will unite again.' [II, 231–3] Some of his dissatisfaction with France, Germany, and Belgium undoubtedly stemmed from his feelings of being so alone. William Donne, who long ago had noticed Fitz's tendency to anticipate loneliness, said in quick empathy with him, 'In one way or another we are always rehearsing the final parting of death.'[5]

It is probable, too, that at the time FitzGerald was prejudiced against everything outside England by the imminent departure of the Cowells for India, in spite of all he had done to dissuade them. Their leave-taking might have been designed as final proof of the brevity of friendship.

Once he had adjusted, a few years before, to the fact that the Cowells had disregarded his advice about going to Oxford, he had settled down to looking forward to the time when all the preliminaries were over and Cowell would be relieved of the tedium of teaching undergraduates by winning a chair in one of the universities, where his time would be devoted to reading and writing, following his own scholarly interests. Somewhere in the corner of this idealized picture FitzGerald thought there would be a place for himself as family friend, learning languages with Cowell, correcting his wife's poetry, bringing Carlyle and Tennyson and

Thackeray to stay, best of all simply sitting by their fire in a comfortable trio discussing literature. 'When shall we three meet again?' was his refrain, and he even sang it aloud.

When the Cowells first left Suffolk, he missed them so badly that he would turn his head away when his train went near Bramford, for fear he should catch sight of the well-loved spire near the cottage where they had lived. 'I think I shall shut myself up in the remotest nook of Suffolk and let my beard grow,' he threatened. [II, 28] He hated the thought of Oxford, where they were so happy without him, but when he finally went there to see them, he found that 'this delightful Oxford' had magically changed its look with their advent, and that he now preferred it to Cambridge, 'which has always a sordid look to me'. The streets of Oxford were wide and clean, 'and the Colleges themselves more presentable on the whole than the unsatisfactory new Gothic at Cambridge'. [II, 124] It was all part of his old habit of merging persons and places in his consideration. Particularly after he began studying Persian there with Cowell, Oxford became as much a part of his life as Bramford had been.

The gloomy joint prophecies of Donne and FitzGerald were fulfilled after Cowell took his degree, for instead of taking up the academic post for which he hoped, for more than a year he had no prospects beyond his casual tutoring. At the beginning of 1856 FitzGerald heard that Cowell had applied for the chair in Modern History and Political Economy at Presidency College, Calcutta. The news, he wrote, made 'my Heart hang really heavy at my side. I *can't* think it can be good – I mean I am so sure you would get on well in England.' Surely, he urged, the Professor of Sanskrit at Oxford would get him a post in England, 'and you teach at Oxford (which you like) meanwhile?' [II, 194–5] When later he heard that the Calcutta professorship had been offered to Cowell, he said he hardly knew whether to laugh or cry, and he tried again to dissuade him from accepting it. When all else failed, he offered to support the Cowells while they waited for a suitable English post. He was always reticent to the point of neurosis in discussing his own financial affairs, but in his effort to hang on to the Cowells he was specific about money:

I *have* it, and shall (without regard to you) take care to have some to spare every Year, so long as the Public Securities hold. I always *must* live well within my Income whatever that be, and whatever Fate has in hand for me (and she will soon open it) – this being my only sense of Riches and great Earthly Luxury: I don't mean the Luxury of hoarding: but to live so as you feel that you can do what you do easily and handsomely, and have enough in the Cupboard for occasional Emergency. On this account, I *always* lay by something: how glad I should be if you would both now and hereafter ease me of some of it, and keep here in England to do so! Would I not – *will* I not – pay a good Sum to keep you both here? What is to become of my Stupendous Learning when you go? I scarce see my old Friends, and make no new ones. I shall die starved of human regard; and besides that shall become a filthy *Miser* if I keep laying by. [II, 213–14]

All the secret FitzGerald is there in the letter: the desperate wish to cling to those he loved; the painful openness about his emotions that he usually tried to avoid; his open-handed generosity with money; the genuine pathos of his loneliness. And, to be honest, something not too far from self-pity. It shows how deeply he was moved that he put it all down in an extraordinary, naked letter that seems one of the most touching he ever wrote.

But it was no use. With what was surely good sense, the Cowells accepted the offer from India. Within a week or two of hearing that they had, FitzGerald had finished writing the prefatory letter to *Salámán and Absál*, in which he took his real farewell of the Cowells. Early in July 1856 he spent a fortnight with them near Ipswich, but a few weeks later he said he could not come on the day of their sailing: 'I think it is best for many reasons that I should *not* go to see you again – to say a Good-Bye that costs me so much.' [II, 236] He wrote frequently to them in India, saying how much he missed them, he welcomed them back to England when they returned in 1864, and in 1867 he helped Cowell get the professorship in 'sordid' Cambridge that he had always predicted for him. Curiously, however, after their return, the Cowells exchanged roles with him, for they sought to preserve the old intimacy as he became increasingly difficult to pin down, either as guest or as host.

The failure of affection was not all his. Mrs Cowell never totally forgot what she had thought was interference when they were deciding on the move to Oxford, and she may have felt that he was intruding too much in their familial privacy, so that going to India was a way of preserving her marriage. Certainly, FitzGerald often found her intractable, and near the end of his life he described her as vindictive. Then in contrition he wrote, 'I mean *implacable* when once she has taken a dislike. It is not often she does so; and, when she does, not on her own account, but others.' She had turned against her own nieces and nephews for being ungrateful to their mother, and also against FitzGerald's brother John, 'who, she thought, alienated me from the Good Faith, by not doing all he jawed about'. None the less, he found her 'quite incapable of Revenge'. [IV, 266] Without being actually vengeful, persons of strait principles may have somewhat harsh views of those who differ from them, as Mrs Cowell no doubt had of FitzGerald.

Of all his personal losses at this period of his life, the most severe was one whose poignancy might have surprised his friends: the death of his mother. He barely mentioned it in his letters, giving only the most factual of details and refusing to dwell on his own feelings, but we have already seen a hint as to how his emotion was worked out in his translation of *Salámán and Absál*, rather than in more overt and expected reactions.

As FitzGerald and his mother both grew older, he had reluctantly learned to admire her spirit, so that what had once seemed flamboyance, even vulgarity, now looked more like courage. She had to give up the famous yellow carriage and sell her matched black horses at Tattersall's, but she still went indomitably to her house in Brighton from her regular home in Ham, where Fitz-Gerald spent longer and longer periods: 'a really lovely place, and neighbourhood, though I say it who am all prejudiced against London.... But the copious woods, green meadows, the Thames and its swans gliding between, and so many villas and cheerful houses and terraced gardens with all their associations of Wits and Courtiers on either side, all this is very delightful. I am not heroic enough for Castles, Battlefields, etc. Strawberry Hill for me!' [II, 55] He even began inviting friends to Ham to meet his mother.

With something approaching gallantry she bore such infirmities of old age as gout, and though it used to keep her awake at night by pain in her hands and feet, she accepted it philosophically and 'felt so clear aloft that she made Night pass even agreeably away with her reflections and recollections' of a long life. [III, 307] Glittering with diamonds or pearls, she still presided at huge dinner parties, and she maintained her special, occasionally embarrassing, admiration of literature and writers. In 1852 Thackeray told of having been 'twice to Richmond where Mrs. FitzGerald receives me with the greatest graciousness, and announces to all her friends that I am the most agreeable of men – that she looks upon me in the light of a son'. To mark her favour she gave him 'a tabinet waistcoat', but it was so ugly that he resolved to 'have it made up and sport it in America and keep the remainder for pincushions'. Before doing so, he wore it once to dinner with Mrs FitzGerald, 'and it was so fine with its emerald and gold that I blushed to wear it'. Whenever he dined with her, she was 'stupendously gracious'.[6]

At the end of January 1855 she died quietly in her sleep of a heart attack 'at her residence in the Royal Crescent, Brighton'. The *Illustrated London News* mentioned her wealth and described her as a 'scion of the ducal house of Leinster; being a Geraldine of that branch which descends from the second son of the first Earl of Kildare'. She had been 'a lady well-known for her high mental accomplishments, and for her patronage of literature and the fine arts (her house being the favourite resort of writers, dramatists, and painters)'. One wonders whether she had ever learned to think of her own son as part of that artistic company.

At his father's death Edward FitzGerald had confessed to Thackeray that he found the black borders of his writing paper inappropriate to his feelings, 'for have I any inward black edge to show?' [II, 52] It is more difficult to pinpoint precisely what his mother's death meant to him, but she had filled a far greater place in his emotions than he liked to admit, both in his love and in something of disapproval that verged on dislike. Both emotions made her death deeply unsettling, but as usual he kept such matters to himself. He had one of her portraits by Lawrence near him ever after, but perhaps characteristically he put it in a cupboard 'for want of room', rather than hanging it openly on the wall. To the end of his life he spoke with special tenderness of the relations between mothers and their grown sons. After Carlyle's death he wrote of how 'one's heart opens again to him at the last: sitting

189

alone in the middle of her Room – "I want to die" – "I want – a Mother."' [IV, 424]

Mrs FitzGerald's body was taken back for burial with her husband at Boulge, where she had fitted in so badly in life. According to one of her son's biographers, her estate was worth nearly a million pounds, and she left £50,000 to each of her younger children, the houses and estates and the bulk of the money to John FitzGerald, who took the surname of Purcell-Fitz-Gerald.[7] Whatever the exact amount he received, Edward FitzGerald referred to it as a fortune, and for the remainder of his life had no further cause ever to worry about money.

CHAPTER IX

FitzGerald's Marriage

The year 1856 was a turning point in FitzGerald's life, because of both external events and what they revealed about aspects of his character that had been submerged before. Shortly after the Cowells left for India, he began thinking of ways to tell his friends the surprising news that at forty-seven he was going to be married, but for several weeks he kept it morosely to himself, hoping that something might intervene to prevent his ever having to make the announcement.

In October Carlyle wrote in delight to congratulate him, saying that Donne's character of Lucy Barton was 'at once credible and superlatively favourable', and that it was impossible to believe that she could be 'other than an eligible Wife'. He professed to have suspected something of the sort from an earlier letter of FitzGerald's, but Donne, when asked about it, had pleaded ignorance, 'tho', he said, there had been for years back some rumour (unfounded, at least quite uncertain, rumour) of the kind, in reference to – the very Lady who now turns out to be the veritable Fact!' [II, 239]

All that month FitzGerald wrote to startled friends, announcing his impending marriage as glumly as if giving notice of a funeral. 'I am going to be married to Miss Barton,' he told Stephen Spring Rice, 'a very doubtful Experiment – long talked of – not *fixt* beyond all Cause and Impediment till lately – and now "Vogue la Galère!"' [II, 239] To young George Crabbe he said, 'I am going to be married – don't congratulate me', and Crabbe thought that he would 'never forget his miserable tones'. [II, 240]

It had been nearly two years since his mother's death, but her estate was not settled until the summer of 1856; in the meantime FitzGerald had continued living as if he had forgotten his commitment to marry Lucy. She, however, followed the fortunes of the FitzGeralds anxiously from afar, and her correspondence suggests that she expected Mrs Cowell to keep her informed of Edward's plans.[1] What, in 1856, actually brought to a head the vague engagement that had been drifting on for seven years is not certain, but it appears, in the absence of other evidence, that before leaving for India Mrs Cowell had taken a hand in seeing that Fitz-Gerald would fulfil his promise to Miss Barton, since the fortune he had inherited from his mother made further postponement indefensible, no matter how reluctant he might be to marry. There is no way of knowing whether she arranged a meeting between Fitz-Gerald and Lucy, whether Lucy wrote to him at her suggestion, or whether he was so gently nudged into action by Mrs Cowell that he scarcely realized what had happened.

It is possible that he was at last moved to renew the relationship by a hint from Mrs Cowell plus a momentary feeling that marriage might be a stay to the apparent transience of his closest relationships. Browne was now back in England, but his wife and children came first, and there was little chance of seeing him regularly. Cowell and his wife were in India, from which they might never return. Both of his parents were now dead, and he was the only one of the brothers and sisters to remain single. His family provided few examples of marital happiness, but at least some of his friends had contented marriages. There was certainly good reason for him to take stock of his loneliness, even to consider marriage, but if he ever thought that Lucy Barton was the answer to his problems, he realized his mistake almost at once.

Fitz asked Allen to thank his wife 'for all her sanguine Wishes – sanguiner than my Expectations!' [II, 238] After all, he said with desperate honesty, 'our united ages amount to 96! – a dangerous experiment on both sides. She at least brings a fine head and heart to the bargain – worthy of a better market.' [II, 240–1] By the time of the wedding he was so frightened of marriage and so angry at feeling he had been manoeuvred into it that he found it hard to say a kind word about his bride.

William Browne was appalled when he heard of FitzGerald's approaching marriage and told him that he was veering towards a precipice: 'Give her whatever you like, except your hand. Make her an allowance.' 'I would cheerfully do so,' said Fitz, 'but then people would talk.' Incredulously, Browne said, 'That from *you*! *you*, who do not care a straw what anybody says about anything!' To which FitzGerald replied sadly, 'Nor should I care, but Miss Barton would care a very great deal. It would be cruel.'[2]

Lucy Barton and Edward FitzGerald were married at Chichester on 4 November 1856 in the church of All Saints in the Pallant. There is no indication that FitzGerald had invited any of his own family or friends, but Lucy's relatives were at the ceremony and came to the wedding breakfast. FitzGerald had refused to wear anything but his usual untidy clothes, his first marital protest against the airs and graces that he thought Lucy had learned while living with the Gurneys. He looked all through the ceremony as if he were being led to his doom, and after the responses he was almost totally mute, breaking his silence only at the breakfast when he was offered blancmange. With a gesture of disgust he waved it away, muttering, 'Ugh! congealed bridesmaid.'

He had been rude enough about Lucy before the wedding; he might fairly be described as savage after the honeymoon, which they unwisely spent in Brighton, a town he had always disliked when staying with his mother. His bride was forty-eight and had injudiciously chosen to dress as if she were a girl, much as his mother used to wear incongruous white satin when she was well over seventy. To him Lucy must have been far more ludicrous than ever his mother was, for she had neither style nor even the remnants of good looks, as Mrs FitzGerald had in abundance. But fashionable Brighton was what she was after, if we are to trust FitzGerald's account of the honeymoon twelve years later. During her time with the Gurneys 'she forgot the plainness and simplicity of the Quakeress and attending Parties, Operas, etc., branched out into the fine, high, intellectual Lady that he found'[3] on marrying her.

Lucy had always been dazzled by the FitzGeralds, and no doubt she had been learning in Norfolk to behave as she thought ladies of the family should. She seems to have had the intention of emulating Mrs FitzGerald, which she thought her husband would welcome her doing. But FitzGerald had spent nearly half a century in rejecting his family's standards, and he had always felt ambivalently about his mother. Now his wife's manners invited a comparison to everything he had disapproved of in Mrs FitzGerald and a contrast with everything he admired. Either way Lucy could not have hoped to win.

Their honeymoon was miserable. FitzGerald had probably never had any sexual experience, and it is almost unthinkable that his wife had. The bitterness, even coarseness, with which he later spoke of her sounds like a thinly disguised transferral of self-loathing, and the physical terms in which he expressed his disgust suggest that what lay at the base of his unwonted lack of charity was his own physical failure as a husband. FitzGerald was not cruel normally, nor was he inclined to speak ill of others, but he had been transformed by an emotion that was fear before the wedding and now was something approaching hatred.

Today we probably overestimate the sexual licence of Victorian men, the hold-over from the Regency and late Georgian period in which many of them came of age; it is too easy to forget that for a man repelled by coarse sexuality with prostitutes before marriage, the only alternative was often ignorance. Ruskin's appalled surprise on his honeymoon at the sight of his wife's body is well known, but there must have been many other men who had reactions similar in nature if not degree; in FitzGerald's case the reaction would have been intensified by his bitter knowledge that he had never wanted to be married in the first place.

According to FitzGerald he and Lucy had made a compact before the wedding 'to see no company, to keep no establishment, and to live very quietly, as being the earnest wish of both', but once they were safely married 'she wanted to stay out, receive friends, and go into society, etc., in fact wishing for everything the very opposite to, as she always knew, his taste and feelings.'[4] Normal pastimes, one would think, and innocent enough if they had not been distasteful to him. To assess the statement, we should consider that once they had separated and she had adequate income to do as she pleased, she lived very quietly indeed, with the majority of her social life passed in Bible readings and lectures, which suggests that FitzGerald's memory had exaggerated her social ambitions. But it may have been more comfortable for him to look back at them with contempt than to remember his own emotional and, perhaps, physical inadequacies.

Since they had not decided where they would finally live, the FitzGeralds went to London from Brighton, to stay in FitzGerald's old lodgings at 31 Great Portland Street. Donne, who broke the news of the marriage to Fanny Kemble, wrote that 'in respect that she is tall and well filled out', his son spoke of Lucy as 'Barton-Barton, conceiving, I suppose, that Baden-Baden means double Baden. However, though there be much of her, it is so much good, and as she and Edward have been intimate friends for at least a quarter of a century, and she has great reverence for him, I am not clear though I have been as incredulous as Thomas and as full of denial as Peter, but that both have consulted and concluded wisely.'[5] The next month he had reason to retract his words, for Lucy went to Norfolk only a few weeks after her marriage, ostensibly to look for a house for herself and her husband but actually to return to the Gurneys, who loved her, she knew. She was away for Christmas, which FitzGerald spent with Donne.

'I want my Wife to learn all she can of Housekeeping, and employ herself in it; I think she is given to Profusion, and her Hand is out of practice.' Once FitzGerald had admired her economy at housekeeping, and this was the first time ever recorded when he complained of inefficiency in a house. When he was offered an armchair as a wedding present, he stipulated that it 'not be a luxurious or ornamental one, but a plain Oak Chair: for I like, and will have, all of the plainest in my House'. [II, 243] It is the voice of the household tyrant; no wonder that Donne called him 'most extraordinary of Benedicks' and said that he distressed 'even Spedding's well-regulated mind' by talking like Bluebeard. Donne was still so far from understanding FitzGerald's behaviour that he thought his friend's remarks were merely ironic and he felt 'so much confidence in Lucy as to believe she'll tame Petruchio, swagger as he list'.

Lucy was away for more than five weeks, during which Fitz-Gerald found rooms at 24 Portland Terrace, dismal enough according to Donne, since their prospect was a cemetery. The sitting room was a dark green that absorbed all the light from the narrow windows, and FitzGerald said '"his contemporary" – which, being interpreted, means his wife! looks in this chamber of horrors like Lucrezia Borgia.'[6]

Instead of joining Lucy immediately when she returned to London, FitzGerald stayed on in his old lodgings for a day or two to write a long letter to the Cowells telling them of the failure of his marriage, which would have never occurred 'had Good Sense and

Experience prevailed instead of Blind Regard on one side'. Until then he had been unable to write to them 'for fear of utterly breaking down' at the contrast of their happiness to his own despair. 'I believe there are new Channels fretted in my Cheeks with many unmanly Tears,' he wrote, and he sat looking at the unpleasing view of Great Portland Street '"remembering the Days that are no more," in which you two are so mixt up'. [II, 245]

The FitzGeralds' new lodgings were kept by Marietta Nursey, daughter of the painter Perry Nursey, a friend of FitzGerald who lived in Great Bealings near Woodbridge. She had never met Lucy before, and she knew nothing but good of FitzGerald. Years later she refused to show her letters from him to his literary executor because they were too private; a friend of hers who had read them said the real reason for her refusal was they proved 'what a brute E.F.G. was to Lucy Barton – and his cruelty after the marriage!'.[7] Letters sent to Aldis Wright when he was preparing an edition of FitzGerald's correspondence and now in Trinity Library, show that at least four other friends destroyed their letters from Fitz-Gerald because of the unkind things he said of his wife. However much one deplores his ferocity, it is hard not to sympathize with him in the pain that he must have felt, changing him temporarily from a charming, thoughtful man into a boorish husband.

Besides referring to Lucy as 'the Contemporary', he spoke of her less attractively but more accurately as 'the Elder' and commented to others on her plainness. Perhaps worst of all were his references to her in letters simply as '*She*'. He was once walking with Stephen Spring Rice in London when they passed the show van of the Corpulent Lady. 'I needn't pay a shilling to see her,' said FitzGerald, 'I can see my own wife any hour.'[8] It was almost as if he were trying to convince himself that no reasonable man could find her anything but repulsive, and that any failure in their relations was her fault not his.

Since his friends were so accustomed to his good humour, some found it hard to believe that he meant what he said. 'Your account,' wrote Fanny Kemble's sister, 'of Edward FitzGerald is very droll, but not comfortable, I think. At least if I was his wife, I should not like him even to play at being bored by me. I think my woman's *feeling* would revolt at that, and my woman's *folly*, at being called the "Contemporary".'[9]

No doubt Lucy realised how much she irritated him, but it is improbable that she ever understood why. Her habit of interrupting him annoyed her husband most of all. He once asked an old friend in Woodbridge if she knew what marriage was: 'I'll tell you. It's standing at your desk all ready for your work, with your brain clear, and then seeing the door open and a great big bonnet asking you to go for a walk with it.'[10]

She never lost either her respect or her uncomprehending love for her husband, and every account of those who visited her after the separation insists on her complete charity about him. In time she no doubt understood more about his emotional make-up than she had when they were together, but her comment about his attraction to other little boys when he was in school (see pp. 43–4) is the only indication that she felt even a touch of resentment at the failure of their marriage. She was indeed insensitive about the feelings of others, and it is a pity that she fastened her affections on someone as incapable of returning them as FitzGerald was.

One of the most perplexing aspects of his treatment of Lucy is that the letters in which other friends wrote about his unkindness to her show so little surprise at his behaviour. His fundamental lack of esteem for women is revealed in a hundred small ways in his letters, but normally his innate kindness was so much stronger than his lack of respect that he avoided saying anything offensive. The only indication that he had always been capable of such conduct comes from a letter to Thackeray when he was only twenty-two, in which he wrote that he was angry with Hume for 'standing up so for polite manners to the ladies – a practice which turns Nature topsy turvy. I have got the character of being rather a brute in society – can't help it; I am worth more, I believe, than any young lady that ever was made, so I am more inclined to tell them to open the door for me, than for me to get up and do it for them.' Then, in typical contrition, he recognized that 'millions of girls have existed a million times more virtuous than I am; and I am ashamed of having said it.' [I, 104] In actual society he was punctilious in his consideration of women, and the passage from the letter is in part a joke, but one suspects that it screened something fundamental in his nature.

During their stay in Portland Terrace FitzGerald had his way about social life, for his letters mention the scarcity of both guests and invitations. Part of their isolation was deliberate, but they were poor company when the 'wretchedness of the terrible mistake he had made was apparent all the time'. W. F. Pollock and his wife invited them to dinner, then came to tea at Portland Terrace; both were 'altogether uncomfortable' occasions. FitzGerald drank wine instead of tea, then walked away from the lodgings with the Pollocks; it was the first time his guests had ever seen him 'very much the worse' for drink.[11] Donne, who was a widower, entertained the FitzGeralds several times, and Fitz's sister, Jane Wilkinson, and her husband invited them to tea. FitzGerald refused several invitations by himself and said that he had declined to walk across the park to see Mrs Cowell's parents for fear of breaking down: 'I think I should flounder into Spooniness if I did – on several accounts. So here we live seeing almost nobody.' [II, 265] Spedding called only once in three months. Even reading Persian was enough to make him regret the happier days when he had gone to Oxford to see the Cowells, with 'Oriel opposite, and the Militia in Broad Street, and the old Canary-coloured Sofa and the Cocoa or Tea on the Table!'.

The lodgings had never been ideal, and they were made worse by unpleasant associations, but FitzGerald would not stir himself to look for others. 'I wish my Wife would go and choose and suit herself, and leave me to find out if it suits me.' [II, 265] In the end inertia won, and they stayed until summer. As he was to do occasionally in later life when he was unhappy, FitzGerald hinted that he was not well and probably would not live long, so that it was hardly worthwhile moving for such a short time.

In May, after a good deal of urging from her husband, Lucy left London for Gorleston near Yarmouth, where she stayed with an old friend as she looked for lodgings. Once she was gone Fitz could potter around the rooms all day, keep the irregular hours that pleased him, and work on a translation of Aeschylus: 'I think I want to turn his Trilogy into what shall be readable English Verse; a thing I have always thought of, but was frightened at the Chorus.... I shall (if I make one) make a very free one; not for Scholars, but for those who are ignorant of Greek.' But he warned Cowell not to be 'alarmed with the anticipation of another sudden volume of Translations; for I only sketch out the matter, then put it away; and coming on it one day with fresh eyes trim it up with some natural impulse that I think gives a natural air to all'. [II, 272]

After a fortnight alone he determined to go to Hertford to see an old friend, but to his apparent astonishment, he 'bungled between two Railroads and got to Bedford', where there was nothing to do except to stay with Browne for another fortnight. Twice since Fitz-Gerald's marriage Browne had come to London to stay with him while Lucy was away. He had always thought her an ambitious woman, and when he saw how unhappy his friend was, he said, 'My dear Fitz I would have kicked you to the Lands End rather than this should have happened.'[12] FitzGerald was now a welcome guest at Goldington, for when Browne had recently come out of the Army, Fitz helped the family out of a financial corner by lending them £6,500. To be there was almost as good as being unmarried again; in the idyllic early summer he 'put away almost all Books except Omar Khayyám!, which I could not help looking over in a Paddock covered with Buttercups and brushed by a delicious Breeze, while a dainty racing Filly of W. Browne's came startling up to wonder and snuff about me.' Rather shamefacedly he confessed that 'Omar breathes a sort of Consolation to me!' [II, 273]

Just as he was leaving London for Goldington, he had received from the author a copy of George Borrow's *The Romany Rye*, which he told Borrow he had been reading 'under the best Circumstances: at such a Season – in the Fields as they now are – and in company with a Friend I love best in the world'. [II, 276]

When he could at last tear himself away to go to Gorlestone, he was reconciled to Lucy's presence by the sight before the house of the 'Vessels going in and out of this River: and Sailors walking about with fur caps and their brown hands in their Breeches Pockets'. [II, 272] A week later, to his 'great gratification', his wife went to Keswick, to attend a Gurney funeral. It was clear to him at last that his marriage must end, whatever the immediate pain. Goldington had been heaven, and he felt like a banished angel at Gorleston.

One evening after Lucy's return the FitzGeralds had a surprise call from George Borrow, who was staying in Yarmouth. Having a guest was no help, for Borrow and his host fell into argument over *Romany Rye* as Borrow drank 'strong Port' and expressed his 'contempt for anyone who *could drink Sherry*', of which Fitz proceeded obstinately to down a great deal. As he had done with the Pollocks, he insisted on walking home with Borrow; coming back from Yarmouth he collapsed by the roadside, where he slept most of the night.[13]

No account survives of the final break between the FitzGeralds, but by 22 August 1857 he was suggesting to the Cowells that in the future they address letters to him to Goldington. [II, 298] It was impossible for him to return to Farlingay, since poor Mrs Smith, the wife of the farmer, had gone out of her mind. For the next three years he was virtually homeless, but he spent his longest periods at Geldestone, Goldington, London, and Lowestoft, with one return stay of several months at Farlingay.

For all the bitterness that he had felt when they were together, his separation from Lucy was remarkably good-natured. There was no question of divorce, and it was much too late for either of them to marry again even if they had been so inclined. He settled £300 annually on her for the rest of her life, more than enough for a comfortable existence, and though they saw one another occasionally over the years and he visited her at least once, the marriage was finished. In the early years of the separation he wrote occasionally to friends who were near Lucy in the various places she lived, asking them to be kind to her. But he wanted no letters from her and, according to her when she was old, he imposed a total embargo on communication. He seems also to have stipulated that she should live somewhere besides Woodbridge, which was not greatly unfair, since she had been away from it so long as to have broken most of her contacts there.

Once he was free of her, FitzGerald was generous about Lucy. He could not pretend that he had greatly admired her, but he seldom blamed her for the failure of the marriage and said repetitively that if there was any real fault in personality, it was his. In the autumn of 1857 he had to write nearly as many letters to friends explaining the separation as he had written the year before to announce the marriage. 'My married Life has come to an end,' he told Mrs Tennyson. 'I am back again in old Quarters, living as for the last thirty years – only so much older, sadder, uglier, and worse! If People want to go further for the cause of all this Blunder than the fact of two People of very determined habits and Temper, first trying to change them at close on fifty – they may lay nine tenths of the Blame on me. I don't want to talk more of the matter, but one must say something.' [II, 313] What he never wavered in was his belief that both were happier apart than together. 'I think you will admit that she is far better off than she was, and as I feel sure, ever would have been living with me.' [II, 556]

Lucy Barton had probably been right in assuming before her marriage that FitzGerald was more like the rest of his family than he knew. However much he fought shy of their values, he often seemed compelled to repeat 'Geraldine' patterns of behaviour. Now he was separated as his grandparents and parents had been, as his brother John and his second wife were, and as the Kerriches were intermittently.

After the separation Lucy made a reasonable life for herself, certainly a more contented one than FitzGerald's was to be. He had seen shrewdly enough that what she was 'pining for' was not particularly a husband but simply 'some one to devote herself to'. [II, 299] For a brief period she acted as nurse for the Brownes at Goldington and was so useful to them that she overcame Browne's objections to her and made FitzGerald fear that he had been replaced in the family's affections. She went for a time to Kent, then tried Brighton more successfully than on her first stay there, and spent her old age among friends in Croydon, where she lived happily, quite without rancour, surrounded by paintings and furniture from her father's house, with a picture of FitzGerald in a leather frame by her armchair. She is said to have believed for years that a reconciliation with him might ultimately be made. At last she became so obese that it was hard for her to move from her chair, but she still welcomed FitzGerald's friends as warmly as if the separation had never taken place. Towards the end of her life her mind was clouded, but her personality remained sunny until her death in 1898. It is impossible not to feel admiration for her, and nearly as difficult not to sympathize with FitzGerald's belief that he had to escape her.

In only one way did Lucy cause trouble for FitzGerald after the separation, and that was surely unintentional on her part. In spite of his understanding that she would live elsewhere, she regularly came for long periods to visit friends in Woodbridge, and probably her generosity about her husband was even more effective in alienating the little town from him than bitterness would have been.

FitzGerald had always been regarded with suspicion because of his eccentric behaviour; if he had insisted on the dignities and rights of his class as his brother John did, even eccentricity might have been overlooked, but his deliberate avoidance of the county families made him seem closer in rank to those who could not forgive him for leaving Lucy, and hence easier to look down on. A letter written in 1865 mentions that he and Richard Jones, the local doctor who was usually Lucy's host when she was in Woodbridge, had not spoken for seven years, and there are other indications that after his marriage FitzGerald was unpopular with the rank and file of the locality, although he kept most of his intimate friends. Even those among them who thought they had to destroy his letters regarded his unpleasant remarks about Lucy as an aberration in his personality, not a true indication of it.

As FitzGerald suggested, one of the few things that helped him through the latter part of his marriage was his study of Omar Khayyám. The copy that he said brought him such consolation when he was staying with William Browne was given to him by Cowell, who had transcribed it from a manuscript he found in the Bodleian Library. It was some time before FitzGerald saw the original, kept among the manuscripts of Sir William Ouseley. He never had the investigative passion of the textual scholar that is satisfied only by pushing back through successive transcriptions until he is as near as possible to the author himself. For him good copies were enough, since it was the literary heart of a work that interested him, not the establishment of its authority. Most of his study of Omar was completed before he ever saw the beautiful little book that had first attracted Cowell's attention with its gold-flecked leaves and brilliant blue decoration.

The poems were enough to keep him absorbed all during the worst days in the summer of 1857. He began corresponding with Garcin de Tassy, the French scholar of Persian poetry, asking him about other manuscripts of Omar's poem, but it was Cowell once more who made the most important discovery for him, this time a supplementary manuscript in the library of the Bengal Asiatic Society in Calcutta.

His letters indicate that what first drew FitzGerald to Omar was the religious – or, rather, philosophical – attitudes of the old Persian poet, rather than his aesthetic qualities, and it is interesting to see how his attention shifted and expanded as he became more familiar with the quatrains. Initially, he told Tennyson, his chief interest in Persian was for its connection with the Cowells in India. 'But also I have really got hold of an old Epicurean so desperately impious in his recommendations to live only for *Today* that the good Mahometans have scarcely dared to multiply MSS of him.' At the time he was living with Lucy in Gorleston, and he could scarcely be said to enjoy '*Today*', but he might never have been in such straits had he been guided by Omar's Epicurean beliefs.

> He writes in little Quatrains, and has scarce any of the iteration and conceits to which his People are given. One of the last things I remember of him is that – 'God gave me this turn for Drink, perhaps God was drunk when he made me' – which is not strictly pious. But he is very tender about his Roses and Wine, and making the most of this poor little Life. [II, 291–2]

In the Ouseley manuscript in the Bodleian there are 158 of Omar's *rubáiyát*, or tetrastichs or quatrains, to give them their most available names in Greek and English prosody. The Calcutta manuscript has 516, and in the French translation by J. B. Nicolas that appeared while FitzGerald's second edition was in preparation, there are 464 more. All three sets contributed ultimately to establishing the tenor of Omar's thought, but the majority of the quatrains in FitzGerald's version are translations of stanzas in the Ouseley collection, or are composite tetrastichs, drawing on more than one quatrain in the original for ideas and images.

A good bit of midnight oil and gallons of ink have been expended on trying to determine exactly how much of his poem FitzGerald took from his sources, but it is a form of scholarly industry that would have startled him, for he never pretended to literal translation, nor would he have been interested in it. His method of composition was to read over the relevant sections several times until their broad outlines were fixed in his mind, then to go for a long walk and work out the stanzas. No doubt when he had written down what he had brought together in his head he compared it to the original, but it was fidelity to the spirit of Omar he sought, not to the text. The result mightly fairly be called an improvisation on Omar's quatrains, rather than a translation, and it is in that light that FitzGerald would have wanted it judged. It has been demonstrated on several occasions that he made outright mistakes in his readings of the originals, but there have been few attempts to show that he mistook Omar's ideas. 'I suppose very few People have ever taken such pains in Translation as I have,' he wrote when he had finished the poem, 'though certainly not to be literal. But at all Cost, a Thing must *live*: with a transfusion of one's own worse Life if one can't retain the Original's better. Better a live Sparrow than a stuffed Eagle.' [II, 335]

One telling example of FitzGerald's 'transfusion' to the text from his own disposition was first suggested some years ago by A. J. Arberry. Shortly after he first came across Omar FitzGerald wrote in delight to Tennyson of the essentially Epicurean nature of the quatrains: 'Drink – for the Moon will often come round to look for us in this Garden and find us not.' [II, 234] As Professor Arberry pointed out, in the back of his mind FitzGerald had the quatrain that later became stanza LXXIV of the first edition, one of the most famous in the whole poem. But 'Omar said nothing about a garden' in the original. By the end of 1858 FitzGerald spoke of the whole poem as 'a sort of Epicurean Eclogue in a Persian Garden' [II, 323], for the image had become so fused to the stanza that he had long since forgotten it was his own, not Omar's:

> Ah, Moon of my Delight who know'st no wane,
> The Moon of Heav'n is rising once again:
>   How oft hereafter rising shall she look
> Through this same Garden after me – in vain!

'FitzGerald already in 1856 conceived the romantic setting of a garden ... three years later the fictitious garden took its place forever in English literature.'[14] When one also considers that the whole first line sprang from the simple words 'O moon' in the original, it is clear how much we owe to FitzGerald's love of the spirit of the text rather than the letter.

But even he could be worried into literality, as in the opening stanza of the first edition:

> Awake! for Morning in the Bowl of Night
> Has flung the Stone that puts the Stars to Flight:
>   And Lo! the Hunter of the East has caught
> The Sultán's Turret in a Noose of Light.

In his notes to the poem, FitzGerald glossed the first two lines: 'Flinging a Stone into the Cup was the Signal for "To Horse!" in the Desert.' He admitted elsewhere that the figure was not in the original, 'but the Image is so pretty and so smacks of the Desert Life – the Pebble thrown into the Cup, and all starting to Horse – that it is worth risking it'. [II, 280–1] Unfortunately, he was nagged by his friends and his conscience until he felt compelled to eliminate what he had invented. He ruined a superbly evocative opening in so doing, and for years thereafter he fiddled inconclusively with the stanza, trying unsuccessfully to find another way of breathing life into the flatness of the original.

For two years Omar's poems dominated the correspondence of FitzGerald and Cowell, and FitzGerald readily acquiesced in the replies that came from India to his hesitant queries about the text. But from the beginning he could foresee differences about the ethics of the poem. 'I see how a very pretty *Eclogue* might be tessel-ated out of his scattered Quatrains,' he wrote in July 1857, 'but you would not like the Moral of it.' [II, 294] The longer they com-municated about the matter, the clearer it became that on the central issue of Omar's religious views they could never be re-conciled. Cowell, whom FitzGerald described as a 'very religious Man' [II, 419], found it difficult to justify his interest in Omar unless his theology could somehow be made to square with con-ventional Christian belief. FitzGerald agreed that some of the stanzas demanded mystical interpretation, but he thought it was impossible to read the other quatrains as anything but 'curious Infidel and Epicurean Tetrastichs by a Persian of the 11th. Century – as savage against Destiny, etc., as Manfred – but mostly of Epicurean Pathos'. [II, 234] It was a philosophy that the free-thinking FitzGerald found completely to his own taste, one that rang 'like true Metal.... "Today is ours."' [II, 262]

He would probably have agreed in principle with the doctrine at any time after he left the university, but it was peculiarly appro-priate for him during the misery of the days before his separation from Lucy, for custom, morality, convention, and formality had, in his eyes, all led to unhappiness because he tried to subdue his natural inclinations to fit them. What is proposed in the poem is not nihilism but the belief that the only certainty is in beauty not spirituality, and to that FitzGerald could easily subscribe.

The question between FitzGerald and Cowell was framed in terms of Sufism, the mystic branch of Moslem thought. They could not agree whether Omar had been a Sufi and, if so, to which party of Sufism he had belonged, since their limits were not easily refined. One of the characteristics of Sufic poetry was its vocabulary of love, for both women and boys, its profusion of roses, wine, and intoxication, expressing in intensely sensual images the otherwise inexpressible holy mysteries. What was immediately in question was whether the imagery in this poetry was solely mystical and allegorical in intent, or whether it was really a glorification of the senses, smuggled in under the label of mysticism.

Cowell thought the problem had a simple answer, the only tolerable one for him: 'By Drunkenness is meant Divine Love.' Nor was he the only authority who believed this; according to FitzGerald's preface to the second edition, J. B. Nicolas 'does not consider Omar to be the material Epicurean that I have literally taken him for, but a Mystic, shadowing the Deity under the figure of Wine, Wine-bearer, etc.'. To this FitzGerald's rejoinder was blunt: 'Omar was too honest of Heart as well as of Head for this.' Omar's worldly pleasures 'are what they profess to be without any Pretence at divine Allegory: his Wine is the veritable Juice of the Grape: his Tavern, where it was to be had: his Sáki, the Flesh and Blood that poured it out for him: all which, and where the Roses were in Bloom, was all he profess'd to want of this World or to expect of Paradise.'*

Perhaps for the first time FitzGerald found himself at loggerheads with Cowell, and at last he had to assert his belief in his own reading of the text. 'I take old Omar rather more as my property than yours: he and I are more akin, are we not? You see all [his] Beauty, but you can't feel *with* him in some respects as I do.... I think these free opinions are less dangerous in an old Mahometan, or an old Roman (like Lucretius) than when they are returned to by those who have lived on happier Food.' [II, 305] With reason he might have added his own name to those of Omar and Lucretius, since he was painfully aware that he had nearly starved on what had nourished Cowell. As the years passed, Cowell became more

---

*Preface, first edition. In later editions FitzGerald modified the curtness of the statement but not his belief.

convinced that FitzGerald was wrong, until at last he was sorry he had ever introduced him to Omar's poetry.

The more one reads FitzGerald the more apparent it becomes that much of his translation was a transformation of material with which he felt strong personal identification. *Salámán and Absál*, for example, was important to him as a psychological projection of his own personality and problems. It is surely not accidental that his most successful work, the one by which his name has survived, should be the one in which he saw himself as clearly as in a mirror. His prefaces to the four editions of the *Rubáiyát* published in his lifetime make it obvious that he felt completely at one not only with Omar's doctrines but with the man himself. There is a flavour almost of self-justification in his conclusion to the preface of the third edition: 'other readers may be content to believe with me that, while the Wine Omar celebrates is simply the Juice of the Grape, he bragg'd more than he drank of it, in very defiance perhaps of that Spiritual Wine which left its Votaries sunk in Hypocrisy or Disgust.'

Over and over FitzGerald spoke of the poem as profoundly sad, a description that is not really corroborated by reading it, since the wit and sparkle of the verse seem held in counterbalance with what he called its 'triste plaisir'.* To Samuel Laurence he described it as a 'desperate sort of thing, unfortunately at the bottom of all thinking men's minds; but made Music of'. [IV, 3] But one suspects that FitzGerald had grown so close to the verse that he believed it to be an exact counterpart of his own emotions.

One aspect of Omar's life that especially appealed to FitzGerald, and with which he clearly identified himself, was that, according to most biographical accounts, he was never employed but spent his life at Naishápúr as a pensioner of the Vizier and the Sultan, 'winning knowledge of every kind, and especially in Astronomy, wherein he attained to a very high pre-eminence'. It was an idealized version of what FitzGerald wanted his own life to be and perhaps also an unconscious justification of what others thought of as his indolence.

Another facet of FitzGerald's version of Omar that needs to be

---

*Probably fewer readers would agree with FitzGerald than with T. S. Eliot, who found on his first reading of the poem that the 'world appeared anew, painted with bright, delicious, and painful colours'.

considered is his deliberate obscuring of the sex of the beloved in the poems. In the original both a woman, or houri, and a youth, are addressed in the love poetry, as was the custom of Omar and his contemporaries. Predictably, FitzGerald obliterates all mention of the youth, but more surprisingly he also eliminates all reference to the beloved as a woman, leaving the sex an open question. It is worth noting that he could not quite forbear bringing the matter to the notice of the reader, by a footnote in his prefaces giving the location of the most overtly homosexual quatrain in Nicolas's translation, mentioning 'la singularité des images trop orientales, d'une sensualité quelquefois révoltante'. Since he leaves so much else from the original out of his translation, the reader feels that it would have been simpler for FitzGerald to have ignored the matter had it not been of some significance to himself. But these quatrains were so personal that he could not remain content with having prudently erased the surface manifestation of his interests, for then he was compelled to call attention to them after all.

Although it was the Epicureanism of Omar that first appealed to him, he was also drawn to the actual form of the *rubáiyát*, not least because they were meant to be epigrammatic, with no logical connection with surrounding stanzas in most cases. In the English version of the stanza form the rhyme is aaba, i.e., lines 1, 2 and 4 rhyme, while line 3 does not. The effect of the lack of rhyme in the third line is to give it authority because of its singularity, what George Meredith once described when he read the poem as the 'march of a king with his train behind him'.[15] The return to rhyme in the last line makes the final syllable even heavier than it would otherwise be, thus preventing any linkage to the succeeding quatrain. The isolation of each stanza makes it an ideal form for setting forth a discontinuous doctrine of the kind that FitzGerald thought characterized the work of Omar, since each perception is self-contained:

> Oh, Thou, who Man of baser Earth didst make,
> And who with Eden didst devise the Snake;
>   For all the Sin wherewith the Face of Man
> Is blacken'd, Man's Forgiveness give — and take!

In this translation FitzGerald retains the five-beat iambic line that he had often used in blank verse, but the rhyme prevents disturbing hints of Shakespeare. Part of this effect is caused, too, by the Oriental imagery, so that when Shakespearean echoes are deliberately introduced, at first they seem slightly intrusive, then become subsumed in what is an older view of the world:

> Ah, make the most of what we yet may spend,
> Before we too into the Dust descend;
>   Dust into Dust, and under Dust, to lie,
> Sans Wine, sans Song, sans Singer, and – sans End!

The reader feels that FitzGerald has at last found the form of translation that allows him to make antique poetry available to his contemporaries without letting Elizabethan language become dominant.

A series of self-contained stanzas presents problems of organization of the whole. Omar himself had no such trouble, since the order of his stanzas was alphabetical, determined by the last character of the rhyme word. FitzGerald was aware that English readers might need a more obvious form of organization, and a few of the stanzas are allowed to fall into connected groups, although most remain independent. It was probably hindsight that made him discover, thirteen years after the first publication of the poem, that Omar's thoughts follow the course of one day: 'He begins with Dawn pretty sober and contemplative: then as he thinks and drinks, grows savage, blasphemous, etc. and then again sobers down into melancholy at nightfall.' [III, 339] Perhaps, but it is an order that most readers do not notice; in any case, FitzGerald had to expand the second edition to give 'Omar's thoughts room to turn in' if the progression was to be noticeable.

His first attempt at translating Omar was in May 1857, when he turned some of the quatrains into 'Monkish Latin' [II, 273], but it was unsatisfactory and within two months he had made his first English translation, this time in paired rhymed couplets of iambic pentameter. [II, 289] By the end of 1857 he had settled on the final version of the stanza and had enough completed to submit thirty-five of the 'less wicked' [II, 419] to John Parker of *Fraser's*, who had agreed in advance to publish them, although he had previously turned down *Salámán*. With an eye to the readers of *Fraser's*, Fitz-Gerald warned him that he 'might find it rather dangerous among his Divines'. [II, 323] After waiting a year for a final decision, he tired of hearing nothing, so he took the manuscript back from Parker, to have it printed privately, as he had done with his earlier works. Before giving it to the printer, he added forty quatrains to what he had shown Parker. It was still a short poem, but he wanted to keep it so, partly in emulation of Gray's 'Elegy in a Country Churchyard', whose brevity he had always admired.

Two hundred and fifty copies of the poem were printed: a thin pamphlet in modest brown paper with no author's name on the title page. FitzGerald retained forty of the copies for his own use, then gave away only three of them. The rest were taken for distribution by Bernard Quaritch, who specialized in Oriental books. It was ready to be sold by 15 February, but it was held up for a month and a half; the British Museum received its statutory copy on 30 March. Copies were sent to most of the literary journals, but there were only two reviews, one a single sentence in the *Athenaeum*, the other a respectable notice by the *Literary Gazette*: 'Nothing can be more dreary than the merriment in which he seeks to drown his despair, and nothing more beautiful than the manner in which he discourses of both.' [II, 337]

After that the little pamphlet of verses sank, apparently never to surface again. But FitzGerald can hardly have noticed, for on the very day that the British Museum received its copy, which was one day before its translator's fiftieth birthday, William Kenworthy Browne died.

CHAPTER X

The Discovery of the
Rubáiyát

Browne's death was of a piece with his life: brave, generous, proceeding directly from his love of sport. Perhaps not uncharacteristic, too, in that a cleverer man might have avoided it. Returning from a day's hunting at the end of January 1859, he was riding a high-spirited mare on which that morning he had asked the groom to put a curb bridle 'that his Mare could ill endure' and a '*high-pommeled* Saddle scarce ever used'. Browne saw a fellow rider punishing his horse and rode up to remonstrate with him, taking his mare too near the other animal, which kicked out at Browne's mount; she reared, lost her footing on the wet turf of the roadside, and fell backwards on her rider, 'crushing all the middle of his Body' as he slipped from the unfamiliar saddle.

Browne lived on for 'two months with a Patience and Vitality that would have left most Men to die in a Week'. FitzGerald was apparently not told of the accident for some weeks, and certainly he was not notified of the seriousness of Browne's condition until only a few days before his death, when he hurried to Goldington to be with his friend. For two days after his arrival he was not allowed to see Browne, then he received a summons to the sick room, a scrawl like a small child's, the last words Browne ever wrote, 'I love *you* very – whenever – WKB.'

FitzGerald afterwards confessed that he had to take a glass of brandy to get up his courage. As he entered the bedroom, the tears came to Browne's eyes and he painfully forced out the words, 'My dear Fitz – old Fel-low' before his visitor broke down. It was nearly impossible to have a conversation with him because he could neither speak nor hear well; ever since FitzGerald met him, he had been deaf in one ear, and the accident had cut off the hearing in the

211

X William Browne, from unfinished portrait
by Samuel Laurence.

other. Everyone around him had recognized for weeks that he could not possibly live, but Browne had continued to believe in his eventual recovery until the last fortnight of his life, when the doctors told him what all those with him already knew. He was bathed in tears as he told Fitz, 'They broke my Heart – but it was necessary.' More often he grieved silently to spare others. 'Once he had his Bed wheeled to the Window to look out abroad: but he saw the Hawthorns *coming into Leaf*, and he bid them take him back.' Throughout his illness he had been sustained by his strong religious belief; FitzGerald could not wish him deprived of any comfort, but it must have been painful to recognize the deep chasm that lay between them in this matter.

Mrs Browne, who had never been strong, was '*inspired*, as Women are, to lose all her own Weakness in his: but the Doctors dread the Effect on her – especially since she is four or five months gone with Child!' FitzGerald admired her selfless nursing of her husband, but it was hard to accept that she was almost constantly at the bedside from which he was kept for fear of tiring the patient. He loitered around the house in case Browne should call for him, and he whiled away the lonely time by looking at the little Crome painting and the hawking picture that he had given to Browne, and at the other pictures they had bought together over twenty years. Among the books were a large number with 'EFG to WKB' written in them, one of them a copy of Digby's *Godefridus*, which had always seemed to him to encapsulate the chivalrous values by which Browne lived. To the inscription in his presentation copy of *Euphranor* he added the words, 'This little book would never have been written, had I not known my dear friend William Browne, who, unconsciously, supplied the moral. E.FG., Goldington, March 27, 1859.'

When it was clear, after two or three days, that Browne would never again call for him, FitzGerald slipped away from Goldington, 'wishing to be alone, or in other Company, when the Last came'. For all his pity for Mrs Browne, he also felt something akin to envy: 'She has her Children to attend to, and be her comfort in turn: and though having lost what most she loved yet has something to love still, and to be beloved by. There are worse Conditions than that.' Of his own condition he said only, 'I . . . have now much less to care about.'

As he left Goldington FitzGerald took away with him the riding crop Browne had been used to carry in London, and Mrs Browne later sent him the snuffbox and the little Stubbs painting he had given to her husband. The summer of the following year, at Mrs Browne's suggestion, he took her sons for a seaside holiday to Aldeburgh, where they 'boated, and rowed, and shot Gulls and Dotterels, and flung stones into the Sea: and swore an eternal Friendship' with a young sailor, 'who, strangely enough, reminded me something of their Father as I first knew him near thirty years ago! This was a strange Thing: and my Thoughts run after that poor Fisher Lad who is now gone off in a Smack to the North.' But he never again went to Goldington, which held too many memories of the 'comely spirited Boy I had known first twenty-seven years ago lying all shattered and Death in his Face and Voice'. [II, 327–47, 371–3] Yet he was homesick for Browne's old home and yearned for 'Bedfordshire, not yet forsaken by the spirit of poetry, where trees are trees (not timber), and tapering poplars – likely enough thirteen in a row – contemplate their doubles in the placid Ouse. But the "dear shepherd" of those fields is gone.'[1] Even London was haunted at every turn by his 'old Companion in its Streets and Taverns', so that he kept away from it as long as possible and never returned with the same pleasure. Gradually he was cutting himself off from other places such as Cambridge where once he had been happy, and he even shunned Oxford and the area around Ipswich because of their association with Cowell before he deserted England.

The published correspondence between FitzGerald and Mrs Browne shows with what amazing candour and unself-consciousness he wrote to her after Browne's death of his love of her husband, in terms that seemed perfectly natural to him although one can easily understand that a widow might dislike them. Naturally, he did not ask her to return the £6,500 that he had lent to Browne, but by 1871, when the debt had been outstanding for some thirteen years, he recalled it, since he understood that Mrs Browne was a rich woman. His tactful letter to her about the matter, written in hope that she would have 'no bitter taste', is the last of his letters to her in the edition of his collected correspondence, and other letters from family friends indicate that she was furious that he had even mentioned the matter. It was a sad end to

214

their friendship. But he never forgot a single detail of his years with Browne. In the last year of his life he recalled his 'rare intuition into Men, Matters, and even into Matters of Art: though Thackeray would call him "Little Browne" – which I told him he was not justified in doing. They are equal now.' [IV, 550]

FitzGerald was less shattered by Browne's death than might be expected, probably because he had already suffered half the pain of loss when he realized that he was no longer at the centre of his friend's existence.

Apart from a few fleeting visits to Boulge, he had not been in Woodbridge since his marriage, nearly two and a half years before. Mrs Smith's illness had made it inconvenient to go to Farlingay, and it was easier simply to avoid the hostility of some of the inhabitants by not appearing in the town. Crabbe of Bredfield had died just at the time when FitzGerald and his wife finally admitted that their marriage was effectually over. With Cambridge, London, and Oxford full of disturbing memories, most of his usual haunts were now denied to him. Two months after Browne's death he went to stay at Geldestone with the Kerriches, and from there he made an excursion to the fishing ports that had provided him with brief periods of pleasure during his marriage, from their likeness to marine paintings with views of the ships and the sea and the sailors with 'their brown hands in their Breeches Pockets'. It seemed an ideal locality to recuperate from his losses, and after another visit or two to confirm his impressions, he went to Lowestoft in November 1859 for a stay of half a year. It was the beginning of the association with the sea for which FitzGerald is most often remembered in East Anglia.

By the time he settled down in 10 Marine Terrace, Lowestoft, 'The Season' was over, so that he was not bothered with its provincial society, and there was 'not a Soul here but the Sailors, who are a very fine Race of Men'. [II, 346–7] Their presence was enough to reconcile him to the cold winds and the dirty yellow water between the town and an offshore shoal. They lived a hard life with great physical courage, in constant danger of being wrecked, often making little money but keeping their sense of fun and good humour: 'When one is in London one seems to see a decayed Race; but here the old English Stuff.' [II, 351] He particularly liked the look of the herring fishermen, who 'really half starve here during

Winter', but he admired all the 'beachmen', as they were known, for their 'half-starving Independence' and their 'wonderful Shoulders: won't take one out in one of their Yawls for a Sovereign though they will give one a Ride when they go out to get nothing at all'. [II, 355] It was their very simplicity and nearness to the primitive that made them so attractive to FitzGerald.

All during his stay in Lowestoft he still ached at knowing he would never see Browne again. Slowly the resolution formed to find a new friend there, and he began searching deliberately among the sailors. In his loneliest evenings in London he had acquired the habit of walking the streets looking for a friendly face or a casual passer-by to whom he could talk. During the solitary winter in Lowestoft, he said, he 'used to wander about the shore at night longing for some fellow to accost me who might give some promise of filling up a very vacant place in my heart but only some of the more idle and worthless sailors came across me'. [III, 40] (Curiously, his confidante on this occasion was Mrs Browne, which indicates his extraordinary unself-consciousness about his behaviour.) To ensure his welcome among the sailors he carried with him a bottle of rum and rolls of tobacco, according to Donne: 'So armed, he spends his evenings under the lee-side of fishing boats, hearing and telling yarns.'[2] At the back of his mind floated a picture of Browne, which he was hoping to match among this wild, often handsome lot of men.

It is no wonder that all the sailors knew him by sight, for even without such remarkable behaviour, he was a distinctive figure on the lonely Lowestoft beach, his obviously expensive but ill-tended clothes thrown on anyhow, his top hat anchored against the sea wind by a scarf tied under his chin, on his face such a curious combination of apprehensive *hauteur* and excessive vulnerability that many of them thought he was mad. No one could have mistaken him for anything but a gentleman, but it would have been hard for the sailors to assign a reputable motive for his walks along the pebbles until he found an upended boat sheltering one or more of their kind. Inevitably he became the butt of innuendoes and jokes for the sailors, who were far more knowing than he. Among them was a handsome, somewhat stolid looking, young man, then only twenty years old, who stood back, silently observing him. Some years later FitzGerald became acquainted with 'Posh' Fletcher, as he told Mrs Browne: 'I asked him why he had never come down to see me at the time I speak of. Well, he had often seen me, he said, among the boats, but never thought it becoming in him to accost me first, or even to come near me. Yet he was the very man I wanted, with, strangely enough, some resemblance in feature to a portrait of you may guess whom, and much in character also.' [III, 40–1] There is little in his succeeding dealings with FitzGerald to suggest that Fletcher suffered from excessive generosity or propriety, and it must have occurred to him that there could be considerable profit from the friendship of an eccentric gentleman more than twice his age, but we know from what happened five years later that he had to take coarse jibes from his friends, so it is not surprising that he stood aloof in 1859, fearing the interpretation the other sailors would put upon his behaviour if he approached FitzGerald.

The rum and tobacco were apparently wasted on the Lowestoft sailors that winter, for FitzGerald wrote of none who had become his friend, but the following summer he employed a 'poor careless Devil' of a sailor, Alfred Hurrell, who subsequently broke into a house and was sentenced to prison for fifteen months. 'But he had Fun in him,' FitzGerald said, 'and the more respectable Men are duller.' [II, 396]

He became so attached to one young sailor from Aldeburgh ('strong as a Horse, simple as a Child') that he invited him to stay. The young man was at 'his turning Point of Life: whether he is to stay with Father, Mother, and Sweetheart, fishing at Aldbro: – or go out in a Square-rigg'd Vessel (humph!) for five or six years, and learn what will qualify him to come home and be a Pilot. This would be best for *him*: but "Father and Mother and Sue" – and even E.F.G. – don't want to lose Sight of him so long, perhaps for ever, some of us.' [II, 391] In order to see the young man FitzGerald was willing to make the trip to Aldeburgh for a 'Smoke with the Sailors', usually with grog in the kitchen of a tavern, but occasionally on Saturday nights they sat drinking and singing in a net-house. FitzGerald was proud of the applause for his own performance of 'Pretty Peg of Derby O!'. His young sailor friend said to him: 'Somehow you know Songs something like ours, only better', which pleased him, as did the 'Childishness and Sea language of these People'. [II, 395–6]

217

The Discovery of the Rubáiyát

Whatever the townsfolk of Lowestoft, Aldeburgh, and Wood-bridge, or the sailors and even his own friends thought about the spectacle of a lonely elderly man consorting chiefly with young sailors, there can be little doubt that FitzGerald was completely guileless and open in his behaviour. Loneliness is seldom attractive, and his was probably graceless and embarrassing to others, but it was never disgusting or sordid, and anything that looked like ugliness to others was surely in the eye of the beholder.

His letters after the publication of the *Rubáiyát* bear resigned witness to FitzGerald's disappointment over its apparent failure, but he was too reticent to express it openly. Probably his frankest statement was to Cowell: 'I hardly know why I print any of these things, which nobody buys; and I scarce now see the few I give them to. But when one has done one's best, and is sure that the best is better than so many will take pains to do, though far from the best that *might be done*, one likes to make an end of the matter by Print.' [II, 335]

It was two years before the poem was 'discovered', the first step to its becoming one of the most popular works of the century. But it was much longer than that before FitzGerald himself knew that his poem had not been still-born. The story has often been told of how the poem was found in a publisher's bin, was puffed by the Pre-Raphaelites and their friends, and at last became one of the standard poems of the language. Because the account involves half of the most important Victorian writers and had such a happy ending, it has been called alliteratively the 'romance of the *Rub-áiyát*', but to make it even more romantic, some aspects have been distorted. In particular it has been tempting to exaggerate the time that passed before the poem was noticed. Actually, only two years before the leading writers of the time were ecstatic about it would seem a short enough time for most other poets waiting for recognition. Even if FitzGerald was unaware of the fact, by 1861 the *Rubáiyát* was well on its way.*

Since few, if any, had been sold, Quaritch put the remaining copies of the poem into the bargain box of his shop for quick sale.

---

*In the past, dispute over exact details has so often led to acrimonious explosions about the inaccuracy of other writers that recounting the discovery of the poem gives one the sense of going on tiptoe through a minefield that has often blown up before; it may be quiescent, but it is not safe to assume so.

The original price had been one shilling, but now they were offered ignominiously for a penny. In the summer of 1861 a young Celtic scholar named Whitley Stokes fished out several copies from the box, kept one for himself, and gave the others to friends, including Richard Monckton Milnes, Richard Burton, and Dante Gabriel Rossetti.

In his turn Rossetti bought copies for both Swinburne and Browning. According to Swinburne's account, which may owe some embellishment to retrospection, he returned with Rossetti the following day to buy more copies and found that the little flurry of sales had caused Quaritch to raise the price to the 'sinfully extravagant sum of twopence'. He secured copies for Edward Burne-Jones and William Morris and took one with him on a visit to George Meredith, where he arrived, as Meredith said, 'waving the white sheet of what seemed to be a pamphlet.... we lay on a heathery knoll outside my cottage reading a stanza alternately, indifferent to the dinner-bell, until a prolonged summons reminded us of appetite. After dinner we took to the paper-covered treasure again.'

Eventually the pamphlet reached John Ruskin, the unofficial apologist and mentor of many of the Pre-Raphaelites. On 2 September 1863 he wrote a letter to the translator, whose identity was still secret, and gave it to Burne-Jones to deliver if ever he discovered the translator's name:

> I do not know in the least who you are, but I do with all my soul pray you to find and translate some more of Omar Khayyám for us: I never did – till this day – read anything so glorious, to my mind as this poem ... and that, & this, is all I can say about it – More – more – please more – & that I am ever gratefully & respectfully yours.

Burne-Jones put away the letter and forgot about it for some years. In 1868 there was a second and enlarged edition, necessitated in part because Quaritch had inadvertently sold most of his stock of the *Rubáiyát* as waste paper. FitzGerald's anonymity had preserved his privacy, but it also deprived him of the pleasure of hearing about the respect of other poets for his work. A third edition appeared in 1872.

Before the third edition was published, there was one shrewd guess at the translator's name, by Fanny Kemble's daughter, who lived in Philadelphia. She wrote directly to FitzGerald, asking about the matter, and he acknowledged his identity, which then became known to a small group of readers in the United States, although it was still a secret in England.

Among the poem's American admirers was Professor Charles Eliot Norton of Harvard, who had first read Burne-Jones's copy in 1868. He helped to spread its reputation in America, among others to J. R. Lowell and Emerson, who paid it a characteristically chilly compliment in saying that it was 'very lofty in its defiance, with rare depths of feeling and imagination'. Four years later Norton was again in England and heard the rumour that the translator of the *Rubáiyát* was 'a certain Reverend Edward FitzGerald, who lived somewhere in Norfolk and was fond of boating'.

Norton sent a copy of the poem to his friend Carlyle, who had said in surprise when told of the rumour about the amphibious parson, 'Why, he's no more Reverend than I am! He's a very old friend of mine – I'm surprised, if the book be as good as you tell me it is, that my old friend has never mentioned it to me.' When he had read it, Carlyle thought that FitzGerald had wasted his time in translating the 'verses of that old Mohammedan blackguard'. Slightly more tactfully, in a covering note sent with Ruskin's letter, he told FitzGerald that he found the 'Book itself a kind of jewel in its way'. Fourteen years had elapsed since he first published it, but at last FitzGerald was beginning to know the pleasures of literary success. No editions of the poem appeared during his lifetime with his name on the title page, but his identity was an open secret in literary circles for the last decade before his death. The poem became even more popular in America than in England. One critic has estimated that by 1929 there had been 310 editions published in the world, and that thirty years later there were 'hundreds and hundreds of editions – how many hundreds no one knows'. And since then, there have been uncounted further editions.[3]

Any work as popular as the *Rubáiyát* acquires a certain critical mystery, one that Ezra Pound hinted at in his *ABC of Reading* when he proposed the exercise: 'Try to find out why the FitzGerald *Rubaiyat* has gone into so many editions after having lain unnoticed until Rossetti found a pile of remaindered copies on a second-hand bookstall.'[4] Pound's factual errors do not obscure the problem, nor does the facile answer that it is always a miracle for a work of serious poetry to become a popular success.

There may be one clue to the answer in the date of the first appearance of the *Rubáiyát*, 1859, which also saw the publication of Samuel Smiles's *Self-Help*, Mill's *On Liberty*, George Eliot's *Adam Bede*, Meredith's *Ordeal of Richard Feverel*, above all Darwin's *Origin of Species*. FitzGerald's work was not recognized at first as such, but we can see in retrospect that it was none the less representative of the distinguishing characteristic of them all, a repudiation of traditional religious morality and the attempt to find an alternative to it.

But nothing could be further than the *Rubáiyát* from the doctrine of work in Smiles or the competition for survival outlined in Darwin. It may be helpful to look again at the names of Fitz-Gerald's 'discoverers': Rossetti, Monckton Milnes, Burton, Burne-Jones, Swinburne, Morris, all of them offering alternatives, some not wholly respectable, both to received religion and to the apparent hardness of the scientific approach offered by Darwin's hypothesis. It would be a mistake to try to huddle them into a group under one label, but it may be said collectively of them that the warm-blooded worship of beauty, 'aestheticism', was offered as a counter-proposition both to the despair that poets like Tennyson recognized as implicit in the survival of the fittest, where the mindless physical world is all, and to the cold spiritual world of the 'pale Galilaean' that Swinburne saw as Christianity, where body is punished to profit soul. It was surely the possibility of a middle way that appealed to FitzGerald's contemporaries in his *Rubáiyát*. But besides the idea of hedonism that seems suggested, FitzGerald meant by 'Epicurean', which he so often applied to the poem, a stricter interpretation of the term, in which man recognises that sense perception is his only guide to knowledge, that his mode of distinguishing choices is by the enlightened pleasure of the senses, and that the best life is a retired one where marriage, the begetting of children, and civic responsibility are no longer para-mount, or even desirable. It was a doctrine of withdrawal that became increasingly attractive in the face of the inhumane society caused by the combination of the Industrial Revolution, intolerant Calvinism, and the theory of evolution.

Not a little of the lure of the *Rubáiyát* was that it tapped the

221

great attraction of the Orient for the Victorians, whether of Persian poetry, Indian philosophy, or Japanese pots, symbols of a world where middle-class conventionality had neither meaning nor validity. In the lushness of the imagery of the poem lay suggestions of sensuality, mystery, satiety, all only hinted at as they are held within the rigid framework of the FitzGerald stanza; it was not unlike the Victorian love of feminine voluptuousness made more irresistible by constraint within stiff confining garments. One suspects that many of his readers were drawn to FitzGerald's work by impulses with which he would certainly have felt little conscious empathy. The very popularity of his translation, however, seems to indicate that he was far more in tune with his contemporaries than he would have guessed.

The long wait for the discovery of the *Rubáiyát* made FitzGerald weary at heart, and he began to feel a 'sort of Terror at meddling with Pen and Paper.... The old *Go* is gone – such as it was. One has got older: one has lived alone: and, also, either one's Subjects, or one's way of dealing with them, have little Interest to others.' [II, 465–6] If publication was not worth considering, it hardly seemed worthwhile writing. He continued to translate Persian in a desultory way, and briefly he considered translating more Calderón, but he published nothing of consequence for six years after the *Rubáiyát*. During 1860 and 1861 he contributed several brief items, concerned with his reading or with local subjects, to *Notes and Queries*; he signed them 'Parathina', of which the translation is 'Along the Shore', which accurately reflects the change in his life.

'Somehow all the Country round is become a Cemetery to me: so many I loved there dead,' he wrote, 'but none I have loved have been drown'd.' [II, 371] Nothing could change the sea, but the countryside was being despoiled progressively: paths were fenced over by the squirearchy and guards set to prevent their use after they had been free to all since history had been recorded, commons were enclosed, trees were chopped down, and the land was systematically bought up by enormously rich families like the Thellussons of Rendlesham Hall and the Tomlines, who were FitzGerald's *bêtes noires*. 'I always like Seafaring People,' he said in justifying his attraction to the uncomplicated, unmercenary beachmen. Even their speech was freer, untainted by the city, more original and poetic, and his literary interests were revived by a sniff of sea air, so that he began collecting examples of the diction of the sailors, which he thought was the backbone of the Suffolk dialect that he had loved ever since his boyhood walks with Major Moor. 'Their very fine old English' was only a manifestation of the superiority of sailing men: 'We have a pretty word here for these fluttering light winds – you will see how pleasantly compounded – "No steady Breeze; but only little *fannyin'* Winds, that died at Sunset," etc.' [II, 397]

His delight in men of the sea led him naturally into sailing on a larger scale than he had undertaken since days on the Channel with his father and his grandfather. In 1861 he replaced a small boat he had on the River Deben with a two-ton, sixteen-foot river boat, sailed by two men and named the *Waveney* after the river on which she was built. 'She'll do all but speak,' said one of the crew in pleasure at her performance.

FitzGerald loved being aboard the *Waveney*, setting out for a sail with a cuddy well stocked with bottled stout for himself and the crew, but he immediately began hankering for a larger craft, one in which he could make short trips to the Continent or to Scotland and which could sleep a few guests. In the spring of 1862 he bought, sight unseen, a yacht that the Woodbridge plumber had found on the Thames at Greenwich; almost immediately he discovered that he had 'one of the biggest owls in Woodbridge (and that is no small thing) to choose and act for me'. The yacht had cost £43, and he paid two men to bring her from London, then discovered that she was nearly derelict and had to be almost entirely refitted. Rather than do that, it was simpler to admit that he had lost his whole investment in the boat.

After a long search for a replacement for the worthless yacht, he finally ordered a forty-three-foot schooner, built in Wivenhoe, Essex, for about £350, which was launched in the summer of 1863. During her building he was afraid he had made another mistake, but FitzGerald loved the new boat when he saw her. Almost immediately he changed her name from the *Shamrock* to the *Scandal*, which he said with feeling went faster than anything else in Woodbridge; her skiff was appropriately named the *Whisper*. She proved awkward in the Deben, 'but then she was to be a good Sea-boat'. For all his love of her, he had few plans for long cruises after all: 'I can't sleep so well on board as I used to do thirty years ago: and not

XI The *Scandal.*

to get one's Sleep, you know, indisposes one more or less for the Day.' Gradually, however, he began thinking of Dover, Folkestone, the Isle of Wight, and the Channel ports of the Continent, 'which will give one's sleeping Talents a *tuning*'. [II, 484]

FitzGerald was quite happy to let his crew sail the boat without his assistance, for watching the white sails and the beacons bothered his eyes: 'as in other Affairs of Life, I only sit by and look on.' [II, 454] He contented himself with good-natured shouts of advice to the helmsman from his own position by the mainmast, where he spent most of his time lying with a book in his hand, perfectly happy at being soaked in a heavy sea. He won the respect of all who sailed with him by knowing nothing of fear in rough weather. Although he took so small a part in their sailing, he was on democratic terms with his crews, calling them by their Christian names and delightedly going aboard other vessels with them to drink rum. He was a good master, asking little for himself and

224

expecting nothing but cold food on board, to save work in the galley. If he kept the crew out over the weekend, he would put into harbour to get them a hot meal. He even made his own bed to save them trouble.

He had always declined to dress grandly for particular occasions, and afloat he maintained the same sartorial indifference, wearing his customary clothing, not 'yachting' costume. Like any other gentleman of the period, he wore his top hat when sailing, in this case tied on to keep it from being blown overboard. Some modern writers have questioned the testimony on the subject of those who sailed with him, saying that a top hat would be manifestly too impractical for the purpose. Contemporary photographs show, however, that men of his class wore it as customary sailing gear; certainly, he would not have worn a common sailor's cap, although he probably took off his hat when the weather was too rough. Around his shoulders was a huge shawl; one of those he owned, a plaid affair, is still worn by the presiding officer at meetings of the Omar Khayyám Club.

But no one could have called him conventional, even when he was sailing. Going ashore in the *Whisper*, he would sometimes be irritated by the slowness and leap into knee-deep water to wade to dry land. Occasionally he was swept off the deck by the movement of the boom in rough weather, which he would forget when he was deep in a book, and more than once he was fished out still clutching whatever he had been reading, quite at his ease once his hat had been retrieved, content to lie down again and let the sea wash over him, since, as he remarked philosophically, he could hardly get wetter.

In 1863 he set out at last for Holland, where he had wanted for years to see the pictures in the Hague. They landed in Rotterdam and put up the boat in a 'sluggish unsweet Canal'. George Manby, a Woodbridge merchant who was his guest on the trip, persuaded FitzGerald to see Rotterdam before going on: 'So we tore about in an open Cab: saw nothing: the Gallery not worth a Visit: and at night I was half dead with weariness.' The following day they went to Amsterdam, where they were in such a rush that they missed two of the pictures they most wanted to see. They arrived at last at the Hague museum, but it was just closing for two days. In 'Rage and Despair' over the Dutch, Manby, and himself, FitzGerald immediately had the boat put out to sea and went back to England without ever having been in the gallery that was the goal of the trip. [II, 489–90]

Each year he kept the yacht under sail for increasingly long periods, taking her along the eastern and southern coasts of England and to the French Channel ports. In Lowestoft he often used her as floating summer quarters. Besides the fun of actual sailing, she provided him with a perfect excuse not to settle down permanently on land.

Mrs Smith, the mistress of Farlingay Hall, whose illness had made FitzGerald leave the house, died at the end of 1859, and he moved back there for the second half of 1860, but it was obvious that her widower was so ill that he would have to vacate the house and that the lodger would have to move elsewhere. The position of Farlingay a short way outside Woodbridge had been been convenient, since it meant that FitzGerald did not have to face the hostility of the townspeople, many of whom were still resentful over his behaviour to Lucy, which became ever more reprehensible as it was endlessly discussed until it was the general opinion that he was either insane or totally without principles.[5]

It was surely a conscious decision to face up at last to his detractors that made him take lodgings in the exact centre of Woodbridge, over the gunshop of Sharman Berry across from the Shire Hall, with his windows overlooking the market place. It would have been hard to find a more conspicuous place to live. He said that he intended to stay there only as he looked for a house in the town, but he remained on that temporary basis in Market Hill for thirteen years: 'I am afraid to leave this poor Lodging, where I do pretty well, though I can scarce store half the things I want away in it.' But he had become acutely aware of his mortality and was afraid that the 'shaking of the Dart over one's Head' might find him in rented rooms: 'I think one should not burden Landlord and Landlady with that.' [II, 434]

The Berrys were 'very kind and attentive'; his two rooms were cramped, uncomfortable, and dirty, but at least the last of these did not worry him. Mrs Berry hired 'at 1s. a week such a Slut as even I cannot put up with', and understandably had trouble keeping servants. FitzGerald's vegetarian diet demanded little of her culinary skills; on one typical occasion his early dinner was pease

226

pudding, potatoes, and a small bottle of Chablis, which he presumably furnished himself. His only complaint about his quarters was that he found the 'Privy quite public'.

Furnishing his lodgings was the excuse for a new orgy of picture buying and restoring: 'I have been playing wonderful Tricks with the Pictures I have: have cut the Magi in two – making two very good Pictures, I assure you; and cutting off the dark corners of other Pictures with *Gold Ovals* – a shape I like within a Square, and doing away with much Black background.' [II, 459] Irreverently he turpentined and rubbed down two paintings that were, at least temporarily, ascribed to Velasquez and Titian. He bought an 'Early Gainsboro'' from Churchyard and quantities of 'large *picturesque* China' to fill any gaps in the already overcrowded rooms, putting them with the pictures, statues, and even a parti-coloured mop that was so agreeable to his 'colour-loving Eyes' that he kept it in his sitting room. By the time he was finished, his rooms were as comfortable – which is to say, disordered – as his undergraduate lodgings or the cottage at Boulge.

The intellectual life of Woodbridge was as sluggish as that of any small market town, and at first FitzGerald was so conscious of the monotonous chimes from the nearby parish church, playing every three hours, that he threatened to hang himself. It was 'Ye Banks and Braes' and 'Where and oh where is my Soldier Laddie gone?' for weekdays, with a dolefully slow version of the 'Sicilian Mariners' Hymn' for Sundays. He had already cut himself off from invitations from people of his own class in the town, but he was not worried about that, and he found his company instead with tradespeople such as the bookseller, John Loder, and a bright young merchant's clerk, Frederick Spalding, whose interests in art and artefacts so commended themselves to FitzGerald that he set him up in business.

Spalding kept a worshipful diary in which he recorded FitzGerald's conversation and his own gratitude to him: 'I am getting selfish about him, I expect. I like him to *myself* best. I feel so at home with him, could ask him anything, could tell him anything.' In return FitzGerald talked frankly of his own family, of his broken marriage, of his disappointed aspirations. When he saw that Spalding's business was not prospering, he burnt the bond for £500 that he had lent to the younger man. 'I feel towards him as I do to no other man,' wrote Spalding. 'But how can he treat me as he does – with his vast knowledge, taste, and abilities, and I half his age?'[6]

The answer to Spalding's question was that he provided some of the intellectual company that FitzGerald missed in the locality, now that Barton and Crabbe were dead. But he continued to have a sense of humour about himself, even in this matter, and after complaining of his boredom in Woodbridge, he added, 'I see, however, by a Handbill in the Grocer's Shop that a Man is going to lecture on the Gorilla in a few weeks. So there is something to look forward to.' [II, 411–12]

Living in Woodbridge meant the danger of running into Lucy FitzGerald. In 1864 she was there twice for long stays, according to FitzGerald, 'though I never came across her'. Two years later she visited the town four times: 'We have different ideas of Propriety, to be sure.' After not having seen her for seven years, he met her in the street: 'I did not look, nor should have noticed her, but she rushed over the way, and put her Claw in mine, and the terrible old *Caw* soon told me. I said, "Oh, how d'ye do, Ma'am; how long have you been here?" I made off. All this is very wrong; but the Woman has no Delicacy: and if one gives an Inch will take an Ell.' [II, 617]

Lodging with the Berrys on Market Hill had one major advantage over living at Farlingay: he was twice as far from Boulge Hall and the FitzGeralds. There was, however, the inconvenience of being within a hundred yards of the Bull Inn, where the coach from Ipswich stopped and let out anyone going to Boulge. FitzGerald's brother John called on him several times a week, often bringing his sons with him; Edward would sit apprehensively waiting for a pause in the cataract of words to bring the visit to an end. He felt an amused love of John, but he never went to Boulge himself, and when the family was congregated there, he knew there would be a 'Levée of People, who drop in here, etc.' [II, 478], so that he had to leave Woodbridge at such times.

John, who seldom found it easy to make up his mind, was trying to decide whether to sell Boulge altogether, but he was to dither over the matter until his death. On one occasion it was put up for auction and the bidding went to £30,000, but John had set the reserve price well above that, so that it would not go out of his hands. Another time he actually negotiated the sale, then worried so much about it overnight that he bought it back the following day. Occasionally he would arrive at the Bull on his return home, ignore the Boulge carriage waiting for him, order a fly instead, then get into neither but walk three miles to Boulge with both conveyances following him; when he arrived home he would complain at having to pay for a fly he had not used. At the Hall he would ring for a footman to tell him the time from the clock at his elbow. Fitz-Gerald said that John broke engagements from the 'feeling of being *bound*' to them, and that all he meant when he said 'D.V.' in accepting them was, 'If *I* happen to be in the Humour'. [II, 612] As his brother observed, John was a 'man one could really love two and three-quarter miles off'.[7]

In 1863 FitzGerald lost the one member of his family whom he loved without serious qualification, his sister Mrs Kerrich, who died at Geldestone. The day of her death he had the only extra-sensory experience recorded in his life. He believed that he had seen from outside the house a clear picture of Mrs Kerrich having tea with her children in the dining room. As he watched, his sister withdrew quietly from the room, to keep from disturbing the children, and at the moment he saw this, Mrs Kerrich died in Norfolk. That he believed in the 'vision' even momentarily indicates how profoundly her death upset him.

He had been assiduous in visiting her in her long illness, but he refused to attend the funeral: 'There will be many Mourners, and I should, I am sure, do more harm than good.' He blamed his brother-in-law for 'having shortened the Life of this admirable Woman' and called him a 'self-Complacent Booby', but he then added with his usual contrition, 'yet he is five hundred times a better Man than myself'. [II, 480] Thereafter, he refused to go to Geldestone, even to see his beloved nieces, adding it to the growing list of places he could not visit because of previous happiness there. He had always hated funerals, and after this he refused to attend even those of his immediate family.

At the end of 1863 came yet another death, to make him feel that his whole past was being cut from beneath him. On the evening of Christmas Day he was walking alone in the dark gardens of the Seckford Almshouses in Woodbridge when he met George Manby, who gave him the news of the death of Thackeray.

I have thought little else than of W.M.T. ever since ... as I sit alone by my Fire these long Nights. I had seen very little of him for these last ten years; *nothing* for the last five; he did not care to write; and people told me he was become a little spoiled: by London praise, and some consequent Egotism. But he was a very fine Fellow. His Books are wonderful.... [II, 509]

At any moment, it seemed to FitzGerald, 'he might be coming up my Stairs, and about to come (singing) into my Room, as in old Charlotte Street, etc., thirty years ago.' [II, 505] For all his sorrow, he refused to subscribe to the Thackeray monument in the Abbey, since he believed that no one should be commemorated there until a full century had proved the permanence of his reputation. [II, 537]

One by one the old friendships were vanishing. That with Tennyson had always been tricky, but it seemed to be disintegrating further. He so disliked the *Idylls of the King* that he said 'they might almost [have] been written by Matthew Arnold.' [II, 340] Although he continued to say how much he gloried in Tennyson's success and how he longed to visit the poet at home, he could somehow never find the time. He was tired of receiving answers from Mrs Tennyson to letters he had written to her husband: 'She is a graceful lady, but I think that she and other aesthetic and hysterical Ladies have hurt AT, who, *quoad* Artist, would have done better to remain single in Lincolnshire, or married a jolly Woman who would have laughed and cried without any reason why.' [II, 538]

When all his oldest friends were slipping out of his life, it hardly seemed worth keeping up newer acquaintances. In the eight years that the Cowells had been in India, he had continued his correspondence with them, and if something of the warmth of close friendship had gone, there was still their shared interest in scholarship to hold them together. But in 1864, when the Cowells came back to England, it was almost as if FitzGerald felt stifled by the renewal of an old intimacy. 'I am afraid you will find me a torpid and incurious Man compared to what you left me,' he wrote, and he began searching for reasons why they could not meet. He told them of his new boat and said they 'must come one day' to see her, but he did not specify when. After they had been in Ipswich for two months without seeing him, FitzGerald wrote that they were 'to have come over here one day, but somehow did not .... we shall meet before long, I doubt not.' When finally Cowell got to Woodbridge, FitzGerald told him the visit was a 'sad sort of Pleasure'. The letters still passed back and forth, but more infrequently and more coolly. His invitations to see the new boat were repeated without a specific date: 'I can't well make sure what day: sometimes I ask one man to go, sometimes another, and so all is cut up.' [II, 560] At last the Cowells had been only five miles away for a year and a half without FitzGerald's having laid eyes on Mrs Cowell.

Once he had been the most enthusiastic of friends, but after the deaths of Mrs Kerrich and Thackeray, a heavy lethargy had settled on him. Even in his correspondence much of the gaiety and spontaneity had disappeared, and for the first time the reader becomes aware of how often he repeated phrases from one letter to another, as if he scarcely had the energy to respond afresh to each new person.

His oddness had become far more than a matter of appearance, although that was eccentric enough. He had always dressed negligently, but now he was slovenly; his plaid shawl sometimes hung off his shoulders and trailed on the ground, with his old top hat wagging on the back of his head. He wore a carelessly tied black silk scarf around his neck, and no ornaments besides his gold watch chain. In the summer he was even seen to take off his shoes and walk barefoot. His whole demeanour was like a deliberate affront to public opinion, as if he were so weary of being distrusted that he was determined to be even more outrageous than the sober inhabitants of Woodbridge thought him. If he was spoken to in the course of one of his solitary walks by a neighbour who had not been introduced to him, he would say brusquely, 'I don't know you!'

For a long time his attendance at church had been little more than a polite observance of social custom, but now he ceased going almost completely. The rector of Woodbridge, the Revd Thomas Mellor, called on him and said, 'I am sorry, Mr. FitzGerald that I never see you at church.' FitzGerald replied curtly, 'Sir, you might have conceived that a man has not come to my years without thinking much on these things. I believe I may say that I have

231

reflected on them fully. You need not repeat this visit.'[8] On another occasion Robert Groome, rector of Monk Soham, near Woodbridge, whom FitzGerald had known since their days together in the Camus Society at Cambridge, preached at the parish church across the street from FitzGerald's rooms and spent the following morning with him. 'I did not venture inside the sacred Edifice,' FitzGerald told a friend, 'but I looked through a Glass Door in the Porch and saw R.G. and heard his Voice (not the Words) ascending and descending in a rather dramatic way.' [II, 470]

The stories of FitzGerald's curious behaviour were no doubt exaggerated in the first place by Woodbridge residents who thought he was nearly insane, and they probably lost little in subsequent transmission, but there is enough objective evidence to suggest that most of them rested on a firm basis of fact, even if they had been given additional trimmings. It was no accident that his nickname among the beachmen of Lowestoft and the disrespectful schoolboys around Woodbridge was 'Dotty'. Sir Sidney Colvin remembered that as a boy he knew well the tall figure of the sad-faced elderly man drifting abstractedly along the roads, a sight so familiar that he was almost disregarded by passers-by.

FitzGerald was in his mid-fifties, but he was already an old man, and the thought of illness and death, like those of his family and friends, was so omnipresent that he determined to get a house of his own to anticipate becoming incapacitated. His eyes, which had never been strong, were failing badly, he had a constant ringing in his ears, and he had to go to London to see a dentist. In 1862, after the death of Mr Smith at Farlingay, he had been offered a chance to buy that house, and he hesitated long over it; it was the 'very most delightful Place' he knew, with 'Gardens *and* Furniture, *and* orderly Servants, all ready to my disposal', but he dared not risk its solitary situation: 'To be alone in the Country – even but a short mile of a Town – is now become sad to me: dull as this Town is, yet people pass, Children scream, and a Man calls "Hot Rolls" which is all less sad than the waving and mourning of Trees, and the sight of a dead Garden before the Window.' [II, 433–4] The days were long past when his cottage at the gates of Boulge had seemed too near to other people.

Unwillingly, he began looking seriously for alternatives to Farlingay. He got as far as having plans made for alterations to the house of the former parson at the end of Seckford Place, and then discovered to his relief that it was too small. He looked at other houses, even made enquiries about servants for them, but decided that 'all the better houses are occupied by Dowagers like Myself.' [II, 426]

It was 1864 when he finally bought a place of his own. An estate at the northern end of Woodbridge, Melton Grange, was parcelled off when it changed hands, and he bought its former farmhouse, a 'rotten Affair' with six acres, for £730. He was not sure what to do with his purchase, but he said he had talked so long of buying that he had to get something, even if he resold it at once. At least, he wrote, 'two or three People have asked to hire, or buy, Bits' of the property, 'so I have risen in public Respect'. [II, 525–6] Within a few months the builders were working on the first of his additions to the old farmhouse, but it was another ten years before he moved in completely and at last called it home.

Grange Farm, as the house was called, had once been two tiny cottages, which still made a small house when thrown together, with three cramped bedrooms above a kitchen, scullery, and sitting-dining room. To this FitzGerald immediately added one large and airy room on each floor and a lavatory. Outside the ground-floor windows he built the handsome garden terrace that still stands. He admitted that he often changed his mind after the builders had begun work on one section and asked them to tear out what they had done, but he was incensed to be given a bill of £1,150 when the addition was completed, half again as much as he had paid for the original house and six acres. He contested the bill as a matter of principle, calling in surveyors, lawyers, and adjusters, and after two years succeeded in having it reduced by £120, which surely did little more than pay his professional fees, but his honour was satisfied because the builder 'will have lost £200 at least by Law expenses, and being out of his money two years – and – *Serve him right*'. [III, 92] It was a brief glimpse of the hardness beneath the surface that sometimes showed when he was angry.

He planted the garden with trees and the bright flowers he loved, had a duck pond put in, bought more land to preserve his view of the river, and furnished the house completely, although he was careful not to hang many portraits on the walls, because he intended that his unmarried Kerrich nieces should use the house for their summer holidays; one of them was epileptic, and he did not want to frighten her with his 'dark Italian Faces', so that she 'would dream of them'.

When the house was complete, he should have taken that as a mark of its transformation into his own property, but he could not summon up courage to move into it: 'I believe I never shall do unless in a Lodging, as I have lived these forty years. It is too late, I doubt, to reform in a House of one's own.' [II, 579] It was more than five years after he bought it that he spent a night in it. He protested that he had no time for the responsibility of running a house, but he actually had that without living there, for he installed a resident couple to care for his nieces and other guests. When all other excuses failed him for not making it his home, he put on another extension of two more rooms in 1871, making it impossible to do more than 'dawdle about my Garden, play with the Cat, and look at the Builders'. What had been a pair of small cottages had now become a handsome and commodious house set in a large garden, far from the bustle of Woodbridge, with only the muffled sounds of Pytches Road to make him feel part of the life of the other townspeople. With great ingenuity and the expenditure of a good deal of money, he had succeeded in recreating all the disadvantages and loneliness that had frightened him out of buying Farlingay. The truth was that he had originally bought the house as a place to die, and it had now become an emblem of his mortality. 'My Chateau', as he liked to call it mockingly, 'is reserved for my last Retirement from the Stage.' [III, 7]

CHAPTER XI

Posh

Among the scrapbooks in the Christchurch Mansion Museum in Ipswich that FitzGerald assembled from his reading is one proving his lifelong love of crime, murder trials, and low life. (Not that his idea of criminals was conventional, for among others he included a picture of his distant relative, Lord Edward Fitzgerald, under which he wrote, 'Noodle'.) In the same volume he pasted a picture of a fighter named Jack Randall on the page facing the likeness of Laurence Sterne. Beneath Sterne's picture, scrawled in FitzGerald's hand, is the laconic legend, 'Compare this Sentimental Beast with the Prize-fighter', with the implication that it would be to the disadvantage of the novelist.

There is no way of knowing when FitzGerald stuck the pictures in the volume, so we cannot be sure whether Randall's likeness is there because it was so reminiscent of 'Posh' Fletcher, or whether FitzGerald included it as a generic face representing what he found most attractive in masculine physiognomy, of which he later found the ultimate, living example in Fletcher. Whichever it may be, there is little doubt that the young Lowestoft fisherman was the embodiment of an ideal that he had entertained for years, certainly since Browne's death. Unfortunately, in time Fletcher proved to be only too human and disappointed FitzGerald, but for a few years he restored a whole central core of emotion to FitzGerald's life and brought back something of his youth; during most of that time the pain he caused was more than balanced by the happiness that FitzGerald felt.

FitzGerald met Fletcher and his father some time in 1864 or 1865, probably at Felixstowe, where the Fletchers had gone to recover a stolen boat. They were introduced by the captain of the

XII FitzGerald (?), by Thomas Churchyard, ca. 1865, oil.

Scandal, Tom Newson. A year or two later FitzGerald wrote that he was 'amused to see Newson's devotion to his younger Friend: he won't leave him a moment if possible: was the first to see him come in yesterday: and has just watched him out of sight.' [II, 603] But there is surely as much of his own feeling for Fletcher as of Newson's in the observation.

The younger Fletcher had just turned twenty-five in the summer of 1864. He was over six feet tall, with broad shoulders, deep chest, and strong arms developed by hauling herring and mackerel nets since he was a boy. Besides a magnificent body, he had a well-set head, with good features, reddish-blond hair and full beard; his blue eyes were a little too pale for the ruddiness of his complexion. It is hard to see in his pictures what it was that reminded FitzGerald so forcibly of William Browne, unless it is the lack of vivacity in both their faces, verging in Fletcher's on the wooden.

He was well liked by the other fishermen while he was still a young man, although he was set apart from them by an apparent sense of superiority in his looks and manner. There is no reason obvious today why Joseph Fletcher was called 'Posh'. The modern meaning of the word would have been apt for his fellows to apply to him: fine, with a deliberate touch of the 'swell'. Unfortunately, that connotation of the word, however appropriate otherwise, seems to have come from our own century.

Fletcher, as we have seen, had been very much aware of Fitz-Gerald in 1859, although he hesitated to approach him on those nights when the older man wandered the shore with a bottle of rum, looking for companionship under the upturned boats. There is no mention of Posh's name in FitzGerald's letters for a year or two after they met, but he must have seen him on his trips to Lowestoft, for by the spring of 1866 their acquaintance had progressed sufficiently for Posh to stay with FitzGerald in Woodbridge for two days. While he was there his host wrote a brief note to the elder Fletcher to tell him of his son's whereabouts, since writing was always a pencil-licking process for the poorly educated young fisherman; in the note FitzGerald spoke jokingly of 'your little boy Posh', indicating both how fond he already was of Posh and part of what had caused that fondness, for he never used 'boy' except in affectionate admiration of the spontaneity and playfulness of his friends, no matter what their age.

Posh already had a 'nice little Wife: and two clean Children; and a tidy Cottage', which stretched his income almost to the breaking point. Nor did his addiction to beer help him financially, for once he began drinking, he would sometimes spend the night at it. 'Not that he is a Drunkard', according to FitzGerald, '(his nice home shows *not*)'; he drank too much only because he was so popular that there were 'many asking him to drink'. And when he was away fishing, Posh could not 'run home to eat, but must stop the gap by a Drink – and of bad beer'. FitzGerald was perplexed to find that his warnings about drink were so ineffective with Fletcher, since he had a 'simple, tender, heart'. [II, 616]

The unself-consciousness of FitzGerald's feelings for Posh is shown by the openness with which he spoke of him constantly, and by his lack of jealousy of the other sailors who were dazzled by him. FitzGerald's captain, Tom Newson, '(who is old, cautious, and has seen enough of Men to distrust them) gives up his whole Love and Confidence to this young Fellow: worships him, one may say; uses me and my Ship in his Behalf; and, as I tell him, has found his Master at last. I am struck and touched with this.' [II, 605] Newson refused any security for money he lent to Posh because he had 'perfect reliance on his Honour, Industry, Skill, and Luck'. FitzGerald told Newson that he had at last 'become possessed of that troublesome Thing: an anxious Regard for some one'. [II, 603] Here, as he so often did, FitzGerald was projecting his own feelings on to others with no apparent awareness that he was doing so. He would surely have been puzzled if he had been told that he was behaving like an infatuated boy. Nearly every letter he wrote in the second half of 1866 mentioned Posh, as if for the sheer pleasure of writing his name, and it often turned up as the object of praise two or three times in one letter.

The least pleasant aspect of his delight in Posh was that it was so often at the expense of Fletcher's maturity; he would tell every detail of what he had done, of his own pride in his good looks, his nobility of heart, his good behaviour, even the moments when he was surprised that Posh had behaved as if he were a responsible adult. It was all too reminiscent of the fondness of a doting parent for his child, boring to others and ultimately to the child himself, who must get some distance away in order to grow up. It is probably significant that years later Posh half-confused FitzGerald's

XIII Joseph ('Posh') Fletcher, ca. 1868.

advice and that of his own parents: 'It was "yew must ax yar faa'er this, an' yew must tell yar mother that, and yew mustn't dew this here, nor yit that theer."'[1] Ungrateful though he undoubtedly was, surely he was correct in feeling that he was scarcely allowed to be his own man, that FitzGerald was constantly trying to transform the simple reality of the sailor to fit an Adamic, even childlike, ideal already formed in his own mind. When they went to Yarmouth to buy a boat together, FitzGerald told a friend that they 'paraded the town', dined in a tavern together, and looked into the church, 'where, when Posh pulled off his Cap and stood erect but not irreverent, I thought he looked as good an Image of the Mould that Man was originally cast in, as you may chance to see in the Temple of *The Maker* in these Days.' [III, 27]

For FitzGerald it was a transparent truth that no man could have an exterior like Fletcher's without an inner nobility to match. 'A young Fellow comes here,' he told Cowell,

> who looks exactly like one of the Phidian Marbles dressed in blue Trowsers and Guernsey Jacket: with a like grandeur of character to line this Outside; only his Hands are those of Michael Angelo's Statues, and he fills up my 'Foksal' like one of the Prophets from the Sistine Chapel. Oh, how much more Gentlemanly than the Gentlemen on the Pier! And how very much more Ladylike than the Ladies there! Simple, good, true, bashful. Well! [II, 604]

When he was not fishing, Posh often came aboard the *Scandal*, either as FitzGerald's guest or as a member of the crew. With him aboard FitzGerald kept re-reading the classics: 'I scarce know why it is that I always get back to Greek (and Virgil) when in my Ship: but so it is. Sophocles has been a sort of Craze to me this Summer.' [II, 608]

All the vitality and youthfulness that had seemed drained from the world came flooding back in the company of 'Sea and Sailors. Why do they revive one's Love of Greek? The Sea talks something of that Language, I think.' [II, 604] Probably the presence of Posh had made FitzGerald more than usually sensitive to the deep-rooted Victorian traditions of strong affection between men in classical times.

Behind his lyrical praise lay an unacknowledged awareness that

Posh was as fallible as his fellows. Once FitzGerald wrote to Spalding, 'At eight or half past I go to have a Pipe at Posh's, if he isn't half drunk with his Friends.' [II, 613] Besides his concern about Posh's love of beer, he was so convinced that Posh was unreliable financially that he not only gave him stern sermons on the subject, but also warned Posh's friends that they should not let him have money without some form of security besides an IOU. When Posh heard of this, he was furious. But FitzGerald was not betraying him: he simply had such an ideal of Posh in his mind that he could not bear for him to be less than the completely unreal person he had conjured up. His letters to Posh are full of well-meant but unintentionally condescending advice. The very first letter he wrote to him that has survived is concerned with prudence in buying nets and the necessity of writing as well as one can. It is no wonder that Posh, who was used to admiration from his fellows, was somewhat resentful of the barrage of counselling and often reacted by doing exactly what he had been warned against.

Posh probably returned some of FitzGerald's affection, and he was sufficiently vain to welcome his admiration. Perhaps more to the point, he knew that FitzGerald was wealthy, rich beyond anything he could imagine for himself, and if he chose to share some of that wealth, Posh could find plenty of uses for it. Certainly, Posh could not have been in doubt about his devotion, either from his actions or, more explicitly, from his words: 'I thought I had done with new Likings, and led a more easy Life perhaps on that account; now I shall often think of you with uneasiness, for the very reason that I have so much Liking and Interest for you.' [III, 5] As he wrote at the end of 1866: 'I tell him he is *the last* I shall ever take to my regard: and that if he turns bad – I shall be eased of all Trouble about him.' [II, 616] But he knew that he could never give up Posh without anguish; he had done so once with Browne, but he could not do so again: 'I seem to have jumped back to a regard of near forty years ago, and while I am with him feel young again, and when he goes shall feel old again.' [III, 41]

Posh had been making a meagre living with a small fishing boat, but he thought he could earn a great deal more with a proper craft. In the autumn of 1866, a few months after he first became intimate with FitzGerald, he borrowed £50 of him and a like amount from Tom Newson, then bought a decrepit herring lugger. When

FitzGerald realized that he could better afford the loan than Newson could, he took over the other half of the debt. But the lugger was in such bad shape that he was in constant terror that it would go down with its owner, and he contracted to have a new one built for Posh at a cost of £360.

In 1866 FitzGerald moored and lived in the *Scandal* at Lowestoft whenever he was not sailing. As long as he was on the craft, he had a good excuse to be near Posh, and he kept her afloat until November despite the paralysing cold that made it even harder for him to sleep aboard, since he had no fire. When at last she was laid up for the winter, he returned to Woodbridge for a week or two, and then came back to Lowestoft lodgings, on the pretext of having to be there while the new lugger was built. He stayed intermittently for the rest of the winter. On the nearly deserted streets of the little fishing town, his public demonstrations of affection for Posh could be deeply embarrassing; once they were walking on the pier on a windy day when a passer-by stopped Posh, as an obvious sailing man, and asked him several questions about the wind and tide. FitzGerald suddenly grabbed Posh by his sleeve and pulled him away, saying to the stranger, 'This is *my* guest.' As Posh said, 'He made me look a complete cake.'[2]

There was good reason for Posh's discomfort, for the other fishermen had often seen FitzGerald wandering the Lowestoft beach looking for companionship, and they could hardly have helped imputing the worst motives to the new friendship when they knew that FitzGerald was setting Posh up with a new lugger. If Posh went off with other fishermen for beer, as he had done so often in the past, FitzGerald would turn up unexpectedly, either to try to get Posh to stop drinking or, if that failed, to join him and the seamen for the evening. Posh was too inarticulate to make the reasons for his displeasure clear, but it would show through as sullenness, and then the whole episode would inevitably be followed by letters of explanation and apology from a contrite but uncomprehending FitzGerald.

If he had not already been made to feel a social pariah because of the break-up of his marriage, he might have been more careful about appearances in his dealings with Posh. He did not make it easy for his friends to understand his relations with an uneducated young fisherman, since he could hardly explain that part of what he liked about Posh was the difference in their ages and social positions. In Woodbridge, where the townspeople were already convinced that he was disreputable, he was tactless in inviting Posh as a guest for two or three days at a time. Once, when Posh was staying at the Berrys' with FitzGerald, Alfred Smith, son of the household at Farlingay, came in and found Posh stretched full-length on the sofa after a large meal. When Smith said that he thought he was taking a liberty, FitzGerald's only reply was, 'Poor fellow! look how tired he is!' Another time he and Posh were walking on the Thoroughfare in Woodbridge and, as they talked, he noticed a woman approaching them and removing her right glove. 'It's my wife!' said FitzGerald. He and Lucy 'met, exchanged looks, held out their hands, but FitzGerald's courage failed at the last moment, and withdrawing his hand he said: "Come along, Posh," and stalked away.'[3]

FitzGerald was quite aware of how much talk about him there was, and though he sometimes seemed deliberately to exacerbate it, as he did when meeting Lucy, at others he understandably felt hounded. One summer when the Cowells were staying in Lowestoft, he was so bothered by the gossip there that he would come to call on them only after dark, and he asked that they should not light the lamps; he sat on the floor with his back to the windows, so that he could not be seen from the street. He was no doubt exaggerating the local curiosity about his movements, but the incident shows how much he thought about it.[4]

Writing letters never came easily to Fletcher, but he soon found that it relieved the tension if he sent a message to FitzGerald at least once a week when they were apart. The answers that came back so promptly were written to 'Dear Posh' or, when FitzGerald was unable to restrain his affections, 'My dear Poshy', or even 'my little small Captain'. [III, 15] They were usually signed with Fitz-Gerald's initials, occasionally by 'the Governor', and mysteriously on one occasion by 'Robertina Jacobs'. When FitzGerald had to be away, he wrote regularly to Posh. Early in 1867 he went to London for two days, but he left his attention in Lowestoft: 'So as I was sitting at Night, in a great Room where a Crowd of People were eating Supper, and Singing going on, I thought to myself – Well, Posh might as well be here; and then I should see what a Face he would make at all this.' [III, 15]

The new lugger left on her first fishing trip in August 1867. She was the major asset in the partnership that FitzGerald now set up with Posh; although he had contributed by far the greater part of the investment and Posh brought only some used nets and gear, they were equal partners as what FitzGerald liked to refer to as fishmongers or herring merchants. He could not resist calling the ship the *Meum and Tuum*, but this was quickly changed by the fortunately uncomprehending fishermen to the *Mum and Tum*. She was forty-five feet long, took a crew of ten with Posh as captain, and was large enough to stay away for two or three weeks at a time while fishing. After one long trip Posh found a note waiting on his return: 'I have thought of you while I have been walking out these fine moonlight nights.... You see I have nothing to say to you; only I thought you might [like] to hear from me whenever you should come back.' [III, 95]

From the beginning FitzGerald had been trying to suppress a nagging worry about Posh's honesty by laughing at the possibility of anything else in his nature: 'If he *should* turn out knave, I shall have done with all Faith in my own Judgment: and if he should go to the Bottom of the Sea in the Lugger – I sha'n't cry for the Lugger.' [III, 36] Just before the new ship was launched, he wrote to Frederick Spalding, who apparently thought he trusted Posh too much: 'No cloven Hoof as yet!' [III, 37] But there were constantly unexplained expenditures that worried him, if only because they demonstrated how unbusinesslike Posh was. When he had to lecture him about the necessity of keeping the accounts accurately, he succeeded only in turning Fletcher silent and resentful.

The first fishing season in the *Meum and Tuum* was so short that a considerable loss was to be expected, and FitzGerald made it up without surprise, although he could not help complaining that Posh was unco-operative: 'You have to puzzle yourself to tell me the little I have to ask, and when you DO tell me, it seems that it is not in a way to make me understand.... I wondered how your grub for eleven men could amount to £160 for four months.' [III, 84] He reported that after the annual reckoning he had told Posh with relief: 'there was *less* to pay than I had expected: and, if he were what I thought, I would rather lose money with him than win it with many others. The dear old Boy got happy: and of course made me angry by coming home rather unsteady after settling the Bills. So I look glum Today.' [III, 75]

Posh was probably only careless, not seriously dishonest, for he had never been taught that his small ways of making money on the side were reprehensible. His stubborn refusal to do as he was asked about the accounts made FitzGerald miserable, for it was incomprehensible that he should continue so irresponsibly, but it was unthinkable that his intentions were fraudulent. After a quarrel FitzGerald, in inevitable repentance that he should have made an innocent, honest young fisherman think he was suspected of deception, would try to re-establish the old footing by being more trusting about the accounts, more liberal with his support of the partnership, even more open-handed in his gifts. He supported Posh and his family while the lugger was being built, bought a house for them, paid the medical bills when the children were ill, equipped the entire crew of the *Meum and Tuum* with life-jackets they hated because he was worried that Posh might drown, and repeatedly backed down without argument when Posh rejected his suggestions for operating the lugger more profitably.

FitzGerald was so spontaneously liberal with his wealth that it would never have occurred to him that Posh might suspect that his free-handedness was an attempt to bind the younger man to him with money. For his own part, Posh was resolved not to be bought, but he could not afford to lose the opportunity to cash in on Fitz-Gerald's attraction to him. It was as if he felt that he was somehow uncontaminated so long as he maintained his ingratitude. Both men were made miserable, but it would be hard to assign blame, for neither was wholly culpable, neither wholly innocent. As Professor Terhune wrote, 'FitzGerald was so diligent in finding excuses for the weaknesses of his hero that he completely spoiled him. The sailor, independent by nature, became headstrong under indulgence.'[5]

In 1868, the second year the lugger was afloat, there was another loss at the end of the season, and again FitzGerald had to pay. The following year there was finally a profit, although only some £35, and Posh wanted to put that back into the purchase of equipment. 'This is the first money we have touched on all our Outlay, after three years loss,' FitzGerald wrote. 'And, as I did not embark in the business for Profit, I did not expect more. But, as I did not know all the anxiety it would cause me about all these people's lives, I believe I shall now try to back out of it, the more so as my Captain certainly wishes (with all regard to me) to be sole Master'. [III, 178–9]

When Posh accused him of meddling in the ship of which he was half-owner, FitzGerald could not resist pointing out the affection he had put into the partnership: 'the anxiety I have [experienced] these two years about your eleven lives is but ill compensated by all these squalls between us two; which I declare I excuse myself of raising.' With touching dignity he defended himself against the charge of spiritual and financial meanness:

> In my whole sixty years, I can with a clear conscience say that I have dealt with *one man* fairly, kindly, and not ungenerously, for three good years. I may have made mistakes; but I can say I have done my best as conscientiously as he can say he has done his. And I believe he has done his best, though he has also made mistakes; and I remain his sincerely. . . . [III, 162]

As captain of the *Meum and Tuum* Posh was paid a regular salary by the partnership before any profits were declared; in effect, FitzGerald had been completely supporting him, but Posh's head was so swollen by the small profit in 1869 that he forgot the entire business would long since have gone under if it had not been bailed out by his partner. He now felt he could afford to keep grey-hounds and drive a smart mare and gig about Lowestoft. Early in 1870 he decided to expand the herring business and, without consultation, bought another lugger, the *Henrietta*, at auction. When he heard about it, FitzGerald put up the money for her purchase with little complaint, but it was becoming obvious that he could no longer continue the partnership. He was convinced that drink was at the bottom of Posh's unbusinesslike habits, and he succeeded several times in getting him to promise to give it up, but the pledges were no sooner made than broken.

'He and I will, I doubt, part Company,' FitzGerald wrote in January 1870; 'well as he likes me, which is perhaps as well as a sailor cares for any one but Wife and Children: he likes to be, what he is born to be, his own sole Master, of himself, and of other men.' [III, 185] The break was made easier by Posh's overweening determination to be sole master; so far he had done well out of the ship, and he could see no reason he would not continue to do so, particularly when he did not have to share the profits. In June 1870 the partnership was cancelled, FitzGerald took over the ownership of the two luggers and let them to Posh at a low rent.

The end of the partnership was not a clean break of the emotional relationship. Posh was somewhat frightened of the responsibility he had been at such pains to assume, and FitzGerald was reluctant to let him sink or swim. As owner of the luggers, he continued to give advice, which was ignored. After one evening together Posh wrote to say he was sorry they had not 'parted Friends', since he had been indeed *'a little the worse* for Drink', which FitzGerald said meant that he had passed out at a public house, slept through the hour for sailing, and found that all the other luggers had gone out ahead of him while he slept. For the first time FitzGerald considered refusing even to let the ships to him and sending back 'his own written Promise of Sobriety, signed only a month before'. But he was afraid that such drastic measures would 'drive him, by Despair, into the very fault' he was trying to cure. There was undoubtedly a good bit of shrewd observation in Posh's mother's remark: 'I tell him he seem to do it when the Governor is here.' [III, 237–8]

The truth was that FitzGerald's affection for Posh was so deep that it took years to die. Before that happened, he determined to have Posh painted by Laurence, so that he might have a portrait to go with the photographs that he had already had made. 'I declare, you and I have seen A Man! Have we not? Made in the mold of what Humanity should be, Body and Soul, a poor Fisherman.' [III, 236] Laurence's reply has not survived.*

By the end of 1870 FitzGerald had decided to sell the *Scandal*, in which he had so often happily followed the *Meum and Tuum* as it set out on a fishing trip; he said merely that he did not intend to sail the following year, but he immediately set about finding other places for his crew, whom he would no longer need. One main reason for his decision, he claimed, was 'these Eyes of mine which

---

*Nor, apparently, has the portrait. Descriptions of FitzGerald's pictures in sales catalogues after his death are too brief to identify the portrait or give any clue as to its disposition. In 1907 Posh himself said that it had been sold to William Hynes, who kept a public house in Bury St Edmunds. Enquiries at the time by James Blyth did not lead to the picture, and Blyth supposed that Hynes was dead and the portrait lost. One would like to think that it may surface again some day, but my own efforts to locate it have been unsuccessful.

will not let me read; and that was nearly all I had to do on board'. [III, 288] The vessel was sold for £200 in the spring of 1871.

As an old man Posh liked to boast about how devoted Fitz-Gerald had been to him, so that one has to be cautious about accepting his account of the final break, which was that at the end of 1873 FitzGerald went to the elder Fletcher's house and cried like a child when he could not find Posh. He wanted to resume the part-nership and left a paper outlining conditions for any further dealings, including a provision that 'Joseph Fletcher the younger shall be a teetotaller.' 'Lor!' said Posh, 'how my father did swear at him when I told him o' that!'[6] Whatever the truth of the story, on the last day of 1873 FitzGerald wrote a coldly furious letter of which the salutation was simply, 'Joseph Fletcher'. He made it clear that he could no longer stand the accusations of unfairness from Posh. 'That you should get such another Boat, is, I am quite sure, the best plan for you and for me also,' he wrote two or three weeks later [III, 472], and on 17 February 1874 both the *Meum and Tuum* and the *Henrietta* were sold at auction. Posh hoped to buy the *Meum and Tuum*, but his bid was too low.

The mare and gig had already been sold, and Fletcher was in dif-ficulties until he got a job as captain of another lugger. From there on his luck went downhill. Many years later he claimed that he had paid off every penny he owed FitzGerald, but that is improbable, particularly as FitzGerald left instructions that in the event of his death the principal of his mortgage from Posh was not to be called in. FitzGerald always defended Posh's morality, saying simply that his background had not allowed him to have the same standards as his own, and that Posh had been right when he said that the behav-iour his patron asked of him was possible only for those born with silver spoons in their mouths.

FitzGerald was deeply hurt by the whole affair, and though he continued to love Posh, he could not easily forgive him. In 1875, when one of Posh's children died, a friend of FitzGerald said that he ought to 'speak to Fletcher, and hold out a hand to him, and bid him take this opportunity to regain his Self-respect. But I cannot suppose that I could make any lasting impression upon him. She does not know *all*.' [III, 557] Two years later he had recovered himself sufficiently to call on Posh in Lowestoft: 'I saw him a few days ago in his house, with Wife and Children; looking, as always,

XIV 'Posh' Fletcher.
   a. ca. 1902.
   b. ca. 1908.

too big for his house: but always grand, polite, and unlike anybody else.' [III, 714] Aboard his lugger his glory was 'somewhat marred; but he looks every inch a King.... This is altogether the Greatest Man I have known.' [IV, 3]

FitzGerald hung the portrait of Posh with his two others painted by Laurence, those of Thackeray and Tennyson: 'the three greatest men I have known', he said, and thought that 'both Tennyson and Thackeray were inferior to him in respect of Thinking of Themselves'. [III, 714]

Posh's maudlin version of their later relations was that when they met on the streets of Lowestoft, FitzGerald would take him by the sleeve of his jersey, pinch his arm, and say, 'Oh dear, oh dear, Posh! To think it should ha' come to this!'[7] If FitzGerald ever wrote again to Posh after the sale of the luggers, his letters have disappeared, but he often mentioned him, always with charity and compassion; one can only admire his dignity and generosity, since he had long realized the ways in which he had been used by Posh. Nor did he shirk recognition of how, in turn, he had been bad for the younger man, for he knew that he had wounded him with an excess of affection. When Posh fell on bad times, he sent money to Mrs Fletcher but never through her husband. He left nothing to Posh in his will, although literally dozens of other friends and acquaintances were remembered. After his death FitzGerald's nieces, the Kerrich daughters, who inherited the bulk of his estate, regularly gave money to Posh.

W. A. Dutt said that in 1906 he occasionally met Posh on the beach at Lowestoft, still looking in surprisingly good health: 'I don't like the man because, notwithstanding all FitzGerald's kindness to him – and he gave him a grand chance to prove himself, at least, something like what FitzGerald imagined him – he is ungrateful, and blames FitzGerald for "spoiling him".'[8] However uncharitable Posh's attitude, he was probably right in thinking that FitzGerald had ruined his life: not as he thought, by withdrawing financial support, but in ever allowing himself to become so deeply involved in a relationship that had neither physical nor emotional future, with a man whose feelings and intellect were inadequate to the situation.

Posh's later history was a sad one. He was never able to stop drinking, and so could not keep the command of the vessels of which he was hired as captain. By the end of the century, when he was over sixty, he was making a shaky living with a shrimping boat at Lowestoft. He was still a solitary, known by the younger beachmen but not close to them. He had apparently been separated from his family, and he was living in a miserable shack on the beach that also housed his boat and tackle. To supplement his income he became something of a beggar; when FitzGerald's friends and relatives gave him money, he wrote laborious letters of thanks, clearly hinting that further contributions would be welcome. At his lowest ebb, he applied to the Kerrich family for more money and was 'returned for answer that, as he had already cost the family £3500, it seemed as though more could hardly be expected'. To FitzGerald's great-niece he seemed, 'as to all FitzGerald's relations, an ordinary, rather tall and clumsy fisherman, the usual type to be seen any day on our East Coast beach. Like many other East Anglians, he had no scruples as to the legality of "besting" a gentleman, though in the long run it turned out that his supposed victim was not as dull as he thought.'[9]

One of the many visitors to Lowestoft who met Posh said he had

XV 'Posh' Fletcher, ca. 1915.

a 'more or less contemptuous appreciation of FitzGerald's great affection for him.' He was doggedly proud of saying that it was his own independence that had brought an end to the partnership, not the wish of his patron. Either through some feeling of his own for FitzGerald or through a shrewd sense that they might in time become valuable, he had kept hundreds of FitzGerald's letters, stored in a bag in his beach hut. Most of them, he said, had been lost, but he sold a good many to the visitors who wanted to talk to him about his former partner, and he posed for their cameras for a small fee. He had become much heavier in old age, and he had the faded, rheumy eyes characteristic of the heavy drinker, but he retained more than a remnant of his youthful good looks. 'One of his most curious traits is that he cannot be made to understand how great a man his old master was. He has been interviewed enough, but still he looks on "Fitz" as a rather eccentric, kind hearted, and perhaps rather exacting man.'[10] In 1907 readers of the *Daily Graphic* subscribed to a fund for his support, and enough was collected to give him seven shillings and six pence a week; he insisted on having ten shillings instead, which the secretary of the fund thought was typical of him. But then, as his contemporaries believed, he was in bad shape from having 'lived like a gentleman' too long.

At the end of his life Posh was admitted to the workhouse in Oulton, a short distance from Lowestoft. For a year or two he continued to spend the summers on the beach, but at last he had to remain permanently within the workhouse, and there he died on 7 September 1915, aged seventy-six.*

---

*Among the letters to Aldis Wright now preserved in the Library of Trinity College, Cambridge, is a very curious one of 20 May 1912, which suggests that FitzGerald was not Posh's last literary friend. Richard C. Jackson, who wrote it, describes himself as 'Walter Pater's "Marius"'. He tells of walking with Pater, presumably in Lowestoft, and meeting Posh, who was begging from passers-by. When he saw him, Pater said to Jackson, 'Stop while I speak to this man.' He walked over to Posh, conversed with him for a time, and gave him a coin as he left. Without advancing any other evidence for thinking so, Jackson makes it clear that Pater knew Posh well, although he cannot understand how they could have met unless Pater had sailed with FitzGerald. The implication of the letter, never stated directly, is that the two men had perhaps met under less reputable circumstances. Since he wrote the letter eighteen years after Pater's death, Jackson may have been confused about details; in any case, the whole matter deserves no more mention than a footnote.

CHAPTER XII

Letters and Readers

The stay of the Cowells in India during most of the period betwen 1856 and 1864 deprived FitzGerald of the inspiration, even of the push, that he needed for extended writing, and their return to England was nearly coincident with the beginning of his long involvement with Posh Fletcher, which absorbed so much of his emotional energy during the 1860s and early 1870s. His great work during that period, the *Rubáiyát*, had of course been started before the Cowells left the country. With one major exception, the most important part of his career as translator was over, and after that the best of his literary talents went into his correspondence.

He would hardly have been FitzGerald if he had completely given up translation, however, and he continued to fiddle with works that had been started long before. In 1856 and 1857, during the worst of his unhappiness over his marriage, he had begun work on a Persian manuscript, the *Mantik-ut-tair*, an allegory of man's search for truth. He intended translating it as a kind of warm-up for the *Rubáiyát*. *The Bird Parliament*, to use FitzGerald's title for it, was a bulky poem of some 10,000 lines. He reduced it summarily to about 1,500, and within a short time he had put it into something resembling final shape. He was, however, dissatisfied with it as being neither Oriental in feeling nor a transformation into something sufficiently personal, and he put it away without committing it to print. For the next decade he worked at it sporadically without managing to alter it appreciably. By the end of 1867 he had reworked it once more, but 'eight years had made little or no alteration in my idea of the matter', although he had 'really condensed the whole into a much compacter Image than the original'. But he remembered 'thinking it from the first rather disagreeable

253

than not', and this too he kept out of print. [III, 74] Several years after his death it was published by his literary executor, Aldis Wright, as part of the complete works, but it has never added much to his reputation.

He returned in 1864 to earlier attempts he had made to translate Calderón's plays *El Mágico Prodigioso* and *La Vida es Sueño*, which he had been working on at the time he published *Six Dramas of Calderon*. Under the titles of *The Mighty Magician* and *Such Stuff as Dreams are Made of*, they were privately printed in the spring of 1865, but once more he felt uneasy about them, and they too remained unpublished until they came out with his collected works after his death.

The finest of his translations after the *Rubáiyát* was the *Agamemnon*, which he had been working on in May 1857 while he was alone in London, after his wife had gone to Norfolk in search of a house. From the beginning he had recognized that the choruses required 'a better Poet than I am to set forth in English', but he intended the work 'not for Scholars, but for those who are ignorant of Greek'. [II, 272] He had undertaken the project after a long conversation in 1856 with Fanny Kemble about the Greek drama. It was originally conceived as an indirect tribute to her, but FitzGerald, as he so often was with other works, was unhappy with the result when it was finished, and he put it away. In 1870 he wrote that he had 'laid it by – took it up once or twice; and last year put it into Type for the purpose of finishing it'. He felt reasonably confident of the dialogue, 'but the Choruses are doubly false to Aeschylus as being utterly without his dark Innuendo style, and poor in any style.... Anyway, it is the very last of all my great Works; good or bad; I now could not finish any other if I had one to finish, much less *begin* one.' [III, 217] No doubt he really felt discouraged about ever writing again, but at the time of the above, he had just determined to break up his partnership with Posh Fletcher, and he was so unhappy that he was not to be trusted in his judgement on other matters.

Agamemnon was privately printed in 1869. In his preface FitzGerald freely admitted that it called for the grand, overreaching language of a Marlowe or a Pope, not his own 'acknowledged transgressions'. 'For to re-create the Tragedy, body and soul, into English, and make the Poet free of the language which reigns over that half of the world never dreamt of in his philosophy, must be reserved – especially the Lyric part – for some Poet, worthy of that name, and of congenial Genius with the Greek. Would that every one such would devote himself to one such work!' It was a variation of his often expressed relief that great poets like Tennyson should make at least one translation of the classics for their own day.

Actually, a modern reader content with a reminder of the noble feeling of the original without worrying about fidelity to the text of Aeschylus will not be disappointed in FitzGerald's reworking of the drama. Something of the dignity of the original, perhaps something of FitzGerald's own dignity of feeling about his life at this time, informs the whole with eloquent gravity untouched by the bombastic stateliness that so often disfigures translations of the tragedians.

Originally FitzGerald had 100 copies of the *Agamemnon* printed, intending to give them to friends if any wanted them. One copy naturally went to Fanny Kemble, and she talked so enthusiastically about it to her friends in the United States that by 1875 Quaritch began receiving orders from America. When he heard of this, FitzGerald sent him half a dozen of his own copies with instructions to give them free to anyone asking for them.

In the meantime, however, the *Rubáiyát* had been reviewed in the United States, then the first of the hundreds of pirated editions in that country was published, and even FitzGerald had to admit that there was a 'little Craze' for the poem among his American readers. 'I believe it is the strong-minded American Ladies who have chiefly taken it up: but they will soon have something wickeder to digest, I dare say.' [III, 389] Within a month of receiving FitzGerald's copies Quaritch had begun advertising the *Agamemnon* for sale with an eye on the American market and promising a new edition: 'The universal interest which has been excited by the marvellous poem called "The Rubaiyat of Omar Khayyam" has created a strong desire on the part of the public to know more of Mr. Fitzgerald and his works.' The new work would 'help readers to a larger . . . acquaintance with the Unknown Poet'. At first FitzGerald was angry and wrote to Quaritch to complain about the revelation of his name, 'but (with his German indelicacy) perhaps he thought he was pleasing *me* by such an Advertisement, and such a *Puff* as makes me ashamed to look at it again'. He believed that it was solely Fanny Kemble who had made his name familiar in America: 'They are a very odd People.' [III, 636–7]

In 1876 Quaritch published the tragedy, identifying the author only as 'the Translator of OMAR KHAYYAM', as FitzGerald had specified, but in his catalogue he printed a tribute from an American admirer, who said that 'Mr. FitzGerald has many admirers in this country' [III, 723–4], thus managing to offend FitzGerald without overtly going against his wishes. 'I am afraid you will only provoke the Jealous Gods,' FitzGerald wrote to him, 'by printing me as if I were a Browning. And the Danger more because of so many of The Gods knowing more of Greek than of Persian.' [III, 652] He was beginning to know both the pleasures and the annoyances of being a popular author, although he did not live long enough to suffer the excesses of either.

Once it became probable that his relations with Posh Fletcher would never be restored to their former intimacy, FitzGerald began repairing his other friendships. Not that he had deliberately neglected his older friends but his emotions had been so occupied with Posh that there had been little left over. The Cowells had visited him briefly at Woodbridge, and they had finally received a definite invitation to sail with him, but he had not gone to Cambridge to see them after Cowell became Professor of Sanskrit there in 1867. All during that time they had corresponded with him, but most of the warmth was gone. In 1871 he tried to restore some of it. 'You know why I don't write to you oftener: that I may not give you more to do than you already have in answering Letters.' [III, 298] When he did go through Cambridge briefly, he failed to call on the Cowells, but he assured them, 'you must believe that I longed so to do. But I did not think it right so to do, when I have so long left so many Friends uncalled upon. It is too late to begin again.' [III, 429]

It had been a long time since he had seen Carlyle, and even their correspondence had dwindled to an annual exchange of letters. They had so lost touch that in 1866 FitzGerald wrote to Chelsea, routinely sending his compliments to Mrs Carlyle, only to have a reply saying that she had died the previous April. It was a fact that he might have known had he read any national newspaper regularly, but a combination of difficulty with his eyes and a real lack of curiosity about the outer world had reduced his periodicals to the

Athenaeum and an occasional local paper. FitzGerald thought age had done nothing to calm Carlyle's extravagance, and that he had become almost insane in his discontent: 'Still his raving is that of Genius: and of a sincere Man too – *that* indeed is his Madness – and I am touched, I say, by his passionate Cries. Also I admire the grand patrician, Coriolanus-like Scorn and Hate of the Rabble that he exhibits; though I think he is too lenient and favorable to the Aristocracy.' [III, 69] But FitzGerald was careful not to let much of his disapproval of Carlyle leak through into his letters; partly, one would guess, because his interest in what the old Scotsman wrote was sufficiently detached for him to feel no necessity to mention his disagreement. Carlyle loved hearing from FitzGerald, even though he could no longer reply easily in his own hand: 'I could willingly accept twelve of that kind in the year,' he said after one annual message, 'twelve, I say, or even fifty-two, if they could be content with an answer of *silent* thanks and friendly thoughts and remembrances. But, within the last three or four years my right hand has become captious, taken to shaking as you see, and all writing is a thing I require *compulsion* and close necessity to drive me into. Why not call when you come to Town?' [III, 116]

But with Carlyle, as with Cowell or Tennyson, it seemed less disturbing to exchange letters than to see him in person. Increasingly FitzGerald thought the *Idylls of the King* no improvement on the *Morte d'Arthur* that Tennyson had read to him in those long-gone days as they boated on Lake Windermere after staying with the Speddings at Mirehouse. He believed that Tennyson would have been better off if he had 'left King Arthur alone from that time forth, instead of turning him into Prince Albert, and otherwise quite failing in the Legendary World, which is best shadowed in the old Prose Romance.' [III, 613] The newer versions seemed to him 'to fail utterly in the one thing wanted – Invention, to make a new and better thing of old Legends, which, without it, are best left alone'. [III, 487] Like many other friends of Tennyson, he laid the blame for the change in his poetry on 'the sympathy of his most Ladylike, gentle, Wife. An old Housekeeper like Molière's would have been far better for him, *I* think.' [III, 487] Probably for the very reason that he felt criticism was not welcome in the Tennyson household, FitzGerald felt perversely driven to mention what he liked least about the recent poetry that his friend had published.

Mrs Tennyson, whose ethereal gentleness of manner concealed a will far stronger than her husband's, sensed FitzGerald's dislike of her and returned it with interest; her method of expressing it was usually to take him up sharply on any criticism of Tennyson's works. After FitzGerald's death she read a magazine article about him and allowed herself one of the few open expressions of her uncharitable feelings ever recorded: 'Pleasant enough but somehow I have not much taste for such reading as you know. Fitz-Gerald is Fitz-Gerald to me after all.'[1] Since Tennyson himself hardly ever answered a letter but left such tasks to his wife and later to his elder son, FitzGerald was finally so disheartened at writing to the poet that most of his letters became empty formalities.

Indeed, a survey of the letters that FitzGerald wrote in the last two decades of his life would indicate that his frankest, most intimate exchanges of correspondence were not with his closest friends. Frederick Tennyson had never been a boon companion, and it is improbable that they saw each other more than a dozen times in the course of their fifty-year correspondence. When he came to Woodbridge in the summer of 1872 for a stay of three or four days, it was the first time they had been together for a decade. They enjoyed talking over old times but knew that they might never meet again, which in no way inhibited the freedom with which they wrote to each other about music, poetry, art, and, of course, Alfred Tennyson. On one subject only FitzGerald was supposed to be muzzled, that of gardens, for Frederick Tennyson told him early in their correspondence that he did not want to hear of anemones, irises, or large red poppies, which characteristically evoked lyrical descriptions of FitzGerald's flowers. With Frederick Tennyson, as with W. F. Pollock, FitzGerald occasionally made pleasantly obscene jokes, although he seldom wrote of such things to other correspondents. In complaining of his writing paper, he once told Tennyson: 'I have determined that this half-quire of paper shall not see my life out at all events. For of all the beastly stuff I ever knew it is the worst. It shall forthwith go to the Privy: and I only hope it may not deceive my fingers there as it does here.' [I, 698] FitzGerald occasionally complained that he wrote two letters to one that he received from Frederick Tennyson, but he took such pleasure in writing to him that he was not worried by that fact, if fact it was.

Since Frederick Tennyson spent most of his adult life living in Italy or Jersey, the natural assumption might be that their meetings were so few because they were seldom in the same country, but it is more probable that they simply found letters the best form of companionship and made little effort to be together. Certainly, physical distance did not account for the scarcity of occasions on which FitzGerald saw Frederick Pollock, with whom he carried on a correspondence comparable to that with Frederick Tennyson in its spontaneity. FitzGerald met Pollock, who was about six years his junior, after he left Cambridge, and from the 1830s until a fortnight before FitzGerald's death they wrote regularly, chiefly about the theatre and about their many friends in common, most of whom were former Apostles, as was Pollock himself. Pollock, who became Master of the Court of Exchequer and then Queen's Remembrancer, was a man who moved in the best social circles in London but seemed always ready to take the time for a gossipy letter to FitzGerald. Yet in London they were more apt to meet by accident than by appointment, and Pollock apparently visited Fitz-Gerald in Suffolk only once, in 1872, two years after he had succeeded to his father's baronetcy.

Like Frederick Tennyson and W. F. Pollock, Fanny Kemble would hardly rate a mention in the index of a book about Fitz-Gerald were it not for the correspondence they carried on for years, chiefly after 1867. They had known each other since childhood but seldom saw each other, largely because Fanny Kemble was so often in the United States. When they met in London in 1879, FitzGerald wrote that he 'had not seen Mrs. Kemble for over twenty years'. [IV, 267] Once they began writing to each other, however, she became his most regular correspondent, and of his letters to her in the last six years of his life some seventy have survived. The subject of their correspondence at first was chiefly literary and theatrical but gradually widened to include almost every subject that interested them both, and when he could find no matter, he would confess the fact so charmingly that it would have been impossible to regret the paucity of his subject:

Is it better not to write at all than only write to plead that one has nothing to say? Yet I don't like to let the year get so close to an end without reminding you of me, to whom you have been always so good in the matter of replying to my letters, as in other ways.

If I can tell you nothing of myself: no Books read because of no Eyes to read them: no travel from home because of my little Ship being vanished: no friends seen, except Donne, who came here with Valentia for two days – *you* can fill a sheet like this, I know, with some account of yourself and your Doings: and I shall be very glad to hear that all is well with you. [III, 304–5]

FitzGerald often complained of the difficulty of reading Mrs Kemble's letters, since she crossed them and also wrote on paper so porous that the ink spread; his own letters were not crossed, but as his eyes deteriorated, he experimented with ink and paper of different colours and thicknesses; the result was that the ink often seeped through the fibres, and today his letters are far harder to read than hers. As the various editors of his correspondence have found, deciphering what he had to say often becomes a process of informed guesswork, particularly in those letters written after he could scarcely see what he had put on to the page.

FitzGerald's correspondence with these three friends might almost have been intended as a substitute for more intimate, more demanding, and ultimately more painful relationships. His correspondence grew because he was at considerable distance from the others, but he had, after all, the money to go to see them or to choose any place in the world to live, and it does not appear accidental that he spent so much of his life in a physically remote spot where a commentary on life became the surrogate for living it. It seems of a piece with his translations in being one artistic remove from what others would think of as reality.

Of the thousands of letters that he received, only a few remain, for he was in the habit of throwing them all away once they were answered. There are some four thousand of his own letters left, and of those most come from the last few years of his life. In part this is to be expected, since it is always the early letters of famous men that disappear before their names are well known, but in his case more than half of the surviving letters were written in the last seventeen of his seventy-four years. It seems an indication of the way, after he was no longer able to read as much as before and particularly after the end of his friendship with Posh Fletcher, that he turned to giving his experience acceptable shape by putting it into letters, with little risk of consequent pain.

The physical immediacy of the accounts of his life in his late letters can easily blind the reader to the fact that they are, ultimately, far from confessional, for he almost never speaks of his deepest feelings, and those must be inferred from what he says of the life around him; there is a final reticence that indicates how little he wanted others to know what went on in his head and heart. But for all that, his correspondence is highly personal, for his own feelings and attitudes can nearly always be determined by a reader with the sympathy and patience to puzzle out the meaning of his statements about the persons and places that become metaphors for his own life. No man can write four thousand personal letters without giving away the personality behind them, try as he will to hide it.

Once when W. H. Thompson apologized for not writing more frequently, FitzGerald asked him never to feel ashamed so long as he wrote at least twice a year, 'to let me know you live and thrive'. But he made it clear that correspondence meant a great deal more to him than that: 'You say my Letters are pleasant ... and they will be so far pleasant if they assure you that I like talking to you in that way: bad as I am at more direct communication.' [II, 477] Most men like writing letters less as they grow older, he told Carlyle, 'and my old friends naturally think that I might go and be with them – much better than writing.' [III, 597] It is our luck that Fitz-Gerald was not among that majority.

One of his frankest statements about the importance to him of writing letters was made to C. E. Norton of Harvard, its openness perhaps deriving from a feeling that the ocean between them made candour safe:

I have nothing of any sort that I am engaged to do: all alone for months together: taking up such Books as I please; and rather liking to write Letters to my Friends, whom I now only communicate with by such means. And very few of my oldest Friends, here in England, care to answer me, though I know from no want of Regard: but I know that few sensible men, who have their own occupations, care to write Letters unless on some special purpose; and I now rarely get more than one yearly Letter from each. Seeing which, indeed, I now rarely trouble them for more. [IV, 111]

With most of his friends, however, his pretence was what he indicated to Frederick Tennyson: 'when I write, it is more to get an answer than for the mere pleasure of writing which some people feel – chiefly Women, I suppose.' [III, 604]

Occasionally FitzGerald took offence at not hearing from his friends, and if they were literary, he often shifted his resentment to their writings rather than their personalities; even so he could not bear to have others criticize them. He used to complain that the only way to get a letter from Spedding would be to ask him for a favour or a loan, in which case the response would be immediate, although he would not otherwise write. Like many of the other friends they had in common, he felt that Spedding had wasted forty years in trying to vindicate Bacon, leaving him '(*I* think) a little less well off than when S. began washing him'. But an attack on Spedding from anyone else provoked instant defence from Fitz-Gerald, couched in the lovable ferocity with which he stood up for friends. Yet he confessed that he 'had not refreshed my Memory with the sight or sound of him for more than twenty years'. [IV, 417]

It is probable that Tennyson's failure to answer his letters contributed to his dislike of his later poetry, but for all his own disparaging remarks about it, he was as prickly as the poet himself about any adverse criticism of it from others. In 1868 he wrote to Pollock in real anger at 'an absurd Article in my old Athenaeum comparing the relative merits of Tennyson and Browning: awarding the praise of *Finish*, etc., to A.T., and of *originality* to B.!'. FitzGerald's own inability to read Browning was proof for him of his mediocrity: 'he is not a rival to A.T. – whom I judge of by his earlier poems (up to 1842). In Browning I could but see little but Cockney Sublime.... Tennyson has stocked the English Language with lines which once knowing one can't forgo.' At Oxford and Cambridge, according to Cowell, 'Browning is considered the deepest! But "this also will pass away." But not A.T.' [III, 111]

It was in part the natural contrast between 'Camberwell Bob' Browning and Tennyson that made him dislike the poetry of the former so intensely. For all its praise by others, he had no intention of reading *The Ring and the Book* when Browning published it: 'I never could read one of his old ones. If the Arts are not beautiful – Music, Painting, Poetry – they are nothing to me.' It surprised him that 'Morris, Browning, and Swinburne should go on pouring out Poem after Poem, as if such haste could prosper with any but First-rate Men'. [III, 730] Because Tennyson himself had qualified admiration and considerable personal liking for Browning, Fitz-Gerald liked teasing him about the other poet: 'Is Mr. Rossetti a Great Poet, like Browning and Morris? So the Athenaeum tells me. Dear me, how thick Great Poets do grow nowadays.' [III, 243] FitzGerald might have felt somewhat chagrined had he known that it was the very poets he liked to denigrate who were the most enthusiastic supporters of his own version of the *Rubáiyát*. But, of course, his strictures on them were less serious than they appeared, and in part they were intended as an indirect compliment to Tennyson, who 'still admires Browning, for a great, though unshapen Spirit; and acknowledges Morris, Swinburne, and Co., though not displeased, I think, that I do not'. [III, 724] It is a sentence that might stand as an emblem of the affection that so often motivated his apparently uncharitable remarks about others, for there was little malice in him.

Part of what did disturb FitzGerald about the contemporary poets he disliked was simply that he thought of them as a group and hence had an exaggerated sense of unity in their theory and practice; he was so constitutionally inclined to individuality that he almost automatically rejected any group with shared artistic theories, whatever those might be. In thanking Fanny Kemble for a paper she had written about the stage, he said, 'I always think that your Theory of the Intuitive *versus* the Analytical and Philosophical applies to the other Arts as well as that of the Drama. Mozart couldn't tell how he made a Tune; even a whole Symphony, he said, unrolled itself out of a leading idea by no logical process. Keats said that no Poetry was worth [anything] unless it came spontaneously, as Leaves to a Tree, etc. I have no faith in your Works of Art done on Theory and Principle, like Wordsworth, Wagner, Holman Hunt, etc.' [III, 595]

Many of FitzGerald's judgements on poetry during the last decade of his life were repeated several times in his letters, as he rolled them around in his head and sought better ways of stating them. This habit of reshaping ideas and incidents for different correspondents grew on him, but it seemed a sharpening of his perceptions rather than lassitude of the kind that had characterized his letters in the early 1860s. One need not claim that his letters are the equals of Keats's to see that he is often reminiscent of the greater poet as he writes, judges, weighs, and then repeats a phrase from letter to letter.

One mark of the spontaneity of FitzGerald's letters in the 1870s is that he wrote some twenty to Frederick Pollock and to the younger Crabbe in colloquial, simple, but not always correct French.[2] 'Que diable! Ce vieux Fitz métamorphose en Français?' begins his first letter to Pollock in that language. 'C'est ce que vous fredonnez entre vos dents, mon cher Pollock, en effleurant ma Lettre. Attendez donc; je vais vous en rendre compte.' [III, 431] Although he knew French well, he was in no sense showing off his knowledge, only writing it as he might play a game, and delighting in the momentary assumption of another language and personality, just as he loved pseudonyms and nicknames for himself. It is the sense of play, the frequent alternation of viewpoint to suit his correspondent, and the constant investigation of the possibilities of language that make FitzGerald's letters a source of literary pleasure that none of his more formal works, even the *Rubáiyát*, can match and that make it a simple statement of fact to say that they are among the great letters in the language. It is useless to come to them for grandeur of statement, even for profundity of thought, but they constantly give us new glances at an affectionate, innocent, cultivated, and enquiring mind.

Along with the spontaneity one finds in the letters of the mid-1870s an increased wistfulness as FitzGerald began to feel old, largely because of his break with Posh and because of the deaths of his brother and sisters. In 1864, the year after Mrs Kerrich's death, his sister Isabella Vignati died, then in 1875 his favourite brother, Peter, who had remained the one relative he was anxious to see, died of bronchitis, murmuring Edward's name three times with his last breath: 'A more amiable Gentleman did not live, with something *helpless* about him – what the Irish call an "Innocent man" – which mixed up Compassion with Regard, and made it perhaps stronger.' [III, 552] There would be no more sailing with Peter as his guest, no surprise visits from him. Alarmingly, FitzGerald was suffering from the bronchitis which had killed Peter after several years of the disease. 'My Day is done,' he told Cowell. 'I have not been very well all this Summer, and fancy that I begin to "smell the Ground," as Sailors say of the Ship that slackens speed as the Water shallows under her. I can't say I have much care for long Life: but still less for long Death: I mean a lingering one.' [III, 592–3] He was not particularly hypochondriacal, but he could easily envision himself being carried off as Peter had been, and he tried to protect his chest from wind and cold to avoid pulmonary trouble.

For more than a decade his hearing had been bad, and when he had a cold he said it was as if a door had been shut between him and all sound. Among the few errands that he considered import-ant enough to take him to London were visits to his 'aurist'. His eyes had never been strong, and they had nearly failed him when he puzzled over the characters in his Persian texts. By 1869 he could hardly see to read: 'I have, I think, broiled my starboard eye with it close to a hot Paraffin lamp these four or five winters: and now, I observe, it can't read by itself, and confuses the sight of its fellow.' [III, 133] His doctor's prescription was of no help, and he began wearing wire-rimmed spectacles with small lenses in colours ranging from pale green to deep blue; several pairs of them are still extant. But even these were inadequate, and on particularly bright days he had to rely on his memory. Once in 1878 he wrote that he had been 'trying yesterday to recover Gray's Elegy ... with shut Eyes. But I had to return to the Book: and am far from perfect yet.' He found spring the least taxing of seasons, since the soft greens of new leaves and grass were soothing to his eyes. For the rest of his life he had to recognize that he would never see well, and he had to resort to readers.

About 1854, when he moved to Farlingay, he had begun asking local boys to read to him, both to rest his eyes and because he was so often amused by the readers. Alfred Smith, son of the Farlingay farmer, was probably the first of the series. For fifteen years there-after he had readers sporadically, then hired them regularly until the end of his life. (Merely to list the occupations of the fathers of five of the boys who read for him indicates the breadth of calling and business then to be found in a small market town: farmer, cabinet maker, butcher, a 'rather drunken Bird-stuffer', and bookbinder.) Since he could normally see print in broad daylight, he tried to read his most difficult books then, and to ask his boys to come in during the early evening to read novels, chiefly those of Dickens, Trollope, Collins, and Scott. The more he knew of the novels of Dickens, the more he admired them, calling their author 'a little Shakespeare – a Cockney Shakespeare, if you will: but as distinct, if not so great, a piece of pure Genius as was born in Stratford'. Given the necessity of having but one of them, he 'would choose Dickens' hundred delightful Caricatures rather than Thackeray's half-dozen terrible Photographs' [IV, 203], and praise could hardly go higher than that. Even the boy readers, he noticed, brightened up over the pages of Dickens.

FitzGerald was good to his young readers, treating them with affection and generosity, but he was also unmaliciously delighted with their mistakes, which he loved to write about, giving the boys nicknames. The cabinet maker's son, for example, read 'her future husband' as 'her *furniture* husband'. Another evening 'he called an *harangue* in the French Assembly a "hangarue." I asked him if he knew what that was; he said he had heard of a *Kangaroo*.' Fitz-Gerald was solicitous of the boys' welfare, as he indicated in describing 'the Blunderer' and his schedule: 'A little Fellow comes to my room every night to read to me from half after seven till nine. By which time he is tired, as well he may, after stumbling at every third word. But he is a nice quiet Boy, and well-mannered; so when nine comes, I give him Cake and Sweet Wine, and send him off to his Bed.' [III, 173] One of the boys who read at the end of Fitz-Gerald's life ate so much that he became 'stupefied and inarticulate' and earned the name of 'my learned Pig'. In the opening lines of 'Gerontion' T. S. Eliot reflects perfectly the mixture of exasperation, affection, and fatigue that FitzGerald felt for his boy readers; it is by no means certain, however, that his subject would have appreciated Eliot's portrait, taken from A. C. Benson's biography of him.[3]

In fact FitzGerald demanded a good deal of the boys; one read in halting Latin, which he was studying in school, and another stumbled through unfamiliar Spanish until he had acquired at least a reasonable pronunciation in that language. FitzGerald was quite as bizarre as the boys, for he usually listened to them wearing his hat, from which he extracted a handkerchief when he wanted it. He put his feet on the fender, kept two candles alight for the readers, grumbled at their mistakes, and commented rudely on the books themselves, ordering the reader to skip passages that bored him. After the reading was over, the boy invariably received a shilling, handsome payment for light labour. FitzGerald's favourite reading, by which he was never bored, was the report of the protracted Tichborne inheritance case, which was prolonged from 1867 until 1874, and of which he knew every detail. After they went on to other employment the half-dozen boys who had read for him over a period of some fifteen years seem to have thought of him with affection, inevitably mixed with incomprehension.

In 1870 FitzGerald's landlady in Market Hill, Mrs Berry, died, but to have a place for the winter when he was spending the summer in Lowestoft, he kept the rooms for several years until Berry wanted to remarry. Her widower was less enthusiastic about his lodger than Mrs Berry had been, and he was inefficient as well. FitzGerald is said to have been annoyed by him and to have written some half-angry verses that came to the attention of Berry and the woman whom he hoped to install as the second Mrs Berry:

> To Mr Berry, Gun-Maker, Market Hill, Woodbridge
> You sent in your Bill, Berry
> Before it was due, Berry
> Your father, the elder Berry,
> Would not make such a Mull, Berry.
> But you being a goose, Berry
> I don't care a Straw, Berry
> I shall just kick your-arsberry
> Till you are black, Berry, and Blue Berry!![4]

The new Mrs Berry brought with her to Market Hill her family by her first husband, and they needed all the room in the house. She appears to have been insulted by what she had heard of the verse attributed to FitzGerald, and she insisted that he move at once. She was a huge woman weighing fourteen stone, and according to FitzGerald her nine-stone husband arrived at his door with her bulk urging him on from behind: 'And you've got to tell him about Old Gooseberry, Berry.' At last poor Berry stammered out, 'And I am told, sir, that you said – you said – I had long been old Berry, but now – now you should call me Old Gooseberry.'[5] FitzGerald's first reaction to the ultimatum was to stay in his rooms until Mrs Berry either took legal action or threw him out bodily, but at last he began looking for another place to live. He insisted that Grange Farm was impossible because he needed it to entertain his nieces during the summer, so he took rooms in the house next to the Berrys, probably choosing it as much to annoy them as for his own convenience, since it lacked even a stairway to the rooms he hired, and they had to be approached by ladder. In fact, he never did move into them, and by the end of January 1874, five months after he had first been given notice to move, he had become reconciled to living in his own house, Grange Farm. From there he never moved until his death.

After a few months at Grange Farm he changed its name to Little Grange, at the suggestion of his friend Annie Biddell. For the rest of his life FitzGerald continued to improvise upon the name, writing some times from his 'Chateau', at others from Littlegrange, La Petite Grange, or Petitgrange, often signing his letters with one of those names or as 'The Laird of Little Grange'. He had been with the Berrys for thirteen years, and in the nine he occupied Little Grange he never quite succeeded in settling down, claiming that he found it lonely when he was by himself, too crowded when his Kerrich nieces were there. As he explained, when they came, 'I give up the house entirely except my one room, which serves for Parlour and Bed: and which I really prefer, as it reminds me of the Cabin of my dear little Ship.' [IV, 30] Occasionally, when there were guests in the house, he would suddenly feel crowded and appear late at night at a nearby public house, carrying his nightshirt and asking for a bed. 'Are you not glad now to be mainly alone?' he asked George Borrow. 'If one ever had this solitary habit, it is not likely to alter for the better as one grows older – as one grows *old*.' [III, 544]

When the weather was possible, he liked to go out in his little boat with his boatman, Ted West; after West's death, he wrote, 'I shall scarce have heart to prowl about our River again, after fourteen years of his Company'. [IV, 32] But boating was only part of his daily routine in Little Grange: 'It wants half an hour of my single Pipe-time: I have been four hours on the River: then after Tea came dear old Doughty for nearly two hours: then Ellen Churchyard for half an hour: then to water my Garden: and still it is but 8:30 P.M., too dark to read out of doors.' As he waited for his smoke, he finished the letter: 'My half hour is – must be – up, I think – yes: positively, those must be the nine o'clock Chimes I hear. Now for a Biscuit: Tumbler of Beaujolais: then a Pipe: then to Bed. Good night.' [III, 693–5]

It was a serene life, but behind the words one can hear the monotonous beat of predictability and boredom that sometimes made him flee Woodbridge in inarticulate terror at the advance of the years and in longing for the passions of the past. And, of course, he fled to Lowestoft.

In the summer of 1874, a few months after the *Meum and Tuum* had been sold and his partnership with Posh dissolved, FitzGerald went for a stay in Lowestoft, ostensibly to make room for his nieces in Little Grange. Like most other places where he had known happiness, then disappointment, Lowestoft seemed at first to have gone downhill: 'It is an ugly place enough: ugly sands, ugly sea, etc.' [III, 514] All during that autumn he shuttled between Woodbridge and Lowestoft. What is surprising is that he returned there at all, rather than shunning it as he avoided London, Tenby, and Bedford after Browne's death. Perhaps he nursed the hope that he could make up his differences with Posh, for he still made enquiries about him, 'my former friend', and said at the end of the year, 'I have not seen him since I have been here.' [III, 533] He wrote that he was glad to return to Lowestoft: 'The little lodging is more to my liking than my own bigger rooms and staircases: and this cheerful Town better (at this Season) than my yet barren Garden.' [III, 547] His consolation was that he had outlived the pain of the separation from Posh: 'What Blunders one has to look back on, to be sure! So many, luckily, that one has ceased to care for any *one*.' [III, 550]

In 1873, after 'many years solicitation from Nieces, Crabbes, and two or three other old Friends' FitzGerald had himself 'Photo'ed' by Cade of Ipswich for the only time in his life. 'The Artist always does three of every Sitter: but my bad Eyes blinked so ... in the Full face, turned toward the Machine, that we only took Copies of the two which turn away.... I call one *The Statesman*: and the other *The Philosopher*.' [III, 401] It tells us volumes about his innate modesty that he found the photographs 'unexpectedly complimentary'. 'They are so good-looking (comparatively) that

a

c

b

XVI FitzGerald, 1873.
a. Discarded sitting.
b. 'The Philosopher'.
c. 'The Statesman'.

upon my honour I shd never have guessed they were meant for me.'[6] Probably no one else found them flattering; far more than FitzGerald recognized, they show the tired, defeated part of his personality that he so seldom allowed to get into his letters. (See plate XVI.)

CHAPTER XIII

Settling Accounts

FitzGerald's last translation was a reworking of Sophocles' *Oedipus Tyrannus* and *Oedipus Coloneus*, 'the two Tragedies united into one Drama under the ponderous alliteration which figures on the Titlepage', *The Downfall and Death of King Oedipus*. The 'First Act', which he called 'Oedipus in Thebes' was privately printed in 1880, followed the next year by 'Oedipus at Athens'. The 'Drama professes to be neither a Translation, nor a Paraphrase of Sophocles, but "chiefly taken" from him: I need scarcely add, only intended for those who do not read the Greek.' [IV, 405]

In what he called his 'perversion' of Sophocles, FitzGerald briskly scours from the original a good many of what he considered its excesses and eccentricities. In a long letter to C. E. Norton (later printed as a preface to the drama), he explained the reasons for many of his changes. [IV, 405–10] The part of Creon is excised from the first 'Act' because his character is inconsistent with that in the second and third parts of Sophocles' trilogy. He believed that the character of Ismene was unnecessary, so she '"disappears from my Playbill" altogether'. Oedipus is presented as a 'man little, if at all, beyond the prime of life' in both parts of the drama, on the grounds that he married young and that he is younger than Creon, who is said to be still 'capable of very active service'. The reader cannot help feeling that FitzGerald is slipping unwarily into the grip of a relentless search for realism that has little to do with these plays. He suggests that if Oedipus is shown as having 'become an old man between the time of his leaving Thebes, and that of his arrival at Athens', Antigone would become a woman too old for Haemon to be enamoured of her. Besides, 'one cannot help asking one's self *where*, in all the little world of Greece, Oedipus could have found Space to wander in all the Time.' One step further, we feel, and FitzGerald will be in a world so logical that the horror of the original will have vanished.

'As for Poetry,' FitzGerald wrote, 'I pretend to very little more than representing the old Greek in sufficiently readable English verse'. He was even more worried about the choruses in Sophocles than he had been in his version of the *Agamemnon*, so instead of translating them himself, he used Robert Potter's old version of them, 'though worthy of a better Interpreter than either of us'. One understands FitzGerald's difficulties, but his changes in the plays indicate how little he really came to grips with the originals, so that this must be counted as one of his least effective works. The dramas of Sophocles from which he worked are too familiar a part of our culture for us to accept the free transmutation of the original material as easily as we can accept even greater liberties in the *Rubáiyát* because few of us know the Persian original.

Two other literary labours he undertook at the end of his life both derived from his wish to make favourite works easily available to modern readers. The first of these was a dictionary of the correspondence of Madame de Sévigné, which he started in a desultory way for his own convenience when he first began reading her letters. In 1875 he wrote to George Crabbe that his command of French would undoubtedly improve, 'ayant si récemment lu avec tant de plaisir des lettres de Madame de Sévigné'. [III, 563] Like most of his passionate friendships, FitzGerald's affair with her was love at first sight. Enraptured, he wrote to Cowell to ask if he knew her letters: 'I never did till this summer, rather repelled by her perpetual harping on her daughter. But it is all genuine, and the same intense Feeling expressed in a hundred natural yet graceful ways: and beside all this such good Sense, good Feeling, Humour, Love of Books and Country Life, as makes her certainly the Queen of all Letter writers.' [III, 593]

For the rest of his life he read her correspondence over and over, quoted tags from her letters, debated whether he should make a trip to Brittany to see her house, Les Rochers, and urged her on every friend who might conceivably be interested. He so loved her 'free thought and speech' that he was vexed he had come to know her so late: 'but perhaps it was as well to have such an

273

acquaintance reserved for one's latter years. The fine Creature! much more alive to me than most Friends.' [III, 671]

Every time he read her letters he added to the annotations he was collecting, and by 1880 he had 'plenty of Notes for an Introductory Argument and List of Dramatis Personae, and a clue to the course of her Letters, so as to set a new reader off on the right tack, with some previous acquaintance with the People and Places she lives among'. (It is characteristic of him to write of her in the present tense in his enthusiasm.) Today his work lies in big boxes in Trinity College Library. He never put it into print: 'I shrink from trying to put such Notes into shape; all writing always distasteful to me, and now very difficult, at seventy odd.' [IV, 336] They were finally published in 1914 by a great-niece as the two-volume *Dictionary of Madame de Sévigné*. From the beginning his only hope was that it would make others return 'to her as for some Spring Music'. [IV, 424]

Another of his loves was Charles Lamb, whose biography he contemplated writing. Instead, in 1878 he had privately printed a calendar of Lamb's life that he had compiled for his own guidance, hoping that it would help convert others to a similar regard for Lamb.

The work to which he gave most time in his old age, perhaps more from stubbornness over the mistaken views of others than from the kind of love he felt for Madame de Sévigné, was an edition of George Crabbe's *Tales of the Hall*. His regard for Crabbe was natural enough, since the poet was born in Aldeburgh and was the father of his friend George Crabbe of Bredfield and grandfather of Crabbe of Merton. The easy humour, pathos, and terror of Crabbe's verse tales was of the 'walnuts and wine' type that Fitz-Gerald most enjoyed in company, and it was a desire to extend that company which led him to make an abridgement of Crabbe's last volume of stories: 'Women and young People will never like him, I think: but I believe every thinking man will like him more as he grows older.' [IV, 5]

In particular FitzGerald wanted to destroy his contemporaries' belief that Crabbe was not funny, a view that he thought Leslie Stephen was guilty of spreading. 'I think I shall do it as well as any one is likely to do,' he wrote, 'though not so well as might be done; but I know not if any one will care for it when done.' He extracted 'all his better Verse ... with as few words of my own Prose as will connect it intelligibly together' [IV, 152], but he was right in worrying about publishers, since in both England and the United States they proved reluctant, although he was willing to underwrite the costs himself. At last, in 1879, he had the edition privately printed, as he had done with so many other works, but it was not until 1882 that Quaritch agreed to take copies for sale. 'I can gain nothing from the Public, whether of Praise or Pelf; neither of which was my object – which was simply to try and gain a few Readers to this awkward old Genius.' [IV, 212] It is improbable that he had more than limited success in his object, even when he brought out a second and enlarged printing with a preface not long before his death. In the letters accompanying presentation copies of this, as well as most of his other late works, he asked that he receive no thanks in return: 'I always maintain it best to say nothing, unless to find fault, with what is sent to one in this Book Line. And so to be done by.' [IV, 322]

Of the four works that occupied him at the end of his life, only his version of Sophocles could be called a translation, however loosely that term is used, but they all had some part in his lifelong desire to bring fine works to a wider reading public, even if that meant their transformation. With apologies for the 'Suffolk Superlative' he spoke with justice of himself as 'one of the "most translatingest" men alive'. [IV, 129]

FitzGerald's thoughts were naturally beginning to turn ever more insistently to the thought of death, particularly following the painful last illness of his brother John. Shortly after his own seventieth birthday in 1879 he wrote to Fanny Kemble:

My Brother keeps waiting – and hoping – for – Death: which will not come: perhaps Providence would have let it come sooner, were he not rich enough to keep a Doctor in the house, to keep him in Misery. I don't know if I told you in my last that he was ill; seized on by a Disease not uncommon to old Men – an 'internal Disorder' it is polite to say; but I shall say to you, disease of the Bladder. I had always supposed he would be found dead one good morning, as my Mother was – as I hoped to be – quietly dead of the Heart which he had felt for several Years. But no; it is seen good that he shall be laid on the Rack – which he

XVII   John Purcell-Fitz-Gerald, 1871.

may feel the more keenly as he never suffered Pain before, and is not of a strong Nerve. I will say no more of this. The funeral Bell, which has been at work, as I never remember before, all this winter, is even now, as I write, tolling from St. Mary's Steeple.

'Parlons d'autres choses,' as my dear Sévigné says. [IV, 202]

John's end was unexpectedly peaceful, and after it FitzGerald wrote to a friend: 'I say nothing of my Brother's death – only that – one's own turn shows so much the nearer. If the end is to be tolerably painless, I think I shall not demur at leaving this World: one has had a very prosperous time of it, and yet that Prosperity supplies one but little to care about now. When I shut the door on seventy years on March 31, I felt the Play was done – except the sad last Act, which must be a short one and one hopes not very tragical.' [IV, 208]

To Fanny Kemble all that he could say of John's death was, 'We were very good friends, of very different ways of thinking; I had not been [inside] his lawn gates (three miles off) these dozen years (no fault of his), and I did not enter them at his Funeral – which you will very likely – and properly – think wrong.' [IV, 211] Winter was not yet over in May of that year, there was 'scarce a leaf on the trees, and a N.E. Wind blowing Cold, Cough, Bronchitis, etc., and the confounded Bell of a neighbouring Church announcing a Death, day after day. I certainly never remember so long, and so mortal a Winter'. [IV, 211]

At the end of the year his sister Andalusia died, leaving only Edward and his sister Jane Wilkinson of the original eight children. After that FitzGerald frequently repeated his conviction that none of his family lived much beyond seventy, which was true, but he said it so often that there is a kind of grim humour in noting the slight irritation with which he regarded each unfulfilled prediction of his own imminent end. Bronchitis had been his steady companion for some years, but in 1880 he had 'pains and heaviness about the Heart.... I shall not at all complain if it takes the usual course, only wishing to avoid Angina, or some such form of the Disease. My Family get on gaily enough till seventy, and then generally founder after turning the corner.' [IV, 378–9]

The death of friends came more often, too. It was hardly a shock when Carlyle died, for he was eighty-six; William Donne was only two years older than FitzGerald, but he had been ill for a long time and did not even recognize his old friends, so his death was something to be thankful for. One of the worst shocks FitzGerald ever suffered, largely because it was so unexpected, was the accidental death of James Spedding in 1881, hardly more than a month after Carlyle died. 'One, not so illustrious in Genius, but certainly not less wise – my dear old Friend of sixty years'. Spedding was knocked down by a cab and taken to St George's Hospital, where he lived for several days, typically exerting more strength in excusing the driver than on his own condition. He was the wisest man he had ever known, FitzGerald said, 'not the less so for plenty of *the Boy* in him – great Sense of Humour – a Socrates in Life and in Death, which he faced with all Serenity so long as Consciousness lasted'. [IV, 404]

'I am rather surprised to find how much I dwell upon the thought of him,' FitzGerald told Pollock, 'considering that I had not refreshed my Memory with the sight or sound of him for more than twenty years. . . . I cannot help thinking of him while I wake; and when I do wake from Sleep, I have a feeling of something lost – as in a Dream – and it is J.S.' [IV, 417]

Although his emotions about death were strong, there was a residual toughness in FitzGerald that kept him bouncing back, a kind of optimism that often came to his aid. Even on the days that he complained about the mournful tolling of the parish church bell as he sat waiting for his brother's death, he could see that his emotions were temporary and even recognize as symbols the very things that most affected him: 'Two of my dear Blackbirds have I found dead – of Cold and Hunger, I suppose; but one is even now singing – across that Funeral Bell.' [IV, 203]

Even as his friends and relatives were dying, he was constantly reassembling those who were left, almost as if he were promoting them into the prominent places in his affections that had been vacated by others. For some time he and Tennyson had been partially estranged because FitzGerald thought he was neglected by his more famous friend, but as early as 1876 the breach between them had been healed – temporarily. In September of that year Fitz-Gerald was sitting in Little Grange when a card was brought in with Tennyson's name on it. Tennyson and his son had been in Norfolk and called in on FitzGerald without warning. 'And immediately it was as if we had parted only twenty days instead of twenty years: with our old Jokes, Banter, Comparisons of Taste, etc.' [III, 705] As the years rolled back, FitzGerald forgot all the tiny occasions of hurt and his old affection for Tennyson surged up. His guests stayed two days at the Bull, where FitzGerald put them up in the belief that they would be more comfortable than in Little Grange. They went to Harwich by steamer, then came back to Woodbridge to sit on the iron bench under the garden trees, where they 'went over the same old grounds of Debate, told some of the old Stories', with the doves fluttering around Fitz's shoulders.

When Tennyson said he still had 'some things on the Anvil', Fitz-Gerald refused to ask more about them, 'for indeed I think he might as well ship his Oars now. I was even impious enough to tell him so.' [III, 711] He could still not resist telling Tennyson what he disliked about his poetry, a tactless habit that forty years of acquaintance had not broken. Much as he longed to be on loving terms with his friend, there was always a perverse imp stirring him to say the very things he knew would irritate Tennyson, and the desire to do so was perhaps strongest when his own poetic powers were at their weakest. Sometimes he seemed to be testing the limits of how far he could go without finally destroying their friendship. 'When Tennyson was telling me of how The Quarterly abused him (humorously too), and desirous of knowing why one did not care for his later works, etc., I thought that if he had lived an active Life, as Scott and Shakespeare; or even ridden, shot, drunk, and played the Devil, as Byron, he would have done much more, and talked about it much less.' [III, 714] Tennyson was not an easy or patient friend, but FitzGerald's behaviour could make him seem remarkably forbearing.

'I suppose I may never see him again,' FitzGerald thought as he watched Tennyson's train pull out. [III, 707] Nor did he. Months, then years, passed with no letters from Tennyson, although Fitz-Gerald wrote often, assuring him, 'I suppose that scarce a day passes without my thinking of you.' [IV, 455] The letters that now came from Farringford or Aldworth, however, were from Hallam rather than Emily Tennyson. Perhaps Hallam's father might have written himself if FitzGerald had been able to restrain his penchant for criticism. Probably he never heard directly from Tennyson again. In 1882 he was in London and heard that Alfred was there as well, 'but in some grand Locality of Eaton Square – so I did not venture down to him'. [IV, 486] To excuse his own procrastination, he insisted he would go once more to see Tennyson 'if he did not live on a somewhat large scale'.

FitzGerald was even more open in his affections than in his criticism and so enthusiastic in their expression that he had trouble understanding more reserved natures such as Tennyson's or even believing that they reciprocated his feelings. As he settled unhappily into accepting that nothing had been changed in their relations by the unexpected visit, Tennyson was actually planning quietly on a celebration of half a century of their friendship. Unfortunately, he moved slowly. His son Hallam came upon a copy of his old unpublished poem 'Tiresias', written in 1833, the period of his poetry that FitzGerald liked most. Tennyson rewrote the poem, then headed it with a long, charming preface, 'To E. FitzGerald', written with the warmth of old intimacy, affectionately addressing his friend:

> Old Fitz, who from your suburb grange,
>   Where once I tarried for a while,
> Glance at the wheeling Orb of change,
>   And greet it with a kindly smile;
> Whom yet I see as there you sit
>   Beneath your sheltering garden-tree,
> And while your doves about you flit,
>   And plant on shoulder, hand and knee,
> Or on your head their rosy feet,
>   As if they knew your diet spares
> Whatever moved in that full sheet
>   Let down to Peter at his prayers...

But Tennyson had put up with Fitz's criticism for so many years that he could not refrain from mentioning it wryly in his account of the discovery and dedication of the poem:

>   ... my son, who dipt
> In some forgotten book of mine
>   With sallow scraps of manuscript,
> And dating many a year ago,
>   Has hit on this, which you will take

My Fitz, and welcome, as I know
   Less for its own than for the sake
Of one recalling gracious times,
    When, in our younger London days,
You found some merit in my rhymes,
   And I more pleasure in your praise.

According to Tennyson he concluded the dedication only a week before he heard the 'tolling of his funeral bell' for the death of Fitz-Gerald, who had of course had no idea of the poem and hardly more of the love with which it was presented. Tennyson did not cancel what he had written, but he added some thirty more lines in closing,

      ... praying that, when I from hence
Shall fade with him into the unknown,
   My close of earth's experience
May prove as peaceful as his own.

There could hardly be a better example of the love that FitzGerald so easily inspired, of the difficulty he put in the way of accepting its return, and of the happiness that he thereby forfeited.

On the whole, however, the last years of his life brought increased warmth to his friendships. His off-again-on-again relations with the Cowells had always been held together by a strong literary curiosity that he shared with Cowell, no matter how attenuated their more personal feelings had become. By 1879 he had recovered all his old warmth, and when they spent some weeks together in Lowestoft, he and his 'delightful Cowell' read *Don Quixote* together every morning. 'If we read very continuously we should be almost through the Book by this time: but, as you may imagine, we play as well as work; some passage in the dear Book leads Cowell off into Sanskrit, Persian, or – *Goody Two Shoes* – for all comes within the compass of his Memory and Application.' [IV, 251] The following spring he was once more in 'our ugly Lowestoft' for ten days, again reading Spanish with Cowell. 'He is a delightful fellow; "a great Boy" as well as a great Scholar: and *She* is as young in Spirit as ever; and both of them very happy in themselves and one another.' [IV, 312]

His friendship with Fanny Kemble had been rekindled years before through letters, but it had been a long time since they had been together before he went to her flat in Queen Anne's Mansions in Westminster in 1879. She had recently lost her sister, Adelaide Sartoris: 'Well, I had not seen Mrs. Kemble for over twenty years; and she wished once more, she said, to see an old friend of herself and her Family', so he called on her daily for four days. [IV, 267] In the intervening years she had developed into a figure far more formidable than FitzGerald suspected from her letters, although he might have had some inkling of the change from the way in which she had ignored his suggestion that after knowing each other for seventy years they might use Christian names in their letters. She scolded him about the old pens he used in writing to her, told him not to put his tumbler on the floor, and lectured him, probably with some justification, about the casualness of his manners. None of it diminished her fascination nor his affection for her, and he returned on several occasions to see her, making for her the trip to London that he was seldom persuaded to undertake for other friends. With remarkable meekness he accepted her corrections and even apologized for his transgressions, as he did after a visit in 1882:

> It is very kind of you to break through your rule of Correspondence, that you may tell me how it was with you that last Evening. I was aware of no 'stupidity' on your side: I only saw that you were what you called 'a little tired, and unwell.' Had I known how much, I should of course have left you with a farewell shake of hands at once. And in so far I must blame you. But I blame myself for rattling on, not only then, but always, I fear, in a manner that you tell me (and I thank you for telling me) runs into occasional impertinence – which no length of acquaintance can excuse, especially to a Lady. You will think that here is more than enough of this. But pray do you also say no more about it. I know that you regard me very kindly, as I am sure that I do you, all the while. [IV, 489]

FitzGerald, who was often moved by the spectacle of family affections that he had known too rarely, was particularly attracted by her loyalty to the memory of her eccentric brother Jack, and by her support of the illegitimate son of another brother.

It was probably too much to think that he could become completely reconciled to his own family, living or dead. When his only surviving sister, Jane Wilkinson, came to England in 1881, they had both softened since the old days when they quarrelled almost as a matter of course when they met. She had been married to a clergyman with a parish near Ipswich, 'a Mr. Wilkinson – made him very Evangelical – and tiresome – and so they fed their Flock in a Suffolk village'. [IV, 12] Because of her strong religious ideas, Mrs Wilkinson had always been very close to her brother John; an oppressively pious diary she kept in 1835–6 shows how often they met to discuss Evangelical tenets and to attend church together. After her husband's death in the early 1860s she had moved to Florence, with the idea, according to FitzGerald, of converting the Roman Catholic Church. When he had not seen her for two decades, he had so far mellowed in his opinion of her as to say that she was 'not at all obtrusively religious: and I think must have settled abroad to escape some of the old Associations in which she took so much part, to but little advantage to herself or others'. [IV, 433]

The meeting was less successful than they had both hoped. Mrs Wilkinson, for all her piety, had no sympathy with her brother's habit of giving money to the poor, and she thought that the lack of ostentation in the way he lived was deliberately adopted to further his charities, 'a style of life which I regret but which put more means in his hands'. When she got to Little Grange, she found him 'terribly altered', his health ruined by living in such a Spartan fashion. With some disappointment she noted the scarcity of contents in his cellar, although 'his little *stores* of wine he had out to make me comfortable'.[1] They talked of old days in France and Wherstead, and when he laid his hand over hers, she felt so close to him that she offered to take care of him if he would come back to Italy with her. To her surprise he responded with considerably less than a qualified acceptance. A week after her departure he wrote to Frederick Tennyson: 'I suppose that she and I shall never meet again: she will not return here, and I could only say at parting that my going to Florence was "not impossible". She is some three years older than I, and likely to outlive me.' [IV, 447] She did indeed outlive him long enough to send her memories to his literary executor, and their faint tone of *de haut en bas* makes one suspect that she thought he had not outgrown his reprehensible boyhood habit of pulling her respectable leg.

283

When he was sorry for himself, FitzGerald liked to present the appearance of a tired old man, unable to face new experience. In 1882 he declined an invitation to London from J. W. Blakesley, and he explained to Donne's daughter: 'you know that I now go nowhere but to the very few old Friends who may wish to see me. . . . I believe that *he* wishes also, for he says so. But – but – he has those about him to whom I am strange.' [IV, 484]

The truth of the matter was that he still enjoyed making new friends, either by letter or in person. His correspondence with Professor C. E. Norton of Harvard began in 1875, although Norton had been an admirer of his for a dozen years before that, ever since he had first read the *Rubáiyát*, reviewed it, and helped to identify its author. Norton was active in suggesting literary projects to Fitz-Gerald that he thought he was well qualified to undertake. Among his English friends were Ruskin, Carlyle, and Burne-Jones, names that often crop up in their correspondence. He and FitzGerald never met, although he invited Fitz to come to Boston. Not surprisingly, FitzGerald was never able to summon up the energy for the ocean crossing.

Norton's friend James Russell Lowell was also a professor at Harvard, and the two men had for a time been joint editors of the *North American Review*. Lowell was the first editor of the *Atlantic Monthly*. FitzGerald thought he was one of the best literary critics alive, felt some admiration for his poetry, and was delighted to annex him as another correspondent. Lowell became American Minister to Spain, then Minister to England, and on at least three occasions wrote to FitzGerald offering to come to Woodbridge to see him, but he was too modest to suggest that he stay for longer than a single day, and FitzGerald was curiously reluctant to have him come for such a short time, telling him that a few hours together would be worse than none. As his editors have suggested, 'FitzGerald's letters to the two Americans contain sustained passages of his best literary criticism garnished with entertaining reminiscence and literary gossip.' [I, 54]

Aldis Wright, Librarian and Vice-Master of Trinity College, was a fellow East Anglian from Beccles, where his father was a Baptist minister. He and FitzGerald struck up an epistolary acquaintance in 1869 over Suffolk vocabulary. Wright, like Norton and Lowell, was scholarly by nature, but unlike them he was primly and academically reserved, which may initially have inhibited his friendship with FitzGerald. In his frequent trips to Beccles from Cambridge, he got in the habit of stopping off in Woodbridge, and finally he spent two or three bachelor holidays a year with FitzGerald. Although Wright was nearly a quarter of a century his junior, Fitz-Gerald deferred to his scholarship while retaining the right to question some of his textual decisions over Shakespeare. He had such unquestioning faith in Wright's honesty and rectitude that he made him his literary executor, not least because he was a 'sound, sensible Editor, dealing not at all in German – or other – Aesthe-tics'. [IV, 447] After FitzGerald's death Wright edited several collections of his letters and works, culminating in the seven-volume edition of 1902–3. It is because of his collecting habits that so much of what FitzGerald wrote has survived and is housed in Trinity Library.

Like Wright, Charles Keene was a bachelor, and like his old friend Edward Cowell, he came from Ipswich. He was a dis-tinguished illustrator and for most of his professional life worked on *Punch*. He was a humorous eccentric with nearly as much learning at his command as Cowell had. He and FitzGerald became friends almost on meeting in 1875. 'C. Keene is a very good Fellow,' FitzGerald wrote of that occasion, 'original, unaffected, and unprofessional, a great reader of old, quaint, Books. He went about the sands playing on a Scotch bagpipe he carries about with him.' [IV, 75] The month before he died FitzGerald wrote to Fanny Kemble to say that his 'grave Friend Charles Keene, of Punch' was coming to stay at Little Grange for a week, 'bringing with him his Bagpipes, and an ancient Viol, and a Book of Strathspeys and Madrigals; and our Archdeacon will come to meet him, and to talk over ancient Music and Books: and we shall all three drive out past the green hedges, and heaths with their furze in blossom – and I wish – yes, I do – that you were of the Party.' [IV, 585] Keene's etching of FitzGerald as an old man seen from the back as he played the organ in the hall of Little Grange is one of the most moving likenesses ever made of him. (See plate XVIII, p. 286.)

FitzGerald was still happy to make new acquaintances, but it is perhaps noticeable that what he had in common with all four of these friends made late in life were scholarly and artistic interests. To identify them in terms of *Euphranor*, they were all of the school of Lexilogus, not Phidippus, more like Cowell than Browne. Wright and Keene were both enough younger than FitzGerald to give him the pleasure he always felt at being with his juniors, but by now he seems to have put behind him his love of youth, physical grace, manly beauty, and the other attributes that he saw, or thought he saw, in Browne and Fletcher.

He must often have thought of Posh when he was in Lowestoft. In 1880 he wrote of going there in terms that suggest the prospect conjured up for him the memory of those lonely nights in the sad months after Browne's death. He had had 'some bronchial cold and cough ever since Christmas ... so possibly I shall not be able to sit about the beach as I used to do, of a night at any rate'.[2] He did manage all the same to spend one evening with Posh, who by now had lost the beard FitzGerald had admired and had only a sailor's fringe under the chin of his increasingly stolid face. It was apparently the last time he ever saw his former partner.

XVIII FitzGerald at 'Minima' organ, Little Grange, ca. 1883, by Charles Keene.

CHAPTER XIV

Boulge Churchyard

Most years FitzGerald tried to go at least once to visit George Crabbe in Merton in Norfolk, and he would perhaps have gone more often if the railway journey had not been so complicated. As the crow flies Merton is less than forty miles from Woodbridge, but by rail it took an entire day and involved no fewer than five changes. In 1881 he decided to make the journey even more lengthy by stopping in Cambridge on the way. It had been thirty years since he had stayed there, although he had gone through it some ten years before. His old terror of returning to scenes of earlier happiness was clearly passing away, and since it was in the middle of the summer vacation, he could 'see the old Place, untenanted, once more – for the last time, I believe'. To Wright he wrote that he hoped to 'take a cup of Coffee, and a Glass of Audit [ale] at your rooms, if you be disengaged and alone: perhaps taking an Evening Stroll in your walks: perhaps a Pipe – one Clean Pipe – afterwards; beside (of course) seeing Cowell, etc.' [IV, 439]

He stayed with Wright in Trinity, where he could look at the grand formality of his old college with stranger's eyes. Wright had rooms in Nevile's Court, 'one side of which is the Library, all of Wren's design, and (I think) very good. I felt at home in the rooms there, walled with Books, large, and cool.' He went several times to be with the Cowells in their house on the Trumpington Road, a 'pleasant lodging with trees before and behind, on the skirts of the town' [IV, 442], and found that he was happy in re-establishing new ties with his old spiritual home, the connections made easier because he was there with friends who had no part in the nostalgia he had felt for the place.

He never again went to Bedford, but in time he forgot his fear of meeting Browne's memory at every corner in London, and in the last five years of his life he visited the city at least as many times. Initially his reasons for going were charitable: to see a friend who was ill, to visit the elderly, or to give money unostentatiously to an acquaintance in need. But the descriptions in his letters usually slide quickly from sickbed to galleries and opera houses, as if they were the real goal of his trips. In 1877, the first time he had been in London for several years, he was appalled by the wet, fog, and slush, he found that the paintings in the National Gallery 'looked very sombre through the November Atmosphere' and decided against a performance of Mozart for fear it would be too 'altered from my remembrances of Sontag and Malibran. I think it is now best to attend these Operas as given in the Theatre of one's own Recollections.' [IV, 88]

But the trip had whetted his appetite for some of the pleasures that he thought he had learned to live without, and two years later he was back, his reactions as vigorous as they had been when he was in his twenties. He dropped into the Lyceum to see Irving's *Hamlet* 'and soon had looked, and heard, enough. It was incomparably the worst I had ever witnessed, from Covent Garden down to a Country Barn.... When he got to "Something too much of this," I called out from the Pit door where I stood, "A good deal too much," and left the theatre'. [IV, 197] A few months later he 'went to morning Service in Westminster Abbey' and sat in Poets' Corner. 'I had not been inside that Abbey for twenty years, I believe; and it seemed very grand to me; and the old Organ rolled and swam with the Boys' voices on the Top through the fretted vault.' [IV, 267]

His love of music remained as passionate as it had been all his life; in spite of his memories of Sontag and Malibran, he could not keep away from the opera when he had a chance, although he still was not fond of oratorios. At the end of 1880 he went to his 'dear old Haymarket Opera' and saw once more the 'several Boxes in which sat the several Ranks and Beauties of forty and fifty years ago ... in which I often figured as a Specimen of both.' He could still remember precisely the spot on

the very corner of the Stage where Pasta stood when Jason's People came to tell her of his new Marriage; and (with one hand in her Girdle – a movement, Mrs. Frere said, borrowed from Grassini) she interrupted them with her "Cessate – intesi!" – also when Rubini, feathered hat in hand, began that "Ah te, oh Cara" – and Taglioni hovered over the Stage. There was the old Omnibus Box too where D'Orsay flourished in ample white Waistcoat and Wristbands: and Lady Blessington's: and Lady Jersey's on the Pit tier: and my own Mother's, among the lesser Stars, on the third. In place of all which I dimly saw a small Company of less distinction in all respects; and heard an Opera (*Carmen*) on the Wagner model: very beautiful Accompaniments to no Melody.... Enough of these Old Man's fancies – But – Right for all that! [IV, 376, 377]

To FitzGerald old melodies were better than new, but he was always willing to experiment. At the time he heard it, *Carmen*, which he thought had 'excellent instrumentation, but not one new or melodious idea through the whole', was only five years old.

While seeing friends in London the year before his death, he tried to 'hear some one opera of Wagner then playing at *my* old Opera House: but my three nights came and went without my doing so. I dare say I should not have stay'd out half ... but I should have heard The Music of the Future – sure to interest one in its orchestral expression, and if no Melody, none previously expected by me.' [IV, 492] He had to content himself with having 'heard but one piece (*not* the March) from Tannhäuser, played by the Brass Band on Lowestoft Pier', which he found delightful as he listened 'with some Sailors at the Inn'.

Lugubriously he told Frederick Tennyson in 1879, 'I never play Organ or Piano now: but I go over some of the old Immortals in my head, especially when wrapt up in the bed clothes.' [IV, 276] Yet the moment he had a musical guest such as Keene, he was back at the keyboard of his Minima organ in the hall, pounding away as joyously as if he were once more an undergraduate in the Camus Society. Because he now had a bad curvature of the neck, it was difficult for him to read music on the stand of the organ, but he had the memories of a lifetime from which to draw the grand melodies he loved best.

Aside from the trouble with his neck, his chief difficulty was with bronchitis, which 'occasionally reminds me that I am not

289

forgotten by him', so that he rather dreaded the coming of winter each year. 'I am better off than many – if not most – of my contemporaries,' he wrote, thinking of five friends who had all suffered strokes in the same year, and in any case 'there is not much [worth] living for after seventy-four.' [IV, 532]

At Little Grange he was taken care of in a somewhat eccentric fashion by an aged pair, John Howe and his wife, for whom he had the amused affection he usually felt for those who worked for him, and he treated them with as much consideration as if they had been his own family. He was so fond of primary colours that when Howe showed up in a blue 'round, short coat like an Eton boy's', he asked Howe's wife to wear a brilliant red skirt and cloak to complete a dazzling palette.

He still liked entertaining his friends, so long as they could accept the simplicity of his hospitality and the muddle in which they sometimes found the house. Like Mrs Faiers before her, Mrs Howe was not a distinguished cook, although it normally made little difference to FitzGerald. In warning Aldis Wright that he would need to know the exact date of his arrival if he were to be fed properly, he said of her, 'My hostess can cook a Chicken nicely enough – and a Sole – though perhaps not both for the same Dinner.' [IV, 528] A luncheon invitation to the daughter of one of his Woodbridge friends read in full: 'Hot *Chicken* today, or cold Tomorrow.'

He seldom went into Woodbridge, more because his old friends had disappeared than because he felt any longer the disapproval of the townspeople. Most of his walking was done on the 'Quarterdeck', a well-worn path above the house, overlooking Pytches Road, where he could rest on the iron seat when he tired. When he walked or weeded in the garden, he would stuff the post into his jacket to be read later, and on one occasion retrieved it somewhat the worse for being stuck to the 'buttered bread for Ducks, etc., in the pocket where I shoved Proof to be read "al fresco" – Damn! – but I'll do so no more'. [IV, 220]

Indoors and out he read as long as his eyes would hold out, then waited patiently for the current reader. His literary curiosity was as keen as ever, and though he re-read the old favourites, he also tried newer books, not always with complete success. He found *Far from the Madding Crowd*, which he picked up 'on the strength of

290

the title', incomprehensible, but it 'contains some good Country Life'. 'Somehow I can't read G. Eliot, as I presume you can,' he told Frederick Tennyson; 'I really conclude that the fault lies in me not in her: so with Goethe (except in his Letters, Tabletalk, etc.) whom I try in vain to admire.' To C. E. Norton he wrote of a 'Paper or two by "Mark Twain"' that gave him some desire to know more of him; 'I know not why up to this time he has been but a Name to me.'

Although he made light of it, his own work was certainly not forgotten. In December 1881 he wrote that 'A week ago the Spanish Ambassador (whose name I now forget) sent me a fine bronze Profile Medal of Calderon from the Spanish Royal Academy, by way of recognition of my Translations.' Modestly he assumed that it had probably been sent at the suggestion of the American Minister, Lowell, but there is no evidence to support the idea. 'Not knowing how to address Ambassadors, I began my Letter of Thanks – "May it please your Excellency!" thinking it best to err on the safe side, especially with a Spanish Grandee.' [IV, 461–2]

Like many writers who were his contemporaries, he was much exercised in the early 1880s with Froude's biography of Carlyle and his editions of his papers. Probably more than worry about Carlyle and Froude lay at the bottom of his interest, since he could hardly help realizing that his own fame was now great enough to make it certain that his papers would be edited after his death and his biography written.

Initially he was disturbed at the publication of Carlyle's *Reminiscences*, which Froude had in print soon after Carlyle's death, and he felt they would 'certainly better have been suppressed, at any rate till the Victims or the Victims' Kinsfolk were out of hearing'. The publication of the biography by Froude, however, so convinced him of the greatness of the work that he offered Froude all Carlyle's letters that he had kept. 'Had not those "Reminiscences" preceded the Biography, I believe others – Critics and Public – would have been of my mind.' Instead of finding Froude an Iago, as some reviewers had done, intent on undermining his Othello, Fitz-Gerald said he 'seems to me to speak of him as he was, nothing extenuating nor setting down (nor hinting) aught in malice.... Yes, I must say again that, whatever Froude may have intended, I not only admire Carlyle more than I did – which was very much –

but that I *love* him now – which scarce entered into my account before.' [IV, 520]

It was an opinion that might have been predicted from Fitz-Gerald's attitude to Lamb when he was thinking of writing his biography and said that he must write about all the horrors of his life 'to show forth what the Man had to suffer'. He often said how deeply he was interested in every detail of Scott's life or of the love of Keats for Fanny Brawne, since it would never have occurred to him that a work of art is in any way separate from the rest of the life of the artist. Six weeks before his death he packed copies of most of his works in a tin box and forwarded them to Aldis Wright at Trinity with an accompanying letter indicating clearly that he expected them to be published eventually.

The day after he had packed off the trunk to Trinity, 2 May 1883, he had to go to London on business; he finished with it in time to jump into a cab with something of his old impetuosity and be driven to the Embankment to see Carlyle's statue there, as well as to walk past the nearby Carlyle house, which he had last visited a quarter of a century before. 'The Statue very good, I thought, though looking somewhat small for want of a good Background to set it off: but the old House! Shut up – neglected – "To Let" – was sad enough to me.' The account of his day's excursion was rounded off with what had become increasingly important to him: 'I got back to Woodbridge before night.' [IV, 587]

When his self-imposed prohibitions against visiting scenes of his happiness in youth and middle age no longer seemed binding, Fitz-Gerald was paradoxically much happier at settling down in the quiet of Little Grange, content to let the rest of the world go its own way. He was noticeably easier with others: he no longer imperiously turned away uninvited callers as he once had done, he no longer held himself aloof from the townspeople (although he certainly did not court them), he no longer felt he had to lecture the young of the parish in good manners when he saw them misbehave. By now his afternoons were full of greatnieces come to eat Mrs Howe's gingerbreads at tea, and he had a long swing fastened to the beams of the old barn, where he welcomed all the children nearby who wanted to come there to play. Once he had been described as having the manners of a dowager duchess with strangers, but now he was simply a gentle old man who was glad to see visitors but was equally content to spend the end of his life with little company save that of his books and his organ.

Early in 1883 Aldis Wright had to go to Bedford, and FitzGerald asked him to find William Browne's grave at Goldington, for he had never seen it. When Wright told him about it, he thanked him sombrely for the search 'on that dismal wet day; for I think you could only have done so from some regard to me'. [IV, 549] In April he made a final version of his will, to be sure that all his 'little pensions and payments' to the indigent of the neighbourhood would continue as they had done in his life; his larger bequests to nieces and to the children of friends were already indicated, and Lucy had been provided for until her death. Just before his death he took a journey he had thought never to make: he went again to Geldestone Hall, which he had not seen since Mrs Kerrich's death twenty years before. By now the house was empty, but the wife of the lodge keeper made luncheon for him and served it to him alone in the room where he had loved eating among troops of nieces and nephews. The last snarl of his life seemed untangled when a few days before his death he received a letter from Posh Fletcher, addressed to 'Mr. Edward FitzGerald, Esq.'; what its message was is not known, but it no longer had the power to disturb him.

On 12 June 1883 he wrote two of the last letters of his life. One was to F. C. Brooke of Ufford, typically making arrangements for the exchange of books and commenting on those he had read. The other letter was to Samuel Laurence; it is pleasant to believe that it was probably the very last of all the thousands he had ever written, for no man could compose a quieter epitaph for himself:

If I do not write, it is because I have absolutely nothing to tell you that you have not known for the last twenty years. Here I live still, reading, and being read to, part of my time; walking abroad three or four times a day, or night, in spite of wakening a Bronchitis, which has lodged like the household 'Brownie' within; pottering about my Garden (as I have just been doing) and snipping off dead Roses like Miss Tox; and now and then a visit to the neighbouring Seaside, and a splash to Sea in one of the Boats. I never see a new Picture, nor hear a note of Music except when I drum out some old Tune in Winter on an Organ, which might almost be carried about the Streets with a handle to turn, and a Monkey on the top of it. So I go on, living a life far too comfortable as compared with that of better, and wiser men: but ever expecting a reverse in health such as my seventy-five years are subject to....

Tomorrow I am going (for my one annual Visit) to G. Crabbe's, where I am to meet his Sisters, and talk over old Bredfield Vicarage days. Two of my eight Nieces are now with me here in my house, for a two months' visit, I suppose and hope. And I think this is all I have to tell you of

Yours ever sincerely

E.FG. [IV, 594]

The next morning he began the first of the six legs of the complicated rail journey to Merton, where he was met at the station by George Crabbe in his dog cart and driven back to the rectory for tea. It had been a hot day, but he complained of being chilly and tired and wore his green plaid shawl until he was within the house. Before tea he uncharacteristically asked if he might wash because the dust of the station at Bury St Edmunds had made him feel 'so dirty', then he brightened up and began talking animatedly of his school days, of which the change at Bury had reminded him, and of the beauty of the remains of the Abbey there. He drank some tea but refused any food.

That evening at nine he asked for a brandy and water, and an hour later he said he would like to go to bed. Crabbe took him upstairs and left him another glass of brandy to help him sleep. He spent a quiet night, but at six in the morning Crabbe heard him moving around his room. 'At ¼ to 8 I tapped at his door to ask how he was,' Crabbe wrote to Wright, '& getting no answer went in & found him as if sleeping peacefully but quite dead.... He always said he should die of disease of the heart and wished so to die.'[1]

On Tuesday, 19 June, when Boulge Churchyard was looking its best on a summer afternoon, FitzGerald was put into his plain earth grave. In the small group that had gathered were Cowell and Wright from Cambridge, Crabbe, who had brought him from Merton, and a number of old friends from near Woodbridge, including 'two or three old Farmers who knew and respected him' from the days when he had lived in Boulge Cottage. But Lucy

FitzGerald, who was staying at the time in Woodbridge, was not there, nor was Posh Fletcher.

In his diary Frederick Spalding wrote, '*I* have lost my dearest and best Friend. I shall ever remember him with Respect, Love, and Gratitude. I shall never know or meet his like upon earth and I heartily thank God that I have known him well, and in a small measure been able to appreciate him.'[2]

Acknowledgements

My primary debt must be to those institutions and persons who have kindly allowed me to publish FitzGerald material, including that in the four-volume edition of *The Letters of Edward Fitz-Gerald*, Princeton, 1980. I am pleased to thank for their generosity the Master and Fellows of Trinity College, Cambridge; the George Arents Research Library for Special Collections at Syracuse University; the Suffolk Record Office, Ipswich Branch; the Cambridge University Library; the Omar Khayyám Club and its Secretary, Mr Charles Hodgson; the British Library, Department of Manuscripts; the Princeton University Press and Mrs Arthur Sherwood; Professor J. E. Kerrich; Mrs Walter Kerrich; Miss Mary Barham Johnson; and Mrs Margaret Sharman. It is a particular pleasure to thank Mrs Annabelle Burdick Terhune, co-editor of *The Letters of Edward FitzGerald* and widow of a previous FitzGerald biographer, for her permission to use material from both the edition of *Letters* and the FitzGerald papers at Syracuse University; her generosity has seemed doubled because I was fully aware that she dissented from some of my views on the subject of this biography. The list of those who have helped me with pictures is given after the list of illustrations (p. 14), and I should like to record my gratitude to them.

I sincerely hope that any copyright owner whom I have failed to trace, or from whom I have inadvertently not sought permission when I should have done so, will accept my apologies.

It would be impossible to list all those persons and institutions to whom I am indebted for advice, help, and generosity too various to specify, but I must single out for special thanks Mr J. H. Dobree, Miss P. Downie, Dr Kenneth Garlick; the John Simon Guggenheim

Acknowledgements

Memorial Foundation; Professor Francis Haskell; Mr Norman Scarfe; Mrs Margaret Uplinger; and Dr J. M. Walker.

Like many other biographers, I owe a great deal to the efforts of my predecessors in the study of my subject's life and writings. I have acknowledged them in many places where the debt is direct, but often their influence has been pervasive rather than specific, and I am happy to indicate my thanks for what they have taught me, in the certainty that living scholars will recognize their own contributions to what I have written, and that earlier ones would have regarded their own work as part of the world of learning on which we all draw.

Notes

As has been indicated previously, numbers in brackets in the text of this book refer to the four volumes of *The Letters of Edward FitzGerald*, eds. A. McK. and A. B. Terhune. To avoid unnecessary clutter in the text, some minor references to that edition have been deleted. These deleted references, as well as dozens of other bits of documentation of comparatively little interest to the general reader, are indicated in the working typescript, copies of which I have deposited in Trinity College Library, Cambridge, and in the George Arents Research Library, Syracuse University, where they may be consulted by interested readers.

The following abbreviations are used in the notes:

Barham Johnson	Letters and transcripts of letters belonging to Miss Mary Barham Johnson
Ganz, Trinity	Material collected by Charles Ganz in preparation for editing *A FitzGerald Medley*; now in Trinity College Library
Spalding	Diary kept by Frederick Spalding of Woodbridge. Transcripts in Arents Library and in the collection of the Omar Khayyám Club
Trinity	Trinity College Library, Cambridge. Largest holding of FitzGerald materials
WAW	W. Aldis Wright, Vice-Master of Trinity College and FitzGerald's literary executor

Reference in the notes is made directly to books listed in the Select Bibliography.

CHAPTER I   FAMILY AND CHILDHOOD

1 Glyde, p. 158.
2 Betham, pp. 258–9.
3 Copinger, p. 239.
4 Journal kept by M. F. FitzGerald, 8.1.41.

5 W. F. Kerrich to James Blyth, 1905, Ganz, Trinity.
6 Betham, p. 259.
7 Jane Wilkinson to WAW, 21.10.83, Trinity.
8 Spalding, 13.10.67.
9 Betham, p. 258.
10 Jane Wilkinson to WAW, 21.10.83, Trinity.
11 Journal kept by M. F. FitzGerald, 24.9.40; 24.11.40; 30.7.40; 20.11.40; 19.7.40; 16.8.40; 7.12.40; 2.4.41.
12 Jane Wilkinson to WAW, 21.10.83, Trinity.
13 Glyde, p. 12.
14 Betham, pp. 260–1. Mrs FitzGerald seems to have written this, although the text is not clear on the matter. I have not located the original.

CHAPTER II   CAMBRIDGE

1 R. H. Groome to WAW, 18.2.84, Trinity.
2 Terhune says that Allen was an Apostle (p. 30), but Peter Allen, the modern historian of the Society, states firmly that he was 'not at all the Apostolic type' (p. 136), which I am inclined to accept, since I have seen no evidence except Terhune's statement that he was even considered for membership.
3 Ray, p. 135.
4 Ray, p. 156.
5 Ray, p. 128.

CHAPTER III   THACKERAY, TENNYSON, AND BROWNE

1 Allen diary, 18.5.30, Trinity, which does not agree with *Letters*, I, 87.
2 Allen diary, 10.12.30, Trinity.
3 Now in Arents Library, Syracuse University.
4 Thackeray: *Letters*, I, 291.
5 Thackeray: *Letters*, I, 172.
6 Quoted, Martin, p. 147.
7 Quoted, Martin, p. 242.
8 Thackeray: *Letters*, I, 200.

CHAPTER IV   MIREHOUSE AND BOULGE COTTAGE

1 To W. B. Donne, 2.1.32 and March 1833, Barham Johnson transcripts.
2 For this and whole episode, see Martin, pp. 197–204, 289–91.
3 Tennyson: *Letters*, I, 134. The text is in part conjectural, since the original at Yale has been partially obscured by a large stain.

4 See Martin, pp. 204, 206–7, 254–6, 270, 282–3, 292–3, 375–7.
5 Donne, p. 47.
6 Donne, p. 24.
7 Thackeray: *Letters*, I, 322, 388–9.
8 To John Kemble, 20.11.38, Barham Johnson transcript.
9 Mary Crabbe to John Glyde (?), n.d., Suffolk Record Office.
10 p. 15.
11 To W. B. Donne, 29.4.47, Barham Johnson.
12 Adams, *Omar's Interpreter*, pp. 44–5.
13 Lamb: *Letters*, III, 220, 224.
14 E. G. Doughty to John Glyde, 19.1.97, Suffolk Record Office.
15 To John Wodderspoon, 15.1.45, British Library, Add. MS 52524, ff. 196b–197.

CHAPTER V   BROWNE'S MARRIAGE

1 To Barton, 10.5.37, Barham Johnson transcript.
2 Wright, I, 190. WAW believed that this assessment was made not by FitzGerald but by a graphologist 'taking' Browne's character from his handwriting. See Terhune, p. 356.
3 Jenkyns, p. 287.

CHAPTER VI   COWELL AND BARTON

1 Ganz, Trinity.
2 Ince, p. 43.
3 Benson, pp. 51–2.
4 Spalding, 5.9.67.
5 Cowell, pp. 59–60.
6 Cf. Cowell, p. 41, and FitzGerald: *Letters*, I, 513, n. 1.
7 Barton: *Literary Correspondence*, pp. 119, 139.
8 Donne, pp. 58–9.
9 Barton: *Literary Correspondence*, pp. 139, 103, 146.
10 Thackeray: *Letters*, II, 94, 166.
11 Thackeray: *Letters*, II, 212, 366, 310.
12 Thackeray: *Letters*, II, 365, 453.

CHAPTER VII   *Euphranor*

1 *The Times*, 5.9.48; 28.12.48; 3.1.49; 18.1.49; 27.4.49; 24.5.49; 22.6.49.
2 To Donne, 22.7.48, Barham Johnson.
3 20.8.48, Barham Johnson.
4 Betham, p. 256.

5 Kerrich, 'Memories', p. 84.
6 FitzGerald: *New Letters*, pp. 170–1.
7 Spalding, 4.5.68.
8 A. M. T. Kerrich to WAW, 11.2.[04?], Trinity.
9 Cowell, pp. 87–91; FitzGerald: *Letters*, I, 685–6.
10 FitzGerald: *Letters*, I, 498–9, 505, 530, 543.

CHAPTER VIII   DEATH OF FITZGERALD'S PARENTS

1 Unidentified newspaper clipping from private collection, referring to 'The East Anglian Daily Times of Friday last'. In view of his father's bankruptcy, the amount may be exaggerated or confused with his legacy on the death of his mother.
2 Terhune, p. 167.
3 Glyde, p. 278.
4 For Carlyle's visit, see FitzGerald: *Letters*, II, 171–83.
5 Donne, p. 198.
6 Thackeray: *Letters*, III, 67–8, 71, 387.
7 Ganz, Trinity.

CHAPTER IX   FITZGERALD'S MARRIAGE

1 Part of their correspondence is in Cambridge University Library.
2 Wright, I, 297–8.
3 Spalding, 4.5.68.
4 Spalding, 4.5.68.
5 Donne, p. 211.
6 Donne, p. 217.
7 E. Ruth Edwards to WAW, Trinity.
8 Brookfield, *Circle*, II, 449.
9 Donne, p. 217.
10 Ganz, Trinity.
11 W. F. Pollock to WAW, 13.9.87, Trinity.
12 Spalding, 4.5.68.
13 Spalding, 13.10.67.
14 Arberry, pp. 4–5, 11, 18. So completely has it taken its place there that the best-known musical setting of the poem derives its title from FitzGerald's interpolation, Liza Lehmann's 'In a Persian Garden'.
15 Clodd, p. 157.

CHAPTER X   THE DISCOVERY OF THE *Rubáiyát*

1 Wright, II, 35–6.

Notes

2 Donne, p. 238.
3 For the 'romance of the *Rubáiyát*' see Terhune, pp. 207–13; Weber, pp. 19–31; FitzGerald: *Letters*, II, 417–18, III, 414–19. There are many other accounts, most of them less accurate.
4 Quoted, Kermode, p. 56.
5 Glyde, p. 249.
6 Spalding, 31.3.68.
7 Wright, I, 314.
8 Wright, II, 89.

CHAPTER XI POSH

 1 Blyth, p. 183.
 2 Wright, II, 106–7.
 3 Benson, pp. 50, 53.
 4 Cowell to WAW, 9.7.95, Trinity.
 5 Terhune, p. 272.
 6 Blyth, p. 186.
 7 Blyth, p. 191.
 8 To WAW, 26.4.06, Trinity.
 9 Kerrich, 'More Memories', pp. 163–4.
10 James Blyth to John Henderson, 17.10.07, Omar Khayyám Club.

CHAPTER XII LETTERS AND READERS

1 Martin, p. 537.
2 Probably rather more correct than the texts in the *Letters* suggest.
3 Kermode, p. 59.
4 Copy from private collection; it is not in FitzGerald's handwriting, which may cast doubt on its authenticity.
5 Groome, p. 91.
6 Ormond, I, 174.

CHAPTER XIII SETTLING ACCOUNTS

1 To WAW, 21.10.83, Trinity.
2 Wright, II, 198; the date assigned (2.3.82) is clearly incorrect.

CHAPTER XIV BOULGE CHURCHYARD

1 14.6.83, Trinity.
2 19.6.83.

Select Bibliography

Unless otherwise noted, the place of publication is London.

Adams, Morley, *In the Footsteps of Borrow & FitzGerald* [1914]
—*Omar's Interpreter: A New Life of Edward FitzGerald*, 1909
Allen, Peter, *The Cambridge Apostles: The Early Years*, 1978
Arberry, A. J., *Omar Khayyam and FitzGerald*, 1959
Barton: *The Literary Correspondence of Bernard Barton*, ed. J. E. Barcus, 1966
Benson, A. C., *Edward FitzGerald*, 1905
Betham, Ernest, ed., *A House of Letters* [1905]
Blyth, James, *Edward FitzGerald and 'Posh', 'Herring Merchants'*, 1908
Brookfield, Charles and Frances, *Mrs. Brookfield and Her Circle*, 2 vols., 1905
Brookfield, F. M., *The Cambridge 'Apostles'*, 1906
Caulfield, Catherine, *The Emperor of the United States of America & Other Magnificent British Eccentrics*, 1981
Clodd, Edward, *Memories*, 1916
Copinger, W. A., *The Manors of Suffolk*, vol. VII, 1911
Cowell, George, *Life & Letters of Edward Byles Cowell*, 1904
de Polnay, Peter, *Into an Old Room*, 1950
Donaldson, J. W., *A Retrospective Address Read at the Tercentenary Commemoration of King Edward School, Bury St. Edmunds*, 1850
Donne: *William Bodham Donne and His Friends*, ed. Catharine B. Johnson, 1905
Dutt, W. A., *Some Literary Associations of East Anglia*, 1907
FitzGerald: *Some New Letters of Edward FitzGerald to Bernard Barton*, ed. F. R. Barton, 1923
FitzGerald: *A FitzGerald Medley*, ed. Charles Ganz, 1933
FitzGerald to His Friends: Selected Letters, ed. Alethea Hayter, 1979
FitzGerald: *A FitzGerald Friendship: Unpublished Letters from Edward*

FitzGerald to William Bodham Donne, eds. C. B. Johnson and N. C. Hannay, 1932

FitzGerald: *The Letters of Edward FitzGerald*, eds. A. McK. and A. B. Terhune, 4 vols., Princeton, 1980

Glyde, John, *The Life of Edward Fitz-Gerald*, 1900

Groome, F. H., *Two Suffolk Friends*, 1895

Hussey, Frank, *Old Fitz: Edward FitzGerald and East Coast Sailing*, Ipswich, 1974

Ince, Richard B., *Calverley and Some Cambridge Wits of the Nineteenth Century*, 1929

Jenkyns, R. H. A., *The Victorians and Ancient Greece*, Oxford, 1980

Kermode, Frank, *Continuities*, 1968

Kerrich, M. E. F., 'Homes and Haunts of Edward FitzGerald', *Blackwood's Edinburgh Magazine*, October 1903, pp. 439–52

—'Edward Fitz-Gerald', *Nineteenth Century*, March 1909, pp. 461–70

—'Memories of Edward FitzGerald', *East Anglian Magazine*, August 1935, pp. 83–7

—'More Memories of Edward FitzGerald', *East Anglian Magazine*, November 1935, pp. 160–5

Lamb: *The Letters of Charles and Mary Lamb*, ed. E. V. Lucas, 3 vols., 1935

Lucas, E. V., *Bernard Barton and His Friends: A Record of Quiet Lives*, 1893

Martin, R. B., *Tennyson, the Unquiet Heart*, 1980

Ormond, Richard, *Early Victorian Portraits*, 2 vols., 1973

Ray, Gordon N., *Thackeray: The Uses of Adversity*, 1955

Tennyson: *The Letters of Alfred Lord Tennyson*, eds. C. Y. Lang and E. F. Shannon, vol. I, 1982

Terhune, A. McK., *The Life of Edward FitzGerald*, 1947

Thackeray: *The Letters and Private Papers of William Makepeace Thackeray*, ed. Gordon N. Ray, 4 vols., 1945–6

Thomas, Denis, *Thomas Churchyard of Woodbridge*, Chislehurst, 1966

Weber, C. J., *FitzGerald's Rubáiyát, Centennial Edition*, Waterville, 1959

Wright, Thomas, *The Life of Edward FitzGerald*, 2 vols., 1904

306

Index

Index

Index

Robert Bernard Martin was Professor of English at Princeton University for a quarter of a century before resigning his position in 1975 in order to give more time to writing. Since then he has been Visiting Professor at Leicester University and is currently Citizens' Professor of English at the University of Hawaii. Among his numerous studies of literature and social history are books about Charlotte Bronte's novels, Victorian comedy, Charles Kingsley, Victorian scandals, and a biography of Alfred Tennyson. *Tennyson: The Unquiet Heart,* published in 1980, won the Duff Cooper Award for biography, the James Tait Black Memorial Prize for biography, the Royal Society of Literature's W.H. Heinemann Award, and the Phi Beta Kappa Christian Gauss Award for Literary Scholarship and Criticism.

Professor Martin is also the author of several pseudonymous mystery novels. Among his other interests are music, architecture, gardening, food, and travel.